T0305228

Debt Default and Democracy

NEW THINKING IN POLITICAL ECONOMY

Series Editor: Peter J. Boettke, *George Mason University, USA*

New Thinking in Political Economy aims to encourage scholarship in the intersection of the disciplines of politics, philosophy and economics. It has the ambitious purpose of reinvigorating political economy as a progressive force for understanding social and economic change.

The series is an important forum for the publication of new work analysing the social world from a multidisciplinary perspective. With increased specialization (and professionalization) within universities, interdisciplinary work has become increasingly uncommon. Indeed, during the 20th century, the process of disciplinary specialization reduced the intersection between economics, philosophy and politics and impoverished our understanding of society. Modern economics in particular has become increasingly mathematical and largely ignores the role of institutions and the contribution of moral philosophy and politics.

New Thinking in Political Economy will stimulate new work that combines technical knowledge provided by the 'dismal science' and the wisdom gleaned from the serious study of the 'worldly philosophy'. The series will reinvigorate our understanding of the social world by encouraging a multidisciplinary approach to the challenges confronting society in the new century.

Titles in the series include:

Debt Default and Democracy

Edited by

Giuseppe Eusepi

Professor of Public Finance, Department of Law and Economics of Productive Activities, Sapienza University of Rome, Italy

Richard E. Wagner

Holbert L. Harris Professor of Economics, Department of Economics, George Mason University, USA

NEW THINKING IN POLITICAL ECONOMY

 Edward Elgar
PUBLISHING

Cheltenham, UK • Northampton, MA, USA

Published by
Edward Elgar Publishing Limited
The Lypiatts
15 Lansdown Road
Cheltenham
Glos GL50 2JA
UK

Edward Elgar Publishing, Inc.
William Pratt House
9 Dewey Court
Northampton
Massachusetts 01060
USA

A catalogue record for this book
is available from the British Library

Library of Congress Control Number: 2018931760

This book is available electronically in the **Elgar**online
Economics subject collection
DOI 10.4337/9781788117937

ISBN 978 1 78811 792 0 (cased)
ISBN 978 1 78811 793 7 (eBook)

Typeset by Servis Filmsetting Ltd, Stockport, Cheshire

Contents

Figures and tables

FIGURES

TABLES

Contributors

Alexie Alupoaiei, Financial Stability Department, National Bank of Romania, Bucharest, Romania

Fabrizio Balassone, Bank of Italy, Directorate General for Economics, Statistics and Research, Rome, Italy

Geoffrey Brennan, Australian National University, Canberra, Australia; Duke University, Durham, NC, USA; University of North Carolina, Chapel Hill, NC, USA

Sara Cecchetti, Bank of Italy, Directorate General for Economics, Statistics and Research, Rome, Italy

Martina Cecioni, Bank of Italy, Directorate General for Economics, Statistics and Research, Rome, Italy

Marika Cioffi, Bank of Italy, Directorate General for Economics, Statistics and Research, Rome, Italy

Wanda Cornacchia, Bank of Italy, Directorate General for Economics, Statistics and Research, Rome, Italy

Flavia Corneli, Bank of Italy, Directorate General for Economics, Statistics and Research, Rome, Italy

Florin Dragu, Financial Stability Department, National Bank of Romania, Bucharest, Romania

Giuseppe Eusepi, Sapienza University of Rome, Rome, Italy

Ernesto Longobardi, Aldo Moro University of Bari, Bari, Italy

Karsten Mause, University of Münster, Münster, Germany

Florian Neagu, Financial Stability Department, National Bank of Romania, Bucharest, Romania

Antonio Pedone, Sapienza University of Rome, Rome, Italy

Andrea Rieck, Federal Ministry of Finance, Berlin, Germany

Ludger Schuknecht, Federal Ministry of Finance, Berlin, Germany

Gabriele Semeraro, Bank of Italy, Directorate General for Economics, Statistics and Research, Rome, Italy

Liviu Voinea, Deputy Governor, National Bank of Romania, Bucharest, Romania

Richard E. Wagner, George Mason University, Fairfax, VA, USA

Preface

In light of the continuing presence of high public debt within many of the members of the European Union, and of the understandable concerns about default that such high levels of debt generate, the European Center for the Study of Public Choice (ECSPC) incorporated a public choice analysis of public debt and debt default into its research program. The chapters presented here are one portion of that research program. A second portion is the book *Public Debt: An Illusion of Democratic Political Economy*, written by Giuseppe Eusepi and Richard E. Wagner, and published by Edward Elgar in June 2017.

These chapters explore public debt along two distinct but complementary analytical paths. One path concerns microeconomic aspects of public debt. Public debt doesn't just happen as some exogenous insertion into society. It emerges through budgetary processes where individuals respond to the costs and gains of different courses of action, with public debt emerging or not in consequence of those costs and gains. This effort to relate public debt to individual rationalities is central to the primary theme of public choice, wherein political outcomes follow an intelligible logic rooted in the universal principle of economizing action.

The second analytical path concerns the systemic properties of rational individuals acting within a democratic system of political economy. In this scheme of analysis, micro and macro are related through the relationship of parts-to-whole. Macro-level observations are not direct objects of policy choice, but rather emerge through interactions among micro-level participants within a political-economic process. Within this scheme of thought, the two levels of analysis are integrated by recognition that efforts to control macro-level outcomes that are thought undesirable must address the micro-level circumstances and conditions that promote public debt as systemic budgetary outcomes.

The book's eight chapters are thus divided into two parts. Part I features four chapters that explore public debt in relation to individual rationality under various circumstances. Part II features four chapters that examine the macro consequences and implications of public debt.

Part I opens with Giuseppe Eusepi and Richard E. Wagner contrasting Antonio de Viti de Marco and David Ricardo regarding public debt.

De Viti accepted Ricardo's equivalence proposition that public debt is future taxation that is equivalent in aggregate magnitude to the taxes that would have been necessary if public debt had not been created. Yet De Viti derives different conclusions about the consequences of public debt, due to his micro-analytic treatment of debt.

Karsten Mause examines the problems that arise when some governments bail out governments that have incurred unsustainable amounts of debt, and explores how appropriate fiscal rules might limit the moral hazard that bailouts promote.

Geoffrey Brennan probes with some challenging questions regarding the relation between governments and individuals, asking whether the ideas about contractual obligation pertain also to governments as they do to private citizens.

Richard E. Wagner closes Part I by exploring the plausible limits to presumptions that the obligations government incur are *ipso facto* obligations that citizens are assumed to have accepted. In short, much depends on the constitutional framework of democracy, much as Antonio de Viti de Marco recognized in distinguishing between cooperative and monopolistic states.

Part II opens with Andrea Rieck and Ludger Schuknecht providing a bridge between the micro-centric character of the chapters in Part I and the macro-centric character of the chapters in Part II. They explore the ability of different institutional mechanisms and processes to limit, or to fail to limit, the creation of public debt.

Ernesto Longobardi and Antonio Pedone examine possible avenues for reducing the relative size of public debt within the European Union. Leaving default aside and avoiding inflation as a means of reducing the real size of debt, this would require some combination of tax increase or expenditure decrease, neither of which is politically palatable.

Fabrizio Balassone and his co-authors explore problems of managing risk with respect to economic governance, which seems to be of particular prominence once the implications that governmental entities are not residual claimants to their actions are taken into account.

Liviu Voinea and his co-authors close the book by examining problems of reconfiguring balance sheets in the presence of high public debt, and especially on how such reconfiguration might affect economic growth.

Acknowledgements

The European Center for the Study of Public Choice (ECSPC) is extremely grateful to Cassa Depositi e Prestiti for its financial support. This book would never have reached the stage of delivery without the assistance of Maria Delle Grotti, permanent secretary to the ECSPC.

Finally, we wish to express our thanks to Edward Elgar editorial staff. We want to make particular mention of Sarah Cook, Karen Jones, Erin McVicar, Sue Sharp, Yvonne Smith, Hayley Stephenson and Alan Sturmer.

Giuseppe Eusepi
Department of Law and Economics of Productive Activities
Sapienza University of Rome, Rome, Italy

Richard E. Wagner
Department of Economics
George Mason University, Fairfax, VA, USA

PART I

Public debt and individual rationality

PART I

1. De Viti de Marco vs. Ricardo on public debt: self-extinction or default?

Giuseppe Eusepi and Richard E. Wagner

INTRODUCTION

This chapter provides new insight into Antonio de Viti de Marco's (1936) interpretation of David Ricardo's (1817) equivalence theorem, for which Robert Barro (1974) provides a modern restatement, holding that an extraordinary tax and a public loan are equivalent. There is a superficial similarity between the two theorists. At a deeper level of examination, however, the two theorists diverge sharply. In this respect, de Viti and Ricardo resemble the two parabolas X^2 and $-X^2$: they share a common origin but point their analytical attention in opposing directions. Ricardo reasoned in terms of macro aggregates and then reduced that aggregate to a representative individual. Within this framework, public debt must be self-extinguishing because Ricardo's representative individual framework prevents an individual from defaulting on himself. The self-extinction of public debt is a built-in feature of Ricardo's purely abstract model where what was in play was a simple matter of double-entry accounting, in which case an extraordinary tax and a public loan must have equivalent present value.

While de Viti accepted Ricardo's aggregative arithmetic, he regarded this arithmetic as a truism that obscured the individual actions and interactions that were occurring at the micro level of action. What de Viti called the cooperative state was but one possible model of political economy that provided more of an analytical foil than a reasonable theory of political-economic experience, as Michele Giuranno and Manuela Mosca (2016) explain in their extensive examination of de Viti's concern with developing realistic models of the state. For de Viti, the cooperative state was actually an anti-political model in the spirit of Carl Schmitt's (1932) recognition of the autonomy of the political in society. It is the state reduced wholly to contractual obligation under voluntarism. In this limiting case, public debt must be self-extinguishing because no one would agree to extend credit to someone without believing that the resulting obligation will be met. At the level of *ex ante* expectation, public debt must be self-extinguishing under an institutional regime within which all political action is voluntary. To be sure, one might doubt whether political action can ever be made wholly voluntary, in which case self-extinction gives way to some form of default, not as reflected in aggregate variables but as reflected in individual expectations.

It is at this point of individual expectation that de Viti's analysis diverges sharply from Ricardo's because de Viti recognized that aggregate variables are derived from individual interactions that themselves occur within particular institutional settings that channel power. Hence, public debt will be self-extinguishing only as an extreme limiting case. Where self-extinction of public debt was built into Ricardo's model, it was only one possibility within de Viti's model. A model that assumes that all collective action is genuinely contractual will necessarily entail self-extinction of public debt. But this outcome is an artifact of a particular model and not a general feature of reality. Even with a cooperative state model, self-extinction can fail if some share of the debt is held externally. In this situation, members of the issuing polity can secure positive wealth gains by defaulting on their obligations to outsiders. To be sure, default would undermine the reputation of the defaulting polity, and so could not serve as a continuing policy. All the same, it is worth noting that a gain that lasts but seven years is worth about half as much as one that would last forever if people discount the future at 10 percent. In other words, the prospect of foreclosing long-term options might be embraced if the short-term gains of doing so are sufficiently attractive. Only if the loan must be re-purchased by domestic taxpayers can default be precluded by theoretical construction.[1] Otherwise, the prospect of default depends on institutionally governed relationships among relevant participants.

Once it is recognized that democratic polities are never fully cooperative, there are numerous paths along which public debt can be repudiated in whole or in part. For instance, the use of debt to transfer cost from some members of a polity to other members is a form of repudiation when judged from a contractual perspective. Repudiation can thus arise even if all debt is held internally, though the presence of external debt widens the possibilities for repudiation. Once we recognize, as de Viti recognized, that democratic states are only incompletely cooperative states, debt will not be extinguished as the contractual framework envisions.[2] Once it is

---

[1] See De Viti (1893).
[2] It goes without saying that this is in a democratic state, not in a cooperative state where defaulting is a clearing transaction only.

recognized that democratic governments are never fully cooperative, public debt becomes a means by which winning groups within the polity transfer wealth from losing groups.

DE VITI VS. RICARDO ON THE EQUIVALENCE BETWEEN TAXES AND LOANS

From a superficial or aggregative point of view, de Viti and Ricardo make similar, if not identical claims about the equivalence between taxes and loans. The equivalence is an accounting identity from the perspective of double-entry accounting applied to some closed entity that contains all of the participants in the public debt transaction. If debt transactions are wholly contractual, as they are within the presuppositions of the cooperative state, public debt leaves all individual balance sheets unaffected. Public debt is not a source of net wealth to any person within the rubric of de Viti's cooperative state. It is easy to see how de Viti could have been described as the 'Italian Ricardo'. For Ricardo, equivalence was treated as an accounting identity, as Robert Barro (1974) explains in his well-cited explanation of how the issuance of government bonds does not increase aggregate net worth, and with Barro's treatment of Ricardo standing in sharp contrast to Keynesian-like claims on behalf of the stabilizing properties of fiscal policy. Subsequent to Barro, a considerable body of literature has arisen over Barro's Ricardian implication about the impotence of fiscal policy. Ricardo is an archetypical macro theorist who reasons in terms of global aggregates, leaving out of analytical sight the micro details from which those aggregates are constituted.

Where Ricardo, like most macro theorists today, theorized in top-down fashion whereby changes in macro variables caused micro variables to take on the necessary accommodating values, de Viti was a quintessential micro theorist. For de Viti, aggregate variables were nothing but statistical reflections of underlying micro-level interaction. De Viti recognized that circumstances could exist wherein an extraordinary tax would be equivalent to a public loan, but this equivalence was not a mere accounting identity. To the contrary, it was a working property of a particular set of institutional arrangements. In particular, these were the institutional arrangements associated with de Viti's model of the cooperative state. With respect to the actual conduct of economic life, de Viti (1893) is manifestly anti-Ricardian, as is Benvenuto Griziotti (1917).[3] It was Buchanan (1958,

---

[3] For a general view, see Eusepi (1989).

1960, 1976) who tried to incorporate de Viti's analysis on public debt into
the specific doctrinal body of the Italian School of Public Finance, and
distinguished the Italian tradition from the Anglo-Saxon tradition on
which the Ricardian equivalence proposition rested.

It is a matter of simple arithmetic to affirm Barro's (1974) claim that the
issuance of public debt does not increase aggregate net worth. Suppose
some volume of taxation is replaced by an equal amount of public debt,
as an act of Keynesian-like fiscal policy. The decrease in taxation is, taken
by itself, an increase in disposable income. The concomitant issuance
of government bonds, however, creates an obligation to increase taxes
in future years to amortize the debt. At the time the debt is issued, an
aggregate balance sheet would show no change in net worth. The asset
labeled 'disposable income' is increased, but that increase is offset by an
increase in the liability denoted 'taxes payable'. As a matter of the simple
arithmetic of double-entry accounting, an increase in public debt cannot
increase aggregate net worth. Such an increase, however, can increase net
worth for some people while simultaneously decreasing it for other people,
with this redistribution having much to do with the creation of public debt.
The validity of this point requires de Viti's recognition to be embraced that
macro-level conditions are generated through micro-level interaction, and
with there being numerous distinct forms that such interaction can take.

Despite Buchanan's emphasis on the central role that public expenditure
had in de Viti's analysis, subsequent Italian scholars mostly failed to extend
and amplify de Viti's scheme of non-Ricardian analysis, and embraced
instead the Ricardian scheme of analysis whereby public debt raises
macro questions that can be addressed without addressing any underlying
micro-level questions. For de Viti, however, macro-level statements must
be reconciled with micro-level actions and interactions. In making this
reconciliation, de Viti recognized the erroneous character of Ricardo's
intertemporal comparison that led Ricardo to conclude that an extraordinary tax and public loan were necessarily equivalent. De Viti recognized that the two could be equivalent, but there was no necessity that they
actually be equivalent. Ricardo's analysis was a simple exercise in macro
aggregation. In contrast, de Viti recognized that macro-level variables
were emergent by-products of micro-level interactions that were governed
by some institutional framework that structured those interactions. To
de Viti, equivalence is a possibility that would arise only if public and
private allocations were equally efficient at the relevant margins of activity.
According to de Viti, the cost has to be analyzed by comparing present and
future utility and 'by reasoning on the difference'. This difference, de Viti
wrote, 'is the new premise of a new problem so that any reasoning dealing
with contributed goods only, without considering public goods that are

provided or dealing with the utility of public goods without referring to costs, would be erroneous' (1898, p. 114). It is precisely with making this mistake that de Viti charges Ricardo.[4]

To avoid Ricardo's mistake required de Viti to develop an analytical framework that enabled public debt to emerge within some institutionally reasonable and plausible system of political economy. De Viti recognized that his purely cooperative state was a limiting idealization that was never fully realized in democratic political systems. On this point, it is perhaps also worth mentioning that de Viti served some 20 years as a member of the Italian Parliament, so his work was informed by some conjunction of theoretical and practical interests. Michele Giuranno and Manuela Mosca (2016) present a careful examination of de Viti's political realism in this respect, which shows that de Viti never confused his limiting ideal of a cooperative state with actual democracies. In this respect, de Viti's (1930) collection of essays characterizing 30 years of political struggles shows clearly that the cooperative state might stand as some model appropriate for the end of history but it was not a reliable guide to understanding the course of historical life.

ACTUAL DEMOCRACY AS SEMI-COOPERATIVE STATE

While de Viti articulated a model of a cooperative state, his interest in doing so created a useful framework for thinking about collective activity in an explanatory manner. In this respect, starting from his first work in public finance in 1888, de Viti sought to place public finance on an explanatory footing, in sharp contrast to the strongly normative or tutorial position it had in the hands of most theorists. De Viti's model of the cooperative state brought forward such commonalities of economic organization through markets as utility, demand, cost, and organization so as to bring those commonalities to bear on the economic organization of collective activity. De Viti (1930) was also well aware that actual democratic arrangements bore but an imperfect resemblance to his idealized model of the cooperative state.

In actual democratic settings there is no necessity that public debt be self-extinguishing. It must be self-extinguishing within the framework of the cooperative state, for the state within that framework had the same properties of consensual interaction among participants as did a market

---

[4] The critique that de Viti addresses to Ricardo regarding his exclusion of benefits can be extended to the Keynesian theory on costs.

economy grounded in private property and freedom of contract. Within a market economy, personal debt is self-extinguishing, which means that personal debt is not an instrument by which a borrower can increase his or her net worth, as against postponing redemption of some liabilities, and paying for that postponement by paying interest. An individual might refuse to discharge a debt, thereby transferring wealth from lender to borrower to the extent that refusal is successful. Within actual democratic polities there are numerous ways that default and repudiation can be baked into the fiscal cake, so to speak. Each of these ways involves one margin or another along which the ideal of the wholly cooperative state is violated, in which case public debt can become a political instrument that allows friends to be rewarded and enemies punished, along the lines that Carl Schmitt (1932) set forth in his analysis of the autonomy of the political in society. This can happen both with externally held debt and with internally held debt.

COOPERATIVE STATE DEFAULT WITH EXTERNAL DEBT

By de Viti's contractual construction of the cooperative state, public debt is self-extinguishing; however, this self-extinguishing feature is a product of de Viti's presumption that the transactions that generate public debt are confined within the state. De Viti's pure cooperative model is an *in vitro* construction consisting of a small closed economy with a small – although not minimalist – government.[5] The extent of politically organized activity depends on the relative efficiency of public expenditures and private expenditures on a project-by-project basis. Under these restrictive conditions, resorting to a public loan is to treat the loan as if it were an intertemporal exchange where the creation of debt is a transaction whereby lenders pay current taxes for borrowers, and with those borrowers discharging their obligations according to the terms of the debt contract. In de Viti's logic, the public loan is a clearing transaction between each member of the cooperative qua producer and each single saver qua consumer. In the end, the public loan is a general clearing account where the net value of both individual and aggregate transactions is zero.

This situation changes once foreigners can buy debt instruments on credit markets. Public debt is no longer confined to the members of a state that issues the debt, as some instruments of public debt can be held by

---

[5]   On the minimalist government see Roth (2002).

foreigners. The opening of the credit market to foreigners can undermine the cooperative state by changing the political dynamics inside the issuing state. No longer does public debt entail the state acting as an intermediary between borrowers and lenders within the state. A foreign subscriber to public debt can do so as an investor, reflecting the reach of an international market in credit instruments. The existence of such a market, however, can bring about the end of the cooperative state because both the automatic self-extinction of public debt and the equivalence between debt financing and tax financing are undermined by the presence of an international credit market which opens a channel of debt default even if the institutional arrangement of the state promotes internal consensus.

To be sure, de Viti seems to follow a different path, along which he tries to extend his cooperative model made up of three individuals with the same income but coming from different sources (liquid assets, landowners and professionals) to the case of external debt. A brief outline of this model would be appropriate before raising doubt on its feasibility. Let's give an Italian flavor to the narrative and assume that Primus, Secundus and Tertius are a landowner, a capitalist and a professional respectively. Let's also assume that Primus and Tertius are taxpayers of the cooperative state and Secundus, who is a foreigner and bond subscriber, is a capitalist who holds his assets in liquid form. De Viti claims that there is no difference between two distinct situations. In the closed credit market, the capitalist lends his money to Primus and Tertius to pay their tax bills, with Secundus paying his tax bill directly to exemplify the equivalence between an extraordinary tax and a set of private loans. In the open credit market, Secundus buys government-issued bonds, with the state using the proceeds to finance state activity in lieu of tax payments by Primus and Tertius.

However ingenious this theoretical construction is, it leaves us puzzled. While in the case of an internal debt Secundus pays his tax bill directly, in the open market where Secundus is simply a subscriber and not a taxpayer, the equivalence between tax and debt vanishes. When the capitalist is a foreigner, more complex mechanisms come into play. Unlike the pure cooperative model, in this case there is a shortage of internal liquidity since the government would be simply unable to levy an extraordinary tax on foreigners. The equivalence between tax and debt requires that there be a genuine choice possible between the two options. This situation, however, is not consistent with market transactions where cooperative relationships are absent. It is precisely the fact that Secundus is not a member of the cooperative polity that renders invalid the identity between producer and consumer on which the cooperative model hinges. As is well known, the non-coincidence between producer and consumer is the presupposition or precondition for the exchange and, hence, also for the exchange between those who lend and those who borrow. This precondition of exchange is not an attribute of the cooperative state. It is rather proper for a competitive state where incomes are not homogeneous, either intra- or inter-generationally.

In the democratic state, government is still an intermediary, as it was in de Viti's cooperative state, save that producers and consumers are different individuals and so are taxpayers and bond subscribers. Hence, when one moves from a single country setting to an international setting, things change dramatically, and differently from what was described in the three-individual examples above. International relationships can be sketched by two extreme profiles. Let A and B denote the two countries under consideration, whose relationships are open to both real exchanges and monetary exchanges. In this open market setting, competition does not concern only A's and B's enterprises, but also the government debt of A and B, which have to sell their bonds. Let us imagine that A's savers find bonds offered by B more palatable and accordingly they buy B's bonds. Assuming an extreme case, all A's savers, or most of them, could buy bonds issued by B's government. This is a likely event in a democratic state where savers maximize their expected results and where the cooperative state presuppositions cannot be applied. By subscribing B's bonds, it is as if A's savers wanted to punish their government, as a sort of voting with their feet. However, a punishment on A's government is not equal to a punishment on A's future generation. And in fact, a punishment on government may generate an advantage for A's future generation. Even in the extreme case in which A's government may default, the future generation could survive thanks to the accrued interest on B's bonds owned by A's savers. This point is an interesting one because it shows the limits of a position *à la* Barro where pure altruism allows insulating government from international competition.

Mutatis mutandis, we would have the same scenario if B's savers did not trust their government and bought A's bonds. On the whole, the two alternatives are able to show not only the limits of Barro's altruism, but also the difficulty that one encounters by extending the presuppositions of the cooperative state to a democratic setting.

The relevance of the distinction between internal debt and external debt, based on the aphorism 'we owe it to ourselves', heralded by Abba Lerner (1943, 1944), has been under vigorous attack by Buchanan (1958), who claims that such a distinction is of a marginal kind since it is contingent on the institutional setting. In particular, Buchanan clarifies that resorting to an external debt allows a larger national gross income, but once interest is deducted, net national income is the same in the two cases. Buchanan's stance is central for also clarifying de Viti's analysis. International indebtedness turns de Viti's governments from intermediaries of producers' and consumers' cooperatives into competitive governments, as political enterprises maximizing their own interests. Thinking of canceling competition between or among governments in order to extend the cooperative model to international relationships is, conversely, to give rise to collusive relationships where governments are not agents of taxpayers, but rather interest groups.

A further clarification is needed here. Intergovernmental competition on available savings makes evident how the aphorism 'we owe it to ourselves' hides competition and ends up by considering the whole debt as it were an internal debt. Differently from de Viti, to whom debt extinction may result from a generalization or democratization process, Abba Lerner conceives of debt as self-extinguished from birth. Hence public debt will never be a problem. To de Viti, in contrast, public debt can generate problems of the form he associated with economic crises (see de Viti, 1898). In framing debt within the general theory of crisis, de Viti emphasizes the evaluation mistakes made by the previous generation. But there is a second aspect in de Viti's thought, which we think is more general, that has been ignored by the literature. This aspect is linked to the change in preferences over time and to the lack of a price mechanism able to quickly capture the disequilibrium between demand and supply, of which the crisis is the result. Debt and crisis intertwine and do not self-extinguish, and may instead lead to default.

DEMOCRATIC STATE DEFAULT WITH INTERNAL DEBT

The relevant officials within a government that shifts from tax finance to loan finance must have concluded that loan finance is less costly from their perspective than tax finance. This might well induce those officials to support expansions in spending that are wasteful when compared to the displaced private alternative activities. If indebtedness were forbidden, those wasteful expenditures would not have occurred. De Viti observes that if this logic regarding public loans were applied to the private loan system, an excessive demand for loans would result because entrepreneurs would not bear personal liability for their losses. This situation is actually not all that far-fetched in contemporary times where many private businesses receive political support and largesse through loan guarantees and subsidies. In numerous ways these days, a good deal of public debt finds its way into the support of nominally private enterprises.

Where de Viti's model of the cooperative state assumes a deep-level homogeneity among the members of the internal polity, de Viti also recognized that actual democratic polities contain no such homogeneity. Hence, there are numerous margins along which public debt can be used to transfer tax burdens from what would have resulted from an extraordinary tax. With respect to taxation, de Viti developed his model of the cooperative state under the presumption that public expenditures were normally financed by a flat tax on income. The basis on which de Viti made this assumption was that the demand for public outputs probably varied in proportion to income. While the relation between income and demand is ultimately an empirical proposition that can be subject to examination, we shall simply accept it here because our interest lies in explaining de Viti's thinking and not in examining the accuracy or plausibility of his assumptions. In consequence, we can assume that what de Viti has in mind by way of extraordinary taxation is a surtax imposed on a pre-existing flat tax. For instance, an ordinary flat rate of 10 percent might be increased to 15 percent through the addition of the extraordinary component of the tax.

If there were no public borrowing, it is reasonable to think, as did de Viti, that some people would discharge the extraordinary component of their tax liability by drawing down their balances on other assets, including cash. Other people would just as surely borrow through private credit channels. In any event, total government revenues would increase through the extraordinary tax, regardless of the extent to which those revenues came from sales of privately held assets relative to privately arranged loans. Whatever the mix, public involvement would be limited to the collection of increased taxes, along with expenditure of those tax revenues. We might further stipulate, in keeping with the tenets of de Viti's cooperative state model, that this fiscal operation is agreeable to everyone. There would be no public debt, and the private debt induced by the extraordinary tax would be self-extinguishing.

Alternatively, suppose that a public loan is issued to finance the added public expenditure. In the previous situation, a set of contractual obligations is created between a set of private lenders and those taxpayers who choose to pay their extraordinary tax by borrowing rather than by selling off other assets. When public debt is created, a governmental entity replaces the set of private creditors. Is this replacement a matter of indifference, or might it have significant consequences? There is good reason to think it will have significant consequences, and in a way that represents a form of debt default. To be sure, default is not limited to some repudiation of existing debt instruments. That is but one manner of default. Within the framework of the cooperative state, default pertains to any operation through which public debt influences individual net worth, regardless of what might happen to some aggregate measure of net worth, for it is individual positions and not aggregate measures that induce action.

Earlier we explained that default on external debt could generate an increase in net worth for internal citizens. It's also possible for internal debt to redistribute wealth among citizens, in which case those who gain through the issue of debt are repudiating their obligations to those who lose from the issue of debt. In this instance, the baseline for judging whether default has occurred is the set of contractual terms that would have arisen within the framework of the cooperative state. Those terms would surely have mirrored the credit market terms that would have emerged when some taxpayers choose to arrange private loans rather than sell other assets. Is it reasonable or plausible to perform the conceptual experiment of replacing a set of private loans with a politically administered loan program, and conclude in Ricardian fashion that nothing of any significance has changed? As an act of creative imagination, anything is always imaginable. As an exercise in plausible reasoning (Polya, 1954), however, it strains all credulity to assert that the replacement of a network of market loans with public debt will have no other effect than to induce changes in individual balance sheets, with some taxpayers incurring a future liability while other taxpayers reduce their present asset holdings.

The officials who guide the activities of democratic entities are not residual claimants to their activities. A private lender who mismanages the portfolio he manages will suffer a decline in net worth, and could even become insolvent and file for bankruptcy. This outcome is impossible for democratic entities. Mismanagement is obviously possible, but it manifests itself as a cost to taxpayers and not as a cost to enterprise managers, reflecting Wagner's (2016) recognition that politics is a peculiar and not an ordinary form of business activity. Furthermore, democratic polities are riven with margins of heterogeneity whereby gains to some people entail losses to others. For instance, de Viti thought in terms of a flat rate of tax on all income. Contemporary tax systems, however, exempt a great deal of income from the tax base. Within the United States, for instance, roughly half the adult population is exempt from the federal income tax. To the extent that borrowing enables an increase in public expenditure within what is clearly a semi-cooperative democracy, debt-financed expenditure will to some extent be self-repudiating and not self-extinguishing.

A SIDEBAR REMARK ON CAPITAL BUDGETING

Fiscal and budgetary scholars often distinguish between current and capital budgeting. The central idea in advancing this distinction is to create a separation between those objects of expenditure that are used up during the current year and those that provide service over several years. The capital budgeting idea would place what are judged to be capital expenditures into separate accounts that are amortized over some suitable number of years. Each year, the appropriate amount for amortization would be transferred to the current budget. Within this budgetary format, current spending would be financed by taxation and capital spending would be financed by public debt. Capital budgeting is often practiced by corporations, and the extension of capital budgeting to governments would seem to be little more than the extension of good business practices to governments.

Once it is recognized that government are *peculiar* forms of business (Wagner, 2016), capital budgeting can easily be misused. The institutional arrangements by which commercial corporations are governed render them as instances of cooperative collectivities in de Viti's sense. This is not the case with democratic polities. Suppose the capital budgeting idea is inserted into a democratic political constitution. The first issue that must be faced is how to distinguish between current and capital expenditures. Not far behind making this distinction is the need to determine the period of time over which capital expenditures will be amortized. Also to be determined is the locus of responsibility and capacity for making these determinations. In modern, large-scale polities, we may be sure that such determinations will not be made by some such abstract notion of 'the citizenry'. They will be made by bureaucratic officials and legislators and in an environment where knowledge is concentrated among intensely interested insiders to the activities in question.

To illustrate in stark relief the problem of inherent ambiguity that capital budgeting entails in democratic polities, consider an agency that is confined by a balanced budget requirement when the head of the agency would like to take his managerial staff on a week-long retreat in some remote venue. The balanced budget requirement would prevent this activity. Such activity might, however, pass muster in the presence of capital budgeting. What would be necessary is to classify the retreat as an investment in enhancing future performance. In this respect, it could be claimed that it is necessary to gain emotional distance from daily organizational activities for management to be able calmly and systematically to evaluate approaches to agency reorganization that would improve future performance. What is in play, then, is a claim that such a current expenditure should be classified as a capital item, so should be incorporated into a capital budget, with the expense amortized over some period of years. While this example might seem a bit far-fetched, it points all the same to recognition that the distinction between current and capital expenditures contains unavoidable margins of arbitrariness. In light of those unavoidable margins of ambiguity, political officials will have margins of action along which they can classify actions to promote their desires.

CONCLUDING REMARKS

Although in democracy government plays an intermediary role, this intermediation is different from that developed in de Viti's cooperative model. In a democratic model, taxpayers and subscribers are not the same and government intermediation is a process that interconnects a share of the population (taxpayers) with another share (subscribers). As we have already seen, while in a cooperative model taxpayers and subscribers are the same individuals, it is not so in the democratic model and also in the case of external public debt. The latter two cases lead us to conclude that there isn't any automatic extinction of the debt. Contrary to the pre-democratic model, where the sovereign debt was a personal debt,[6] in the democratic model, where the parliamentary assembly creates public debt in the name and on behalf of taxpayers, public debt also raises ethical issues. While the Ricardian equivalence theorem is not a good fit for the democratic model, de Viti's non-equivalence theorem is a good fit because it also incorporates the expenditure side into his model. De Viti does not conceive of public debt as an ordinary rational problem, for he associates public debt with extraordinary economic crisis. Thus, economic crisis raises intertemporal and not intergenerational issues because public debt is not shifted to future generations. But we believe that the economic crisis/debt is at once de Viti's strong point and his Achilles heel. The crisis, in fact, is not so much the result of an intentional project of transferring costs to future generations as it is the inexorable outcome of politically directed choices inside institutional arrangements that escape the confines of the cooperative state.

To de Viti, the economic crisis has, in fact, its origin in a wrong evaluation of the investments that have yielded lower levels of benefits than expected. However, this is only part of the story. De Viti conceives of the crisis as a failure in investments presuming that all public expenditures financed through debt are employed in investments without considering that the government has a proclivity to wasteful expenditures, for it is guided by the conviction that public debt is less costly than an extraordinary tax and even an ordinary tax.

---

[6]   On this see Eusepi and Wagner (2012).

REFERENCES

Barro, R. (1974), 'Are government bonds net worth?', *Journal of Political Economy*, **82**: 1095–118.

Buchanan, J.M. (1958), *Public Principles of Public Debt*, Homewood: Richard D. Irwin.

Buchanan, J.M. (1960), '"La scienza delle finanze": The Italian tradition in fiscal theory', in J.M. Buchanan, *Fiscal Theory and Political Economy: Selected Essays*, Chapel Hill: The University of North Carolina Press.

Buchanan, J.M. (1976), 'Barro on the Ricardian equivalence theorem', *Journal of Political Economy*, **84**: 337–42, pp. 24–74.

De Viti de Marco, A. (1888), *Il Carattere Teorico dell'Economia Finanziaria*, Rome: Pasqualucci.

De Viti de Marco, A. (1893), 'La pressione tributaria dell'imposta e del prestito', *Giornale degli Economisti*, **6** (2) (January–March): 38–67, 216–31.

De Viti de Marco, A. (1898), 'Contributo alla teoria del prestito pubblico', in *Saggi di Economia e Finanza*, Rome: *Giornale degli Economisti*, pp. 61–123.

De Viti de Marco, A. (1930), *Un Trentennio di Lotte Politiche*, Rome: Collezione Meridionale Editrice.

De Viti de Marco, A. (1936), *First Principles of Public Finance*, London: Jonathan Cape.

Eusepi, G. (1989), 'Buchanan's critique of the neoclassical model and the rediscovery of the Italian tradition in public finance', *Rivista Internazionale di Scienze Economiche e Commerciali*, **36** (9): 801–22.

Eusepi, G. and R.E. Wagner (2012), 'Indebted state versus intermediary state: Who owes what to whom?', *Constitutional Political Economy*, **23**: 199–212.

Giuranno, M. and M. Mosca (2016), 'Political realism and models of the state: Antonio de Viti de Marco and the origins of public choice', working paper, Dipartimento di Scienze dell'Economia, Università del Salento.

Griziotti, B. (1917), 'La diversa pressione del prestito e dell'imposta', *Giornale degli Economisti e Rivista di Statistica*, **54** (3): 313–34.

Lerner, A.P. (1943), 'Functional finance and the federal debt', *Social Research*, **10**: 38–51.

Lerner, A.P. (1944), *The Economics of Control*, New York: Macmillan.

Polya, G. (1954), *Mathematics and Plausible Reasoning*, 2 vols, Princeton: Princeton University Press.

Ricardo, D. (1817 [1951]), *The Principles of Political Economy and Taxation*, Cambridge: Cambridge University Press.

Roth, T.P. (2002), *The Ethics and the Economics of Minimalist Government*, Cheltenham, UK and Northampton, MA, USA: Edward Elgar Publishing.

Schmitt, C. (1932) [1996]), *The Autonomy of the Political*, Chicago: University of Chicago Press.

Wagner, R.E. (2016), *Politics as a Peculiar Business: Insights from a Theory of Entangled Political Economy*, Cheltenham, UK and Northampton, MA, USA: Edward Elgar Publishing.

2. Governing the market for sovereign bailouts

Karsten Mause*

2.1 INTRODUCTION

In their best-selling book *This Time is Different: Eight Centuries of Financial Folly*, Reinhart and Rogoff (2009) present a long list of historical examples of sovereign debt defaults. To avoid this potential outcome, in the wake of the 2007/2008 financial crisis the European Union (EU) member states Greece (2010), Ireland (2010), Portugal (2011), Spain (2012) and Cyprus (2013) were bailed out by other EU member states. The figures in brackets indicate the starting year of the respective rescue operation. With the exception of Spain, the aforementioned countries also received bailout loans from the International Monetary Fund (IMF). There is a public debate and a vast amount of politico-economic literature discussing various instruments of fiscal governance that may be suitable for preventing solvency problems and future bailouts of countries and (sub-)national jurisdictions. Following the advice of constitutional economists (for example, Buchanan and Wagner, 1977; Brennan and Eusepi, 2004), in many countries fiscal rules such as public spending limits, balanced budget rules or public debt ceilings have been established at the (sub-)national level (for cross-country reports, see Burret and Feld, 2014; Bova et al., 2015). Essentially and implicitly, this literature discusses the issue of how to regulate the 'demand side' of the 'market' for sovereign bailouts. As will be explained in more detail below, in this context the term 'sovereign bailout' means that a sovereign nation state is rescued from bankruptcy in some way by another actor. In other words, this bailout operation averts a 'sovereign default' of this state (often also called 'sovereign debt default'; Panizza et al., 2009).

* The author is grateful to Bruno S. Frey, Friedrich Gröteke, Andrea Rieck, Jennifer Rontganger, Ludger Schuknecht and the participants of the European Center for the Study of Public Choice (ECSPC) 2016 Conference at Sapienza University of Rome for their useful comments and suggestions.

The present chapter complements the aforementioned strand of research by pointing out that – from a politico-economic perspective – there may not only be a demand for a bailout by financially distressed countries but, at the same time, there are actors such as other countries, central banks or international organizations, such as the IMF, which may decide to (not) offer a bailout to countries in financial difficulties. More specifically, inspired by institutional economic research on the governance of (non-)market transactions (for example, Kasper et al., 2012; Ostrom, 1990; Williamson, 1996), this chapter discusses the relatively neglected issue of how to regulate (or 'govern') the 'supply side' of the market for sovereign bailouts. Should it be left to the discretion of potential rescuers such as the governments of other countries, the governing boards of central banks, or decision-makers of international organizations to respond to the question of whether 'To bail out, or not to bail out'? Or should there be (constitutional) rules that regulate the supply of sovereign bailouts by defining specific conditions under which a potential rescuer is allowed to offer a bailout? In this context, one may also ask from the viewpoint of 'normative individualism' as applied in Constitutional Political Economy whether the citizens in a rescuer jurisdiction in their role as 'the ultimate sovereigns' (Buchanan, 1991, p. 227) should have a say in this matter.

The chapter proceeds as follows. Section 2.2 defines the 'market' for sovereign bailouts. Section 2.3 discusses the possibilities and limitations of regulating the supply side (that is, governments, central banks, international organizations) of this market. Section 2.4 discusses whether the citizens of potential rescuer jurisdictions should have a say in the matter under investigation via a bailout referendum. Finally, section 2.5 provides some concluding remarks.

2.2   THE MARKET FOR SOVEREIGN BAILOUTS

There are basically three types of actors with the instruments to bail out a country. There may be a 'sovereign bailout' (as defined above) by other jurisdictions, by central banks, or by international organizations such as the IMF – or by all three types of actors together (which has happened, for example, in the EU since 2010). Other jurisdictions may rescue a certain country from going bankrupt, for instance, (1) by injecting money in the form of monetary subsidies; (2) through lending money with favorable credit conditions; (3) by putting up a guarantee of payment of loans; or (4) via purchasing government bonds newly issued by the financially distressed country at a lower interest rate than the capital market would demand. In contrast to such rescue operations, 'normal' institutionalized fiscal transfers between countries (for example, the redistribution mechanism within the EU's budget) are usually not denoted as bailouts in the public finance literature. Another form of sovereign bailout is that an international organization such as the IMF offers financial assistance (for example, IMF bailout loans) in order to prevent a sovereign default of a country. Moreover, a country may be rescued by 'its' central bank. The latter can help to reduce a country's debt burden basically in two ways. First, by setting a lower interest rate in the respective currency area, thereby expanding the money supply and, in so doing, trying to inflate away (real) debt (that is, trying to reduce the real value of debt by inflation). Second, by buying the bonds of an indebted jurisdiction at a lower interest rate than the capital market would demand; this would also lead to an expansion of money supply and, potentially, inflation (see, for example, Rieck and Schuknecht, 2016 for more details). These rescue operations are easy to accomplish when a country's government has direct access to 'its' central bank (we return to this in section 2.3.2).

At this point one may wonder why some economists and other critical observers take a skeptical, if not hostile, view toward sovereign bailouts. Someone rescuing someone else is usually seen as a very positive and very welcomed activity in many everyday life contexts. However, in the context of sovereign bailouts there is the (potential) problem that such a rescue operation under certain conditions may change the incentives of the actors involved in the 'bailout game' in a manner that increases the likelihood of future fiscal crises and bailouts. For instance, if the government of a jurisdiction can expect a bailout then this may weaken this government's incentive to run a sound fiscal policy. In other words, a government with bailout expectations 'may have weak incentives to conduct [its] fiscal policies in such a way as to minimize the risk of bailouts' (Wildasin, 2004, p. 252). This potential problem is discussed under the keywords 'moral hazard problem' (for example, Persson and Tabellini, 1996) and 'soft budget constraint problem' (for example, Rodden et al., 2003) in the public finance literature. However, a more-or-less explicit bailout guarantee may not only affect a jurisdiction's behavior – in the eyes of potential creditors such a guarantee is a strong signal that lending money to this particular jurisdiction is nearly risk-free. That the creation of bailout expectations is not only a theoretical issue can be illustrated with the examples of German fiscal federalism (Baskaran, 2012; Fink and Stratmann, 2011) and the European Economic and Monetary Union/Eurozone (Blankart, 2015). In both cases, bailout expectations on the part of jurisdictions (and their citizens) as well as capital-market participants to some extent – and alongside other explanatory factors – explain why some German states (for example, Bremen) and some member countries of the Eurozone (for example, Greece) got into financial difficulties in the past.

Against this background it is not surprising that there is much politico-economic research focusing on the issue of how to design the institutions in a country or a 'club' of countries (such as the EU or the Eurozone) in a way that creates incentives for (sub-)national governments to run a sound fiscal policy. The latter can be expected to reduce the likelihood of fiscal crises and bailouts. There is, for instance, a large body of theoretical and empirical literature that analyzes the design and effects of (constitutional) fiscal rules such as public spending limits, balanced budget rules or public debt ceilings (for surveys, see Mause and Groeteke, 2012; Burret and Feld, 2014; Bova et al., 2015). Complementing this research dealing with the issue of how to reduce the *demand* for future bailouts, in the next section we will take a closer look at the actors on the *supply* side of the market for sovereign bailouts, which under certain conditions may be willing to rescue financially distressed countries. As sovereign bailouts may have serious side-effects such as the 'moral hazard problem' and the 'soft budget constraint problem' sketched above, the discussion particularly focuses on whether there are actors and institutional mechanisms having the power to control the 'bailout supply' by governments of foreign jurisdictions (2.3.1), central banks (2.3.2) and international organizations (2.3.3) as potential rescuers.

2.3   THE GOVERNANCE OF THE SUPPLY SIDE OF THE BAILOUT MARKET

2.3.1   Foreign Governments as Potential Rescuers

As mentioned above, one important type of player in the 'bailout game' is jurisdictions that have the financial power to bail out other jurisdictions. In the simplest case, the government of jurisdiction A has the exclusive power to decide whether or not another jurisdiction should be bailed out by A. If citizens of jurisdiction A are dissatisfied with their government's bailout decision, then they can – provided that A is a well-functioning democracy (including freedom of speech, freedom of assembly, press freedom and so on) – use their voice option in the sense of Hirschman (1970). That is, dissatisfied citizens/taxpayers may, for example, (1) write angry letters to the editors of newspapers; (2) publish their critical comments in social media and the online forums of different media; or (3) participate in anti-bailout demonstrations. If many people are dissatisfied with their government's bailout decision then this may result in a significant decrease in government popularity and may reduce that government's chances of getting re-elected (Kirchgässner, forthcoming; Lewis-Beck and Stegmaier, 2013). As another form of voice, dissatisfied citizens may simply punish the government of A in the next election for their bailout decision. And, of course, dissatisfied citizens may make use of their exit option in the sense of Hirschman (1970; 1993): that is, they may 'vote with their feet' and emigrate to another jurisdiction.

If we assume in line with public choice theory (Downs, 1957; Mueller, 2003) that governments are interested in getting re-elected, then such governments will carefully weigh the political costs and benefits of their decision to bail out another jurisdiction. In this context, a government has to check whether the aforementioned potential responses of citizen-voters to a bailout decision are really endangering this government's re-election. How many citizens of jurisdiction A will really invest time, energy and money to exit to another jurisdiction due to the bailout decision by the government of A? Citizens that are dissatisfied with this specific government decision may appreciate many other factors that make living in jurisdiction A a great pleasure. Likewise, a government confronted with the question 'To bail out, or not to bail out' may estimate how many of its citizens will really invest time, energy or even money by using their voice option. Maybe the government of A will be able to convince many of the citizen-voters who are currently dissatisfied with the bailout decision that this particular decision is necessary and will not significantly harm the welfare of jurisdiction A. And if, prior to the next election, there should still be a fraction of the electorate that are dissatisfied with government A's decision to bail out another jurisdiction, then it is questionable whether this single issue will be the pivotal issue (alongside unemployment, environmental concerns, and many other issues or policy areas) that leads to that government's replacement.

In many real world democracies, governments thinking about bailing out other jurisdictions do not only have to evaluate the impact of this decision on the voting market but also have to take into account that there might be other political institutions within a society's system of checks and balances that have the power to veto a government's bailout decision. That is, there might be other actors that act as '*veto players*' in the sense of Tsebelis (2002). For example, since 2010 the Members of Parliament (MPs) in the German national parliament (*Bundestag*) had several opportunities to vote on the various 'rescue packages' for Greece and other EU countries. In all of these decisions a majority of MPs voted in favor of Germany's participation in these bailout operations. More precisely, the German government had already agreed to be part of these operations, but this agreement had to be ratified by the national parliament – which was rather unproblematic as the national government in the German political system is usually backed by a majority in the national parliament; though it should be mentioned that also a number of MPs from opposition parties voted 'pro bailout' and a number of MPs from government parties voted 'contra bailout' (see Degner and Leuffen, 2016 for more details).

Moreover, the German Federal Constitutional Court (*Bundesverfassungsgericht*) as an additional potential veto player did not stop the participation of Germany in the EU's bailout policy. In 2014 this court refused several constitutional complaints against Germany's participation in the so-called European Stability Mechanism (ESM). This permanent 'bailout fund' (or 'rescue facility') was established in 2012 by the Eurozone member countries. The claimants had argued that Germany's participation in the ESM, which is located at the supranational EU-level, violates the German national parliament's constitutionally guaranteed budget autonomy. However, in its 2014 decision the German Federal Constitutional Court argued that Germany's ESM participation is in accordance with the German constitution as the national parliament's participation and control rights in the ESM – according to the court – are sufficient. It should be mentioned that more than 37 000 claimants (legal scholars, members of parliament from various political parties, and other citizens) joined one of the aforementioned constitutional complaints (namely, the complaint 'Europe needs more democracy'). This constitutional complaint was the largest complaint in the history of the German Federal Constitutional Court established in 1951.

It should also be noted that the 2014 decision of the court confirmed its 2012 'express decision', in which a complaint of an opposition party in the German national parliament (the Green Party) against Germany's participation in the ESM was refused. After the constitutional court's 2012 decision, Germany was the last of the 19 Eurozone countries to ratify the ESM at the national level. In eight countries the ESM was ratified by parliament and in the remaining countries by parliament plus the second chamber. In no country did the citizens have the opportunity to vote on their respective country's participation in the ESM in a referendum. Finally, it should be mentioned that an additional potential veto player located at the supranational EU-level – the Court of Justice of the European Union (CJEU) – in 2012 refused a complaint against the ESM submitted by an independent MP in the Irish parliament (see Feld et al., 2016). In line with other critical observers in Germany and other EU countries, this MP argued that the bailout fund ESM violated the so-called 'no-bailout clause' in the EU treaties (we return to this clause below).

As we have seen, in many real world jurisdictions there are already mechanisms such as the *re-election constraint* (that is, voters' voice/retribution option) as well as potential *veto players* (for example, parliaments and constitutional courts) that may influence or even block a government's decision to bail out another jurisdiction. These mechanisms are part of the governance of the supply side of the market for sovereign bailouts. Consequently, it may not only be the financial power of a jurisdiction that determines whether or not it is able to bail out other jurisdictions – but there may be politico-institutional factors that make it difficult or even impossible for a jurisdiction to supply a bailout. The strongest form of regulating the supply of a bailout would be to establish a constitutional rule which prescribes that jurisdiction A is not allowed to bail out other jurisdictions. As briefly mentioned above, the EU treaties contain such a *'no-bailout clause'*:

> The Union shall not be liable for or assume the commitments of central governments, regional, local or other public authorities, other bodies governed by public law, or public undertakings of any Member State, without prejudice to mutual financial guarantees for the joint execution of a specific project. A Member State shall not be liable for or assume the commitments of central governments, regional, local or other public authorities, other bodies governed by public law, or public undertakings of another Member State, without prejudice to mutual financial guarantees for the joint execution of a specific project. (Art. 125(1) Treaty on the Functioning of the European Union, TFEU).

As pointed out by Ostrom (1990) and other political economists, in real world settings it is often not sufficient to have certain rules but there must be someone who enforces these rules and who sanctions breaches of these rules. To illustrate, in the EU context, the aforementioned 'no-bailout clause' has not in fact prevented Greece and other EU countries from being bailed out by their fellow member states since 2010 (see also Vaubel, 2012). And the Court of Justice of the European Union in a 2012 decision interpreted that the permanent *bailout* fund ESM is in accordance with EU law and compatible with the *'no-bailout* clause' in Article 125 TFEU.

In summary, citizen-voters/taxpayers that are dissatisfied with a government's decision to bail out another jurisdiction have the power to 'punish' this government by using the mechanisms of voice and exit sketched above. In the extreme case, they may throw this government out of office *ex post*, that is, in the next election if the dissatisfied voters are in the majority.[1]

---

[1] According to Popper (1999, p. 94), '[t]here are in fact only two forms of state: those in which it is possible to get rid of a government without bloodshed, and those in which this is not possible. [. . .] Usually the first form is called "democracy" and the second "dictatorship" or "tyranny". [. . .] Any government that can be thrown out has a strong incentive to act in a way that makes people content with it. And this incentive is lost if the government knows it cannot be so easily ousted.'

However, in Germany and other representative democracies, citizen-voters do not have the power to prevent their government *ex ante* from bailing out another jurisdiction – as long as the constitution of the potential rescuer jurisdiction is not changed in a way that allows citizens to vote on the potential bailout in a binding bailout referendum (we return to this possible direct-democratic mechanism in section 2.4). And if we assume that the new government fulfills the bailout package granted by the previous government (that is, the latter leaves a 'policy legacy' in the sense of Rose, 1990), then dissatisfied citizens staying in this jurisdiction have to live with this policy legacy.

Citizens with a preference for 'no bailout' may pin their hopes on the separation of powers in their jurisdiction: that is, they may hope that the jurisdiction's parliament (that is, their elected representatives in the legislature) gets the opportunity to vote *ex ante* on the bailout deal negotiated by government as the executive branch. However, as illustrated above by the German case, it is by no means clear that the majority of parliamentarians would vote against the particular bailout even if many or the majority of people in this jurisdiction have a preference for 'no bailout'. Likewise, it is by no means clear that a constitutional 'no-bailout clause' would prevent a bailout. The executive and legislative branch may ignore this constitutional rule – and the responsible constitutional court (the judiciary) may formulate an *ex post* statement of grounds in which the judges explain why this rule violation was/is still in accordance with the constitution (see again, for example, the German case mentioned above). In the end, citizens/taxpayers with 'no bailout' preferences staying in the rescuer jurisdiction have to live with the bailout.

This, however, may not be the end of the story. Citizens with 'no bailout' preferences, for instance, may overcome the collective action problem in the sense of Olson (1965) and found a political party whose candidates try to get in office in order to get the 'no bailout' preferences existing in this society represented in government or at least in parliament. The latter has happened, for example, in Germany where the political party *Alternative für Deutschland* (AfD = Alternative for Germany) was founded in 2013 as an explicit response to Germany's bailout policy. In the 2014 European Parliament elections, the AfD won 7 out of the 96 German seats in the European Parliament. After the 2017 German national elections, the AfD entered the German national parliament for the first time: the party received 12.6 percent of the votes, was the third biggest party (after CDU/CSU and SPD), and won 94 out of the 709 *Bundestag* seats; in the 2013 *Bundestag* elections, the AfD narrowly missed the 5 percent electoral threshold (AfD vote share = 4.7 percent).

Furthermore, at the time of writing (September 2017), the AfD had about 28 000 members and held a total of 152 seats scattered across 13 of the 16 German state parliaments. This equals a rate of 8.3 percent of all 1821 seats in German state parliaments (see Grimm, 2015 for more details on this party). Moreover, it is safe to say that the EU's 2010-and-beyond bailout policy to some extent – and alongside other explanatory factors – explains the rise of Euroskeptic political parties in other European countries as well (Kriesi and Pappas, 2015; Judis, 2016). The recent developments observable in Europe's political landscape illustrate that bailout decisions may have unintended and unforeseen side-effects.

2.3.2 Central Banks as Potential Rescuers

As mentioned in section 2.2, another important type of actor on the supply side of the market for sovereign bailouts is central banks that have the financial power to bail out countries. In many real world settings, the central bank of a country (for example, the Swiss National Bank) or the central bank of a currency area covering several countries (for example, the European Central Bank, ECB) are deliberately designed as politically independent institutions (Fernández-Albertos, 2015). This political independence shall, among other things, prevent a jurisdiction's government from being able to use the central bank and its monetary policy instruments for fiscal purposes; for example, when a government instructs 'its' central bank to 'print new money' in order to purchase government bonds (that is, 'monetization' of government debt). However, this political independence *could* be used by a central bank (a) to bail out the 'home' country for which this bank is responsible or (b) to bail out a 'foreign' country. To preclude a central bank from using its political independence for bailout operations, one might establish a 'no-bailout clause' in the rules regulating this bank's behavior. An example is the 'no-bailout clause' in Article 123(1) TFEU:

> Overdraft facilities or any other type of credit facility with the European Central Bank or with the central banks of the Member States (hereinafter referred to as 'national central banks') in favor of Union institutions, bodies, offices or agencies, central governments, regional, local or other public authorities, other bodies governed by public law, or public undertakings of Member States shall be prohibited, as shall the purchase directly from them by the European Central Bank or national central banks of debt instruments.

As recent EU history tells us, it cannot be ruled out that central bankers ignore or 'reinterpret' such a 'no-bailout clause'. For example, critical observers in Germany and other EU countries interpret the 'unconventional measures' carried out by the ECB in recent years (for example, the ECB's policy of 'quantitative easing' via purchasing government bonds of a number of heavily indebted EU member states) as a violation of the 'no-bailout clause' in Article 123 TFEU which actually forbids the monetary financing of EU member states (Vaubel, 2012). Of course, people who have the impression that the ECB (1) is violating the 'no-bailout clause' in EU law and (2) is moving beyond its mandate (that is, making *monetary* policy in the Eurozone) with its government bond purchase program (easing the *fiscal* sorrows of some EU member states) may appeal to a national constitutional court or the CJEU. Currently, the German Federal Constitutional Court has to deal with complaints against the ECB's aforementioned 'quantitative easing' program (namely, the ECB's sovereign-bond-buying scheme). It remains to be seen whether the judges will decide that the ECB (1) went beyond its monetary policy mandate, and (2) violated the 'no-bailout clause' (see Feld et al., 2016 for more details).

It is clear that a violation of this clause is only a problem for EU citizens/ taxpayers with 'no bailout' preferences. However, what has to be taken into account in this context is that central banks – unlike democratically elected governments – are non-elected actors (Vibert, 2007). Whether citizens 'like' the decisions of a central bank (that is, the 'popularity' and 'voting market' issue) does not matter for the bank and its employees. In other words, a central bank's bailout decision is a typical 'low-cost decision' in the sense of Kirchgässner (2008, p. 140): 'The decision of the single individual is irrelevant for the individual himself, but it is highly relevant for a single other individual (or for a group of other individuals)' (see also Kirchgässner, 1992; Kirchgässner and Pommerehne, 1993). What could happen, however, is that dissatisfied citizens might protest against a central bank's policy. In extreme cases, such protests may even include assaults on employees of a central bank. Less dramatically, the government of a certain jurisdiction may try to influence a politically independent central bank's behavior by replacing important decision-makers of this bank after these employees' respective term of office. And there may be countries in which politicians or other society members use 'unconventional measures' to get rid of central bankers (Chivers and Kramer, 2006).

In any case, though it might sound a bit fatalistic, recent EU history tells us that it is in fact a mission impossible for elected politicians, citizen-voters and constitutional courts to *immediately* prevent a politically independent central bank (here, the ECB) from exerting some kind of bailout operation although it might not be explicitly labeled as a 'bailout'. And even if after such an operation a constitutional court should find out that this operation was illegal, it can be expected that it is practically impossible to claim back the public money already transferred from the rescued jurisdiction.

2.3.3 International Organizations as Potential Rescuers

Apart from the EU, there are other international organizations which may offer a fiscally distressed EU member state or countries outside this club of European countries a bailout. As mentioned above, the IMF has contributed a share to the bailout packages for Greece, Ireland, Portugal and Cyprus. Moreover, there are the Paris Club (a group of creditor countries) and the London Club (consisting of private creditor banks) who from time to time (try to) negotiate a debt relief for heavily indebted countries (Sturzenegger and Zettelmeyer, 2006). In this context, it should also be noted that the budgetary problems facing many countries in the wake of the recent financial crisis have fueled the debate on the necessity and adequate design of sovereign bankruptcy procedures (see Fuest et al., 2016 for an overview). To date, there exists no sovereign insolvency law, either for the member states of the European Union or for other nations – but informal institutions exist, like the aforementioned Paris Club and London Club that offer a forum for negotiating a sovereign debt relief. Moreover, formal insolvency rules exist at the sub-national level. There are, for example, bankruptcy laws for municipalities in the USA and Switzerland (Blankart, 2011; Duff, 2010).

Without going into the details of these insolvency proceedings, it should be noted that they are designed to offer a highly indebted municipality a 'fresh start' via a 'reorganization of debts', which means not going into liquidation, as is often the case for bankrupt private-sector enterprises.[2] However, from a politico-economic perspective, the possibility that a country could indeed go bankrupt and the existence of legal rules that determine what to do in this situation could have an influence on the supply side of the market for sovereign bailouts: because a sovereign insolvency law may be a measure that (a) possibly reduces the likelihood that other rescuers such as foreign governments (see section 2.3.1) and central banks (2.3.2) offer a bailout, and (b) possibly prevents political activism and discretion in the creditor countries.

Why should the existence of an insolvency law make it more difficult for potential rescuers to carry out a bailout? The government of jurisdiction X has to explain to the public why the citizen-taxpayers in X should rescue the highly indebted jurisdiction Y, which is subject to an insolvency law

---

[2] See Duff (2010, p. 50), referring to the US case: 'The purpose of chapter 9 is to provide a financially-distressed municipality protection from its creditors while it develops and negotiates a plan for adjusting its debts. Reorganisation of the debts of a municipality is typically accomplished either by extending debt maturities, reducing the amount of principal or interest, or refinancing the debt by obtaining a new loan.'

which means (a) that Y is liable for its debts and (b) that there are legal rules prescribing how Y and its creditors (who made a risky investment decision) have to act in such an emergency situation. A central bank faces a similar barrier to a bailout since it has to explain to the *'classe politique'* and the public why – notwithstanding an existing insolvency procedure – the bank is rescuing Y and its creditors. Moreover, potential creditors, expecting that a bailout is less likely due to the bankruptcy law, can be expected to run a more careful lending policy toward jurisdiction Y since their outstanding debits will be (partially) lost if Y becomes insolvent (Blankart and Klaiber, 2006, p. 53; Sutherland et al., 2005, p. 36). This, in turn, constrains Y's borrowing activities: the closer Y moves to the 'bankruptcy abyss', the more difficult it gets to find someone who is willing to give (further) credit. Hence, an insolvency law (combined with a low or no bailout expectation) works in the same direction as the capital-market mechanism which, under certain conditions, disciplines a government's borrowing behavior (Lane, 1993).

Clearly, under real world conditions policymakers and central bankers might find more or less convincing justifications as to why they perceive a bailout to be necessary, which prevents a bankruptcy and the insolvency proceedings. And it is likewise an empirical question, which can only be addressed on a case-by-case basis, whether the vision of an (un)ordered default has a deterrent effect on political decision-makers in a fiscally distressed jurisdiction. A re-election-oriented and/or fiscally conservative government can be expected to take precautionary measures (such as increasing taxes, cutting expenditures, liquidation of assets) in order to remain liquid and prevent an insolvency with its potential negative effects on society, the economy, government's popularity and re-election chances, and individual government members' reputation (Blankart et al., 2006, pp. 567, 571). There may, however, also be governments that do not care about the possible social, economic and political costs of a bankruptcy – for instance, because of including government members who have options to make their living outside the political business and/or outside their jurisdiction. To illustrate, it became public that several Greek politicians, while the bailout/insolvency negotiations were under way, transferred considerable amounts of private money abroad (see Makris, 2012).

2.4 TAKING CITIZENS' BAILOUT PREFERENCES SERIOUSLY

In line with the principle of 'normative individualism' as applied in Constitutional Political Economy, one may argue that the citizens of a 'rescuer jurisdiction' in their role as 'the ultimate sovereigns' (Buchanan, 1991, p. 227) should have a say in the issue of whether 'To bail out, or not to bail out' via a binding bailout referendum *before* a potential bailout. A bailout is costly for the rescuer jurisdiction, and the resources spent by the latter are no longer available for alternative uses. The costs of a sovereign bailout have to be borne by the citizens of a rescuer country and especially its current and future taxpayers. As the question at hand may be of great importance to a rescuer country's present and future, the instrument of a mandatory and binding bailout referendum could be explicitly integrated into a country's constitution regardless of whether or not this country's political system already includes direct democratic institutions.

Some may object that hosting such a referendum is impossible in Germany and other 'advanced democracies' as the citizen-voters are 'too stupid' to understand the 'complex' mechanisms, instruments, consequences and so on, included in a bailout package. Simply letting citizens vote 'yes' or 'no' on a bailout deal – so the argument goes – is definitely 'too dangerous'. For example, German Chancellor Merkel and other prominent politicians in Germany in their public statements during the negotiations about bailout packages for various EU countries warned that 'If the Euro Fails, Europe Fails' (Wright, 2012). Other leading politicians in the EU even spoke of the danger of wars in Europe if Greece and other EU countries were not rescued from bankruptcy. The current problem in the EU is that nobody knows with certainty what will happen after a sovereign debt default of a country such as Greece. Many politicians, economic experts and other observers expect that this would cause spillover effects onto other Eurozone/EU member states (for example, capital-market reactions; sovereign defaults of other countries; the return of some Eurozone countries to national currencies; breakdown of the Eurozone; and so on) as well as political and social side-effects (social unrest, secessions from the EU, wars and so on).

Given the unpredictable consequences of a 'no bailout' decision, the EU member states, the European Central Bank and the International Monetary Fund have done everything in recent years to avoid a sovereign default of Greece and other EU countries. And given the danger that the majority of citizens in Germany and other countries would possibly vote 'no' in a binding bailout referendum, public policymakers in Germany and other countries have not offered their citizens the opportunity to vote in such a referendum. However, the history of sovereign debt defaults demonstrates that countries are able to recover from sovereign defaults after a period of time which, admittedly, may be painful for many society members (Reinhart and Rogoff, 2009). Apart from the societal costs of a default to be expected in the short- and medium-term, a default may offer a country a fresh start – and all actors affected by the default (for example, governments, citizens, government-bond holders) may possibly learn from this event to be more careful in financial affairs in the future. And if Greece or another EU member country really should suffer from famines, epidemics or other societal problems after a sovereign default, then it can be expected that Germany and other countries that have denied a sovereign bailout will provide (financial) assistance. By contrast, a sovereign bailout may nurture the expectation in the bailed-out country (and in other fiscally distressed countries) as well as on the capital market that there will be a sovereign bailout again in the future. This potential effect is discussed in the politico-economic literature under the headings 'moral hazard problem' (for example, Persson and Tabellini, 1996) and 'soft budget constraint problem' (for example, Rodden et al., 2003).

With respect to the aforementioned claim that 'ordinary' citizens lack the expertise to decide on the 'expert issue' at hand, it should be mentioned that it is by no means clear that political representatives are better informed than the 'average' citizen. For example, in September 2011 the members of the German national parliament had to vote on whether the existing Eurozone bailout fund should be enlarged. A survey among a small sample of politicians (N = 25 MPs) conducted by journalists in the House of Parliament revealed that many of the MPs interviewed were poorly informed about the bailout fund (Teevs, 2011). Moreover, it can be expected that the announcement of a binding bailout referendum would trigger a lively public debate on the pros and cons of a bailout, which possibly leads to a better informed electorate (cf. the general discussion of this argument in Benz and Stutzer, 2004; Frey and Stutzer, 2006; Frey et al., 2011).

This argument can be illustrated, for example, with the 2014 Scottish independence referendum (result: 55.3 percent of Scots against leaving the UK; turnout: 84.6 percent). The relatively high turnout rate indicates that many people in Scotland understood what was at stake in the referendum. And both the 'yes' and the 'no' camp pushed their respective arguments into the public debate and the media. Likewise, as the public debate about the 'rescue packages' for Greece and other EU countries in Germany and other 'rescuer countries' indicates, there is already a lively public debate on the pros and cons of further bailouts for Greece; however, so far the Germans and the peoples of other 'rescuer countries' have not had the opportunity to vote on this issue in a binding referendum.

According to a representative public opinion poll conducted in January 2012, a majority of Germans at that time were 'against bailout payments for over-indebted EU countries': 40.1 percent said they are 'somewhat against', and 20.9 percent are 'strongly against' such payments (N = 4499 respondents; see Bechtel et al., 2014). This survey suggests that a majority of people in Germany as a 'rescuer country' would vote against further bailouts for Greece in a referendum. However, participating in a public opinion poll is 'cheap talk'. The case of the 2014 Scottish independence referendum illustrates that public opinion might change when people have to make a 'yes'/'no' decision that has real consequences. In this context, it should be mentioned that due to the broad news coverage on this issue, many people in Germany have understood that the bailout packages for Greece, among other things, rescued many German citizens, banks and firms that invested their money in Greece. Hence, it can be expected that many citizens would carefully assess to what extent their own fate (savings, job, old age pension and so on) is interconnected with the fate of Greece, before they would vote 'yes' or 'no' in a binding Greek bailout referendum.

2.5 CONCLUSION

It should have become clear that the only way to make sure that the bailout preferences of the citizens/taxpayers in a rescuer jurisdiction, who have to bear the costs of a bailout, are really taken seriously *before* a potential bailout is to establish the instrument of a mandatory and binding *ex ante* bailout referendum in this jurisdiction's constitution. If one accepts 'the normative premise that individuals are the ultimate sovereigns' (Buchanan, 1991, p. 227) in this jurisdiction then this referendum must necessarily be mandatory and binding for the jurisdiction's government. Otherwise it would be possible for the government simply to ignore the citizens' bailout preferences. More specifically, without such a referendum there might be the possible case that a majority of people in a society were against a certain bailout of another jurisdiction. However, the citizens' political representatives who determine this jurisdiction's official bailout policy – for whatever reason – do not necessarily have an interest in this majority view among the citizens of this jurisdiction: that is, the executive and legislative branch in this society may form a 'pro-bailout coalition', regardless of what 'their' citizens think about a particular sovereign bailout.

That the latter is not only a theoretical possibility has been illustrated above with Germany's bailout policy during the EU's recent crisis. The German/ EU case also illustrates that even a constitutional 'no-bailout clause' does not necessarily prevent a government from granting a sovereign bailout to another jurisdiction, when the judiciary (here, the responsible constitutional court) decides that this bailout – in the 'exceptional' case at hand – is in accordance with the constitution for whatever reason. So, to avoid the citizens' bailout preferences from simply being ignored by a 'pro-bailout coalition' consisting of a society's executive, legislative and judiciary, a mandatory and binding referendum prior to a potential bailout is indispensable.

However, this is not the end of the 'governing the market for sovereign bailouts' story. Because even if a majority of citizens in a jurisdiction vote against a bailout in a binding referendum, that jurisdiction's government is not necessarily tied to the 'no-bailout mast'. Although offering a sovereign bailout may no longer be possible for this national government at the domestic level, this government may use its membership in international organizations such as the IMF in order to circumvent the binding referendum result at home by negotiating a bailout deal for a certain country in the international political arena.

Moreover, a successful 'no bailout' referendum in a country is certainly not binding for the politically independent central bank managing the currency of this country. This central bank may bail out another country by buying government bonds of this country, for example. Due to its political independence, the central bank is in a position to bail out another country, regardless of what citizens and the '*classe politique*' in the country that has delegated the monetary policy competence to this politically independent bank think about this particular bailout. And even if a central bank is subject to a constitutional 'no-bailout clause', then this does not necessarily prevent that central bank from granting a sovereign bailout to another country. As the case of the European Central Bank mentioned above illustrates, the constitutional court responsible for enforcing this 'no-bailout clause' may decide that this bailout – in the 'exceptional' case at hand – is in accordance with the constitution for whatever reason.

Consequently, there might be a country in which even a successful 'no bailout' referendum does not prevent citizen-taxpayers from having to bear the costs of a sovereign bailout granted (a) by their government via this country's membership in international organizations, and/or (b) by the politically independent central bank responsible for managing this country's monetary policy. While some '*loyal*' citizens in this specific case may simply accept that political decision-makers and central bankers for whatever reason have ignored what the majority of citizens want, other citizens may use their *voice* option in the sense of Hirschman (1970) and punish the bailout government in the next election. Alternatively these citizens may found a new political party to get their no-bailout preferences represented (see, for example, the case of the party 'Alternative for Germany' founded in 2013; Grimm, 2015). By contrast, citizens do not have the power to hold central bankers (as unelected agents) accountable. Moreover, dissatisfied citizens may think about using their *exit* option in the form of (a) emigrating to another country or (b) letting at least their money 'emigrate' to another country.

To conclude, this chapter has argued that – following the principle of normative individualism – the citizens in a rescuer jurisdiction should get the opportunity to vote on the question of whether 'To bail out, or not to bail out' another jurisdiction in a mandatory and binding referendum before a potential bailout. Whether the political decision-makers in a certain jurisdiction, which could become a rescuer jurisdiction in the future, like and implement the referendum mechanism proposed above is, of course, another issue. Likewise, it is questionable whether the result of such a bailout referendum would have an influence on the bailout policies of politically independent central banks (for example, the ECB) and international organizations (for example, the IMF) as potential rescuers.

REFERENCES

Baskaran, T. (2012), 'Soft Budget Constraints and Strategic Interactions in Subnational Borrowing: Evidence from the German States, 1975–2005', *Journal of Urban Economics*, **71** (1), 114–27.

Bechtel, M., J. Hainmueller and Y. Margalit (2014), 'Preferences for International Redistribution: The Divide over the Eurozone Bailouts', *American Journal of Political Science*, **58** (4), 835–56.

Benz, M. and A. Stutzer (2004), 'Are Voters Better Informed when they have a Larger Say in Politics? Evidence for the European Union and Switzerland', *Public Choice*, **119** (1–2), 31–59.

Blankart, C.B. (2011), 'An Economic Theory of Switzerland', *CESifo DICE Report*, **9** (3), 74–82.

Blankart, C.B. (2015), 'Swiss Role – What the Eurozone Could Learn from Switzerland', *CESifo Forum*, **16** (2), 39–42.

Blankart, C.B. and A. Klaiber (2006), 'Subnational Government Organisation and Public Debt Crises', *Economic Affairs*, **26** (3), 48–54.

Blankart, C.B., E.R. Fasten and A. Klaiber (2006), 'Föderalismus ohne Insolvenz?', *Wirtschaftsdienst*, **86** (9), 567–71.

Bova, E., T. Kinda, P. Muthoora and F. Toscani (2015), *Fiscal Rules at a Glance*, Washington, DC: International Monetary Fund.

Brennan, G. and G. Eusepi (2004), 'Fiscal Constitutionalism', in J.G. Backhaus and R.E. Wagner (eds), *Handbook of Public Finance*, New York: Springer, pp. 53–76.

Buchanan, J.M. (1991), 'The Foundations of Normative Individualism', in J.M. Buchanan, *The Economics and the Ethics of Constitutional Order*, Ann Arbor: University of Michigan Press, pp. 221–9.

Buchanan, J.M. and R.E. Wagner (1977), *Democracy in Deficit: The Political Legacy of Lord Keynes*, New York: Academic Press.

Burret, H.T. and L.P. Feld (2014), 'A Note on Budget Rules and Fiscal Federalism', *CESifo DICE Report*, **12** (1), 3–11.

Chivers, C.J. and A.E. Kramer (2006), 'Russian Bank Reformer Dies After Shooting', *New York Times*, 15 September, p. A3.

Degner, H. and D. Leuffen (2016), 'Keynes, Friedman, or Monnet? Explaining

Parliamentary Voting Behaviour on Fiscal Aid for Euro Area Member States',
  West European Politics, **39** (6), 1139–59.
Downs, A. (1957), *An Economic Theory of Democracy*, New York: Harper & Row.
Duff, J.C. (2010), *Bankruptcy Basics*, 3rd edn, Washington, DC: Administrative
  Office of the US Courts.
Feld, L.P., C. Fuest, J. Haucap, H. Schweitzer, V. Wieland and B.U. Wigger (2016),
  *Dismantling the Boundaries of the ECB's Monetary Policy Mandate: The CJEU's
  OMT Judgement and its Consequences*, Berlin: Stiftung Marktwirtschaft/
  Kronberger Kreis.
Fernández-Albertos, J. (2015), 'The Politics of Central Bank Independence',
  Annual Review of Political Science, **18**, 217–37.
Fink, A. and T. Stratmann (2011), 'Institutionalized Bailouts and Fiscal Policy:
  Consequences of Soft Budget Constraints', *Kyklos*, **64** (3), 366–95.
Frey, B.S. and A. Stutzer (2006), 'Direct Democracy: Designing a Living
  Constitution', in R.D. Congleton and B. Swedenborg (eds), *Democratic
  Constitutional Design and Public Policy: Analysis and Evidence*, Cambridge:
  MIT Press, pp. 39–80.
Frey, B.S., A. Stutzer and S. Neckermann (2011), 'Direct Democracy and
  the Constitution', in A. Marciano (ed.), *Constitutional Mythologies: New
  Perspectives on Controlling the State*, New York: Springer, pp. 107–19.
Fuest, C., F. Heinemann and C. Schröder (2016), 'A Viable Insolvency Procedure
  for Sovereigns in the Euro Area', *Journal of Common Market Studies*, **54** (2),
  301–17.
Grimm, R. (2015), 'The Rise of the German Eurosceptic Party Alternative für
  Deutschland, between Ordoliberal Critique and Popular Anxiety', *International
  Political Science Review*, **36** (3), 264–78.
Hirschman, A.O. (1970), *Exit, Voice, and Loyalty: Responses to Decline in Firms,
  Organizations, and States*, Cambridge, MA: Harvard University Press.
Hirschman, A.O. (1993), 'Exit, Voice, and the Fate of the German Democratic
  Republic: An Essay in Conceptual History', *World Politics*, **45** (2), 173–202.
Judis, J.B. (2016), *The Populist Explosion: How the Great Recession Transformed
  American and European Politics*, New York: Columbia Global Reports.
Kasper, W., M.E. Streit and P.J. Boettke (2012), *Institutional Economics: Property,
  Competition, Policies*, 2nd edn, Cheltenham, UK and Northampton, MA, USA:
  Edward Elgar Publishing.
Kirchgässner, G. (1992), 'Towards a Theory of Low-Cost Decisions', *European
  Journal of Political Economy*, **8** (2), 305–20.
Kirchgässner, G. (2008), *Homo Oeconomicus: The Economic Model of Behaviour
  and its Applications in Economics and other Social Sciences*, New York: Springer.
Kirchgässner, G. (forthcoming), 'Voting and Popularity', in R. Congleton,
  B. Grofman and S. Voigt (eds), *The Oxford Handbook of Public Choice*, Oxford:
  Oxford University Press.
Kirchgässner, G. and W.W. Pommerehne (1993), 'Low-Cost Decisions as a
  Challenge to Public Choice', *Public Choice*, **77** (1), 107–15.
Kriesi, H. and T.S. Pappas (eds) (2015), *European Populism in the Shadow of the
  Great Recession*, Colchester: ECPR Press.
Lane, T.D. (1993), 'Market Discipline', *IMF Staff Papers*, **40** (1), 53–88.
Lewis-Beck, M.S. and M. Stegmaier (2013), 'The VP-Function Revisited: A Survey
  of the Literature on Vote and Popularity Functions after over 40 Years', *Public
  Choice*, **157** (3–4), 367–85.

Makris, A. (2012), 'Venizelos: More Politicians and Relatives Took their Money Abroad', *GreekReporter.com*, 24 February, available at: http://greece.greekre porter.com/2012/02/24/venizelos-more-politicians-and-relatives-took-their-mon ey-abroad/. Accessed 30 September 2017.

Mause, K. and F. Groeteke (2012), 'New Constitutional "Debt Brakes" for Euroland? A Question of Institutional Complementarity', *Constitutional Political Economy*, **23** (4), 279–301.

Mueller, D.C. (2003), *Public Choice III*, Cambridge: Cambridge University Press.

Olson, M. (1965), *The Logic of Collective Action: Public Goods and the Theory of Groups*, Cambridge: Harvard University Press.

Ostrom, E. (1990), *Governing the Commons: The Evolution of Institutions for Collective Action*, Cambridge: Cambridge University Press.

Panizza, U., F. Sturzenegger and J. Zettelmeyer (2009), 'The Economics and Law of Sovereign Debt and Default', *Journal of Economic Literature*, **47** (3), 651–98.

Persson, T. and G.E. Tabellini (1996), 'Federal Fiscal Constitutions: Risk Sharing and Moral Hazard', *Econometrica*, **64** (3), 623–46.

Popper, K. (1999), 'On the Theory of Democracy', in K. Popper, *All Life is Problem Solving*, London: Routledge, pp. 93–8.

Reinhart, C.M. and K.S. Rogoff (2009), *This Time is Different: Eight Centuries of Financial Folly*, Princeton: Princeton University Press.

Rieck, A. and L. Schuknecht (2016), 'Preserving Government Solvency: A Global Policy Perspective', *CESifo DICE Report*, **14** (4), 71–81.

Rodden, J., G.S. Eskeland and J. Litvack (eds) (2003), *Fiscal Decentralization and the Challenge of Hard Budget Constraints*, Cambridge, MA: MIT Press.

Rose, R. (1990), 'Inheritance before Choice in Public Policy', *Journal of Theoretical Politics*, **2** (3), 263–91.

Sturzenegger, F. and J. Zettelmeyer (2006), *Debt Defaults and Lessons from a Decade of Crises*, Cambridge, MA: MIT Press.

Sutherland, D., R. Price and I. Joumard (2005), 'Fiscal Rules for Sub-Central Governments: Design and Impact', *OECD Economics Department Working Paper* No. 465.

Teevs, C. (2011), 'Euro-Votum im Bundestag: Denn sie wussten nicht, worüber sie abstimmen', *SpiegelOnline*, 30 September, available at: http://www.spiegel. de/wirtschaft/soziales/euro-votum-im-bundestag-denn-sie-wussten-nicht-worue ber-sie-abstimmen-a-789405.html. Accessed 30 September 2017.

Tsebelis, G. (2002), *Veto Players: How Political Institutions Work*, Princeton: Princeton University Press.

Vaubel, R. (2012), 'The Political Economy of Sovereign Bailouts in the Eurozone', in J. Brodsky (ed.), *Today's World and Václav Klaus. Festschrift in Honour of Václav Klaus, President of the Czech Republic*, Prague: Fragment, pp. 323–8.

Vibert, F. (2007), *The Rise of the Unelected: Democracy and the new Separation of Powers*, Cambridge: Cambridge University Press.

Wildasin, D.E. (2004), 'The Institutions of Federalism: Toward an Analytical Framework', *National Tax Journal*, **57** (1), 247–72.

Williamson, O.E. (1996), *The Mechanisms of Governance*, Oxford: Oxford University Press.

Wright, T. (2012), 'What if Europe Fails?', *The Washington Quarterly*, **35** (3), 23–41.

3. Political obligations: is debt special?

Geoffrey Brennan

INTRODUCTION

My brief in writing this chapter has been to focus on debt in its *ethical* aspects. There are lots of questions that one could ask in this connection. Is public debt bad? If so, why? Would debt default be so dreadful? After all, one might think, if debt itself is bad then the long-term effects of debt default might be to inhibit public debt, and therefore it would be good in the longer run. Is there a tension here (as in some other policy areas) between short-run considerations of minimizing the risk of immediate crisis and longer-run considerations of securing a stable and responsible fiscal order? Are these issues primarily 'economic' or are they also (or perhaps predominantly) 'political'?

I think these are all interesting and worthy questions. But I want to begin by saying something rather more abstract and conceptual about how we might understand the 'ethical' dimensions of debt, because I think that debt, and debt default specifically, raises ethical questions in two very different senses. On the one hand, there are the directly 'normative' questions – about what we ought to do. On the other, there are questions about the role that the ethical beliefs of ordinary players play in determining social outcomes in relation to debt. The first set of questions concerns issues in applied moral philosophy; the second might be described as issues in moral anthropology – or perhaps moral psychology.

This second set of questions is often occluded in conventional economics, and frankly, public choice theory has not done a great deal to remedy the situation. And this is so even though public choice theory from the very outset diagnosed the relevant difficulty. Let me elaborate.

One of the core tenets of public choice theory has always been its critique of the so-called 'benevolent despot' model of government. One way of expressing this critique is to observe that the motivations ascribed to 'policy-makers' and to 'policy-takers' in conventional policy analysis are widely (and perhaps wildly) divergent. The model of individual response to various policies typically assumes that all policy-takers are self-interested optimizers, altering their behaviour only when (and to the extent that) it comes to be in their interests to do so. By contrast, policy-makers are assumed to be orchestrating those behavioural responses to policy so as to promote the public interest (the benevolence aspect), and, moreover, to be doing so quite independently of all political/electoral considerations (the despotic aspect).

The 'despotic' aspect of this challenge can be met by including in the analysis of policy an account of the policy formation process – and especially those aspects of it that reflect democratic procedures. So, for example, many public finance textbooks these days include a chapter or two on 'positive' models of electoral competition and perhaps its policy upshots. But the spirit of such inclusion is often enough that 'electoral constraints' offer just another factor to be taken into account in the overall 'social welfare maximization' process.[1] It is worth underlining in this connection that what most political theorists would regard as representing the carrier of the normative aspirations in the political setting (namely the democratic process itself) is in this 'electoral constraint' formulation treated *as* a 'constraint' – serving only to inhibit policy-makers from doing the good that their policies are presumed to do!

As to the motivational asymmetry aspect, public choice theorists have responded largely by extrapolating the 'policy-taker' motivational model – the model of *homo economicus* – to policy-makers: *everyone* was assumed to be self-interested. Now, it is a simple analytic truth that motivational asymmetry can in principle be resolved by assuming any *common motivational picture whatsoever*. So, everyone (including specifically policy-takers) might be taken to be motivated by the *public* interest. Or more plausibly, everyone can be modelled as having a combination of private and public interest in whatever proportions seem most realistic. There is nothing special analytically speaking in this choice about the limiting case of *homo economicus*.

So, one interpretation of the 'benevolent despot' critique – the interpretation I favour – is that we ought to recognize that both policy-makers and policy-takers have some ethical motivations: both are bound

---

[1] An interesting example of this manoeuvre lies in the literature on the independence of central banks. The central bankers (mostly economists, so good guys just like us) are taken to pursue good monetary policy because electoral processes cannot reliably do so: hence the need for 'independence'. Democratic processes are introduced explicitly into the analysis; but the motivational asymmetry remains in place – (independent) central bankers pursue the public interest while ordinary citizen-voters pursue their private interests. Just for the record, I make this observation not because I reckon it represents a decisive case against central bank independence, but rather to encourage economists and others to generalize somewhat their observations that central bankers do not exploit their powers exclusively for their own ends!

Debt default and democracy

by notions of 'good and bad' and 'right and wrong', which have some impact on their behaviour and are perhaps bound too by norms of conduct that do not automatically reduce to ethical categories[2] – whether as bureaucrats or politicians or voters or consumers or producers or CEOs or university professors. There is of course no reason to think that those conceptions of 'good' and 'right' will perfectly track moral truth (or the 'public interest'). But once we have conceded that the 'ethical precepts' that people actually recognize are behaviourally relevant, then it seems important to the *explanatory* enterprise to investigate the content of those ethical precepts and use this expanded account of human motivations to make more accurate predictions about how real humans will actually behave. This is not soppy sentimentalism: it is just good social science![3]

And as I shall try to argue, the ethical views that inform relevant decision-makers in relation to public debt play an important role in any plausible analysis of public debt as a phenomenon. I reckon, for example, that the relevance of such ethical views is central in Buchanan's treatment of issues relating to the debt problem (as he perceived it) – and as I shall argue shortly in relation to the very *existence* of sovereign debt. Consider for example the general argument laid out by Buchanan with Richard Wagner in *Democracy in Deficit* (1977). In a suitably stripped down version, the story there is that there was a time when the 'old-time fiscal religion' embodying balanced budget norms held sway over US fiscal behaviour. But with the onslaught of Keynesian thinking (and what Buchanan regarded as mistaken views of public debt incidence), that old-time fiscal religion was discarded: deficit financing, and the accumulating debt it gave rise to, became entirely respectable in relevant policy circles and among a credulous voting public. This was a peculiar legacy of the impact of Keynesian thinking on prevailing fiscal *norms*. In other words, the central factor in explaining exploding sovereign debt was a change in norms – in the ethics that relevant decision-makers (and/or voter-citizens) carried around with them.

When Buchanan (1987) came to focus on debt *default* specifically, a central role again was played by ethical constraints – those that Buchanan

---

[2]   Norms of etiquette exemplify. These norms create in those subject to them an inclination to act as the norm requires; but no one thinks that, in laying a table, placing knives and spoons on the right and forks on the left of the diner is a *moral* issue.

[3]   Economists are often reluctant to accept this claim. They want to be 'hard-nosed' or 'tough-minded' for its own sake. But surely one thing that the experimental evidence shows (say, 'ultimatum experiments' or experiments involving contributions in prisoner's dilemma and public goods games) is that pure pay-off maximization isn't the only thing that motivates behaviour! It just seems perverse to persist in pretending otherwise!

thought should probably be jettisoned. His argument in that setting can be summarized in terms of several propositions:

1. Governments are disposed to exploit 'debt illusion' whereby citizens excessively discount the future tax liabilities associated with debt financing.
2. This is true for democratic as well as for more despotic governments.
3. One mechanism for reducing reliance on public debt lies on the supply side. Specifically, if governments were more prone to default on the debts undertaken by their predecessors, then debt-holders would factor into their investment decisions the riskiness of debt instruments.
4. So, more extensive debt default would reduce the capacity of current governments to undertake debt financing; and this would on balance be a good thing.

In a paper (Brennan and Eusepi, 2002) expressly designed to engage the Buchanan reasoning, Giuseppe Eusepi and I argued that debt default is an inappropriate method for applying fiscal discipline to governments: that it is unjust to debt-holders, parties who are not primarily responsible for inappropriate fiscal decisions; and that it fails to distinguish between legitimate and illegitimate uses of debt-financing, because the current set of citizens will always have an incentive to default on debt if default is regarded as a legitimate option. If debt has a perfectly legitimate role to play in best practice public finance, then one would ideally want to institute provisions that protect against bad use but allow good use. More liberal default options would, if they had the effect envisaged by Buchanan, simply throw the baby out with the bathwater. Of course, this claim presumes that there *is* a baby; and either that there are available more nuanced mechanisms of control or, if there are not, that the bathwater is sufficiently obnoxious that it's better to throw it out even if the baby goes as well.

In principle, this latter possibility is perfectly imaginable, and indeed is staple fare in the public choice/constitutional economics tradition. The fact that an institutional arrangement is not perfect does not imply that it is not optimal. Markets with externalities may be preferable to political provision; imperfect decision rules for collective decisions (those that fall well short of unanimity) may nevertheless be the best available; fiscal systems without a debt option may be superior to those that have unconstrained access to debt (or vice versa) and either might be optimal, even though neither is perfect. Such propositions flow simply from the recognition that ethics is a matter of 'optimizing subject to constraint' (a thought that comes naturally to the economist).

In any event, it is worth underlining one important implication of

Buchanan's focus on debt default, which is that public debt is only feasible *at all* if current governments carry (or more accurately are believed to carry) a commitment to fulfil the commitments of their predecessors. In other words, public debt presupposes that pre-commitment by government is possible. If that were not so, if governments routinely repudiated the debt commitments of their predecessors, then no one would be prepared to hold government bonds. There would be no market in sovereign debt and hence no debt crisis. In other words, the fact that there is public debt at all reflects a belief on the part of bond-holders that future governments will service and redeem the debt more or less as stipulated; and that belief, I want to argue, is equivalent to the belief that governments are constrained by certain fiscal norms – certain ethical presuppositions. The point is worth spelling out in a little detail.

Consider a government in some notional 'initial' period where there is no debt. Its capacity to float debt at all depends on a belief on the part of purchasers of the debt instruments that they will be repaid. But what makes that belief rational? Since the government itself is the agency that is supposed to supervise the enforcement of contracts, government will have the power in the next period to repudiate the debts earlier contracted. Of course, if repudiation were to inhibit the government's own capacity to contract (further) debt in the current period, that would be a reason not to repudiate. But for the repayment undertaking to be credible, the government in each successive period must leave 'enough and as good' debt creation capacity for all its successors: otherwise, each potential debt-holder can rationally anticipate the point at which it will pay a government to repudiate – namely that point where the savings from nullifying existing debt claims are greater than the value of the debt increment available in that period. And backward induction ensures that the only possible equilibrium time path for debt is one in which that point never comes. This will, I think, allow a small amount of debt in a growing economy; but none at all in a static one.

In any event, this is not the environment that Buchanan assumes. He seems to be taking it that contracts entered into by the contract-enforcer have some weight. (Precisely how that assumption fits with his Hobbesian assumptions about the way in which anarchy operates and his general presumptions in relation to arguments for government, I shall not here enquire, except to note that some enquiry might be called for.) Buchanan thinks that debt is sustained – or not – by ethical considerations that bear on the behaviour of governments. And his enquiry into the 'ethics of debt default' is, I take it, an attempt to persuade people that the ethics in question might be defective. Without the assumption that governments are ethically constrained to service and redeem the debt undertaken by prior governments, Buchanan thinks that there would be negligible debt (apparently, his preferred scheme). In other words, setting aside the question of whether debt financing might be good or bad, Buchanan is assuming that there exists some mechanism that will induce governments to service and redeem debt entered into by its predecessors (that is, that bond-holders are not irrational). And that 'mechanism' is an ethical commitment to abide by contractual obligations, even when it is not in the current government's interests to do so.

Of course, without some similar ethical input – a propensity to follow rules and behave in a broadly trustworthy fashion in relation to undertakings entered into – it is not clear how any constitutional government at all would be possible, or how the entire analytic apparatus of constitutional contractarianism can get off the ground. Buchanan is rather coy about what precisely he is helping himself to by way of the normative commitments of constitutional calculators (ordinary persons) and it is not clear that he is everywhere consistent in his application of motivational assumptions. But in the debt case, the working assumptions seem clear enough (and indeed, the theme runs through all his work on debt and deficits): people are ethically constrained in their behaviour, and the content of the ethical norms they follow is an important determinant of what policy outcomes emerge.

Here then seems to be what we must believe about the ethics of governments.[4] They must feel inhibited about breaking contractual commitments (even though there is no external enforcer of those contracts). And just as being trustworthy can, in the right circumstances of disposition transparency/translucency, be a disposition that individuals may rationally possess, so governments being trustworthy (in much the same sense) can be to their advantage. It will allow them to keep promises made (or taken to have been made) such as those that relate to constitutional government – and more relevantly here, those relating to debt servicing and repayment.

And on the face of it this seems to create a puzzle.[5] Because as public choice reminds us, 'government' is just a linguistic shorthand for the individuals that figure in the policy-making process – the bureaucrats and

---

[4] By referring to the 'ethics of governments' I do not mean to reify governments. Government can be construed as a set of individuals – politicians, bureaucrats and voters – all locked together in a well-specified structure, and it is these individuals whose ethical attitudes determine what is ethically permissible.

[5] Actually more than one puzzle. One is to set out precisely what government could look like in a world where they could make no credible pre-commitments whatsoever. In Chapter 4 in this volume Richard Wagner draws a distinction between private and public debt. One aspect of that distinction is that in the private case repayment is externally enforced by government; in the public case, there is no external enforcement: *'quis custodiet ipsos custodes'*, indeed!

politicians and advisors and in a democratic system the voters, and the relations between them. It is going to be problematic to attribute to those various players, ethical commitments that we have some reason to think they do not possess.

It is this 'puzzle' to which I now turn.

ETHICALLY CONSTRAINED CITIZENS?

On the face of things, politicians seem to be breaking promises all the time. They commit in their electioneering to all kinds of extravagant policies, which they conveniently forget once they achieve office (if they do). I understand that in Britain public questionnaires about the trustworthiness of various professions reveal that politicians clock in just below 'used car salesmen'. Since used car salesmen used to be regarded as the classic example of shiftiness, this rating must be counted as something of a negative accomplishment for the politicians.

And it's not just when in electioneering mode that the issues arise. Governments sign on to international agreements from which they subsequently defect. Witness the Stability and Growth Pact of the EU. The 3 per cent limit on deficits might have been a nice idea, but it seems to have been treated at best as an aspiration, to be broken whenever it is in the national interest to do so. And it has been broken not just by the renegades of the Eurozone but by the stalwarts, when their domestic politics required it.

In the Australian case, it is a signatory to the international Agreement on Refugees, which requires that asylum-seekers that enter national territory have to be received by the accommodating country if their credentials are valid. But Australia has treated that subset of asylum-seekers that arrive by boat (a special category, apparently) by shipping them off to very miserable accommodation elsewhere – with the stipulation that they will not, whatever the decision on the validity of their asylum-seeker status, be allowed to settle in Australia. (Australia does, though, I understand, make it possible for those asylum-seekers to contact their relatives and friends back home – presumably to spread the word that Australia is not a good destination to aspire to. Quite apart from the country's international obligations, which it agreed to and urges other nations to fulfil, the idea of using severe 'punishment' of so-called 'illegal immigrants' to deter other potential asylum-seekers seems objectionable in itself and a gross violation of natural justice.)

Some political commentators in Australia (and elsewhere) have suggested a two-tier structure for electoral promises. The idea is that any politician can, if she chooses, sign a contractual undertaking to implement a promised policy if elected. The thought is that subsequent violation of that contractual undertaking would render the candidate liable to impeachment or some sanction beyond whatever electoral fall-out there might be from non-fulfilment. I myself regard the provision of any such opportunity with horror. I reckon the pressure on candidates to sign up to their electoral promises would be very considerable; and that all sorts of policy fantasies would be foisted on the citizenry as semi-unbreakable commitments. The current arrangement, in which politicians can show us what good people they are by promising us the moon, although hardly edifying, is not likely to be improved by making it the case that they have to deliver the moon, post-election day.

In one sense, politicians are electioneering all the time. The process of getting re-elected is a matter of retaining one's standing in the polls; and though public opinion on such matters is highly febrile (after all, 'a week is a long time in politics') and so it does not mean a great deal how one's popularity stands until the days immediately prior to election, nevertheless it's always better to be ahead than behind. Even if popular opinion is a random walk through time, the random walk always starts from where you are. A 'handy lead in the polls' is indeed 'handy'!

On a standard view of the public choice approach to such issues (if a slightly old-fashioned view, as I like to think), the central driver of public opinion is what politicians *do*; each voter is conceived to be a buyer in a public policy space in which political agents are the sellers. On that view, what politicians *say* is of no independent account. It is only in so far as what is said is an indicator of future policy that it matters at all. Note two features here: first it is future *policy* that matters; and second it is *future* policy. This second feature is just an upshot of standard accounts of individual rationality: bygones are bygones. Of course, if past action is positively correlated with expected future action, then the past may carry information about what it is reasonable to expect in the future. But it is only in so far as that is so that the past can matter. Voting could never on this view rationally be retrospective as such. Punishing candidates/parties for poor performance or failed promises *for its own sake* could never make sense on this view.

As I have argued extensively in the past, I believe this instrumental view of voting behaviour involves a serious misconception. I will not rehearse here the underlying logic of my preferred 'expressive voting' account.[6] But I reckon that it is perfectly rational for individuals to treat democratic elections as a kind of popularity poll. That is, it is by no means irrational

---

[6] See, though, Brennan and Lomasky (1993).

for me to vote for a candidate because I like what I see of her, because I think she's a decent person, or because I like the sound of her voice or her rhetorical style.

Again, the current US primaries are instructive in this regard. What is it, one might ask, that explains Donald Trump's attractiveness to (many) Republican voters? His election promises? His banning Muslims from entry to the US? His reconstruction of the Berlin wall along the Mexican border? It seems doubtful. It also seems doubtful that such policies promise significant material benefits to the voters in question. Surely, what explains Trump's success is that the relevant people like what he says. They like his style. They positively admire the fact that he speaks his mind (such as it is), that he actually voices all those politically incorrect (and worse, sometimes positively outrageous) thoughts that they might themselves have. Of course, this does give democratic political process the feel of a reality TV show – but I believe that that 'feel' is one element in its real nature.

The public choice picture of electoral politics as a quasi-market process in which candidates 'buy' support by promising goodies to their potential supporters is at best a very partial picture. A better metaphor in my view is that candidates are trying to *woo* voters – and if that involves promising the moon, then such 'promises' simply reveal the intensity of the candidate's enthusiasm for the beloved. To elevate this kind of extravagant undertaking to the status of a genuine bargain offer is to mistake its essentially poetic character. To treat such undertakings as one side of a potential contract – and in that spirit to introduce contract-like institutions into the electoral process – would invite disaster. It would be disastrous because 'binding' contracts to fulfil extravagant (and even impossible) undertakings are likely to be used if they are available. Part of the electoral competitive process would become a race to demonstrate 'levels of commitment'. A candidate who tries to reveal his goodwill and generous spirit by extravagant statements of intentions can hardly respond to a challenge from a rival to translate such extravagant statements into genuine contracts by saying: 'well, I didn't really mean it!'. It seems highly likely that too many such extravagances would become contractualized, and that does not seem to me like a good recipe for sound policy.

My central message here is that, if we understand electoral processes as having an ineluctable tendency towards the poetic, if we see candidate speech as an attempt to reveal the candidate's dispositions and character rather than laying out a genuine policy manifesto, then we recognize an important difference between campaign 'promises' and what we might think of as 'policy contracts'. This is of course not to say that there are no such things as policy contracts. When a government moves to implement a policy programme that will take time to put in place and will bear fruit only if those affected by it believe it to be in place for a reasonable time period, then it will need to have access to quasi-contractual machinery. Some kinds of undertakings require a capacity on the part of government to pre-commit. But we undermine rather than support that capacity if we try to exploit it beyond its limited capacities. Or so it seems to me.

BACK TO DEBT

One instance where government needs that capacity to pre-commit is in relation to debt financing. Buchanan's thought – to reduce the promises to bond-holders to the status of other kinds of specifically electoral promises – is to undermine the government's capacity to pre-commit more generally. And my view is that that would have disastrous consequences.

I think that this has become a more pressing issue given what I take to be the emergent problems relating to climate change. Actually, I think the Paris Agreement was a significant accomplishment in this area, largely because of the participation of the US and China – two very big players – but even if countries fulfil their Paris commitments, there is a gap between what is promised and what is estimated to be the level of carbon emissions necessary to stabilize atmospheric carbon concentrations at a level that will produce no more than a 2°C increase in average global temperatures. I do not here wish to engage in detailed argument about carbon emissions and the threats they pose. But I do need to say a little.

I am not a scientist. I have no grounds for disputing what I take to be a broad scientific consensus that carbon concentrations above current levels constitute a serious problem. The way I think about the normative imperatives surrounding this issue involves seeing the problem in part as one of insurance. Even those sceptical about the science cannot be certain that the science is wrong. And if the scientific consensus is right, it seems clear to me that there is a serious *risk* that the climatic upshots of increased atmospheric carbon concentrations will be bad and a small chance (perhaps 5 per cent) that they may be totally catastrophic (by which I mean the possible elimination of human life on earth).[7] To me,

---

[7]   These are issues of high speculation, but it doesn't take much of an exercise of imagination to recognize that 'catastrophes' come in degrees. If September 11 was a catastrophe (3000 dead) or WWI was a catastrophe (20 million dead) or WWII (60 million dead), what would we make of an effective return to the situation of human life as at 1700 AD (by evolutionary standards very high) which involved a population of fewer than 700 million (the elimination of 90 per cent of the current population) and an average standard of living around one-sixteenth of the prevailing one. It could well be that climate change will have effects that are 'off the charts'.

that suggests that carbon emission reduction is a prudent course if we can manage it at not too horrendous a cost (which relevant evidence suggests we now can). There are two problems in doing this, however. One (the more important) relates to the global public goods nature of the problem: it is simply not in the national interest of any country (even very large players like the US) to reduce its carbon emissions unilaterally. There is a classic prisoner's dilemma problem in play here, and it is not clear, given our prevailing political institutional structure, that we will be able to solve it (however catastrophic the failure turns out to be).[8] I think this is an aspect of the problem that is insufficiently emphasized by much of the economic literature on climate change, which, like the Stern report (2006) (or the Weitzman (2009) critique), focuses on what level of carbon emissions-reduction is currently 'optimal' for the world, rather than why the problem is as serious as it is.

The second issue – also political – involves the inter-temporal aspect, by which I mean the scientist's consensus that the worst features of increased carbon emissions will not begin to appear for perhaps a century or more (at which point, given the lags in the atmospheric/climate interaction, it will be too late to do anything about it). It takes an effort of imagination to see the consequences of acts that lie so far into the future. And as in relation to the debt itself, it is always tempting for incumbent governments to 'pass the buck' to their successors – to leave to the next government the nasty work of imposing short-run costs on current voters in return for benefits that won't appear for perhaps a century. I do not think that this inter-temporal challenge is as deep a problem as the free-rider one, but it is part of a package that makes climate change an especially severe problem for political institutions (at least as currently constituted). Of course, there is also a positive side: current governments can always announce carbon emission reduction policies that will take effect in the medium future, and to promise targets that successfully demonstrate their 'green credentials' while actually imposing minimal costs in the current term.

I have said that climate change is a little like the debt problem in this inter-temporal aspect. But I also think that debt is part of the solution to this problem. After all, no one disputes the claim (at least as far as I know) that the use of public debt financing to fund projects that will yield their benefits to future rather than present generations is a legitimate exercise. The anxiety is that, currently, debt is being used to fund projects that yield their benefits in the present at the expense of future taxpayers. There are two reasons for the public finance consensus around legitimate uses of

---

[8]   If any country can buy itself (and its citizens) a bit more time by not contributing to a collective effort, then it will focus on adaptation rather than emission reduction.

debt. The first is that it seems 'fair' (in the way that all benefit taxation might have a claim to be fair): those who benefit pay. The second is a political economy point: namely, that if future benefits are not funded by debt then the current generations of taxpayers may not be prepared to undertake the relevant expenditures. Shifting the cost to those who benefit makes the proposal more likely to receive political support.

To be honest, I think this latter part of the argument is often overstated. It is part of a general cluster of 'self-interest' assumptions that, as already indicated, I regard as dubious. I have no doubt that the current generation cares about the next generation – at least in the minimal sense that parents care about their own children and their grandchildren (and possibly by extension, their grandchildren's grandchildren). So if the current generation can collectively vote for a policy that will ensure that the transfers they make to their grandchildren will be in the most efficient form (the right mix, that is, of private and public benefits), they will have an incentive to do that. But of course, any country making a significant reduction in its carbon emissions provides benefits not just to the grandchildren of *its* citizens but also to the grandchildren of the entire world's population. If we want to offer maximal protection to our own grandchildren, the best strategy may well be to pass on to them more private goods, so that they are better equipped to adapt and respond to a less hospitable climate. But that is just to restate the free-rider problem. As I see it, it is this free-rider problem rather than the long horizons involved in the climate change threat that is the major challenge.

Nevertheless, I do not believe the situation is hopeless. Perhaps the situation would be hopeless if countries' governments routinely acted strictly in the interests of their citizens. But they do not. Government is, as Hume used to insist, based on 'public opinion', not on national interest. And it is perfectly conceivable that public opinion might insist on policies to restrict greenhouse gas emission, even though that is not the best course for any individual country. Already, we see (some) local governments proudly announcing emission targets by 2030, say – even though that local government's emission reductions will have a negligible effect on atmospheric conditions. That kind of 'green politics' can be expressively very effective: voters may cheer for 'good policy' even when the policy in question is good strictly from the world's point of view!

At the same time, voters may be yet more inclined to vote for such policies if those policies do not appear to cost very much. It's probably the case that it is easier to get electoral support for small sacrifices than for heroic ones. And this is where there may be an important role for public debt. Policy-makers (or more accurately policy-sellers) can make it rather more likely that current generations of taxpayers will support climate-oriented policies by funding a significant proportion of the policies in question from debt. And that choice can be defended in the case of climate change on the basis that those who stand to benefit will be those who pay.

John Broome (2012) makes much of this kind of point in his recent *Climate Matters* book. He observes that if carbon emissions are (or will without current action soon be) at an inefficiently high level, then it will be possible to reduce the inefficiency without imposing a 'sacrifice' on anyone (as compared with the business-as-usual alternative). And he recommends aiming for 'efficiency without sacrifice' as the appropriate pragmatic way of 'getting the political process started'. As he sees it, an important element in securing 'efficiency without sacrifice' is to shift the cost of current policies to the future generations who will benefit – and public debt financing of current emission reduction policies (subsidies for sustainable energy and so on) appears as a major element in any such strategy. If he is right, then access to (additional) sovereign debt across the world may be an important element in the 'saving of the earth'.

Unfortunately, scope to use public debt for such purposes has been compromised by the levels of debt already set in place for much more dubious purposes. Once debt/GDP ratios reach significantly high levels, scope to raise further debt is limited. Since many countries already have debt/GDP ratios well in excess of 100 per cent (even without including the implicit debt associated with unfunded social security obligations), there does not seem scope for further significant increases in debt without hikes in interest rates and increased current budgetary costs. So at least one means of making carbon emissions policies more attractive electorally is closed off. And as I see it, that is a serious matter.

At the same time the problem of excessive debt would hardly be solved if the moral norms that support governments in fulfilling their contracts were made weaker. Encouraging a more relaxed attitude towards debt default would simply sweep off the table one mechanism for making carbon emissions policies more politically palatable.

SUMMARY

My argument in this chapter involves three general (and apparently disparate) claims:

1. Trying to explain social phenomena without appeal to the ethical norms that are one significant factor in individual behaviour is generally a mistake – and is especially a mistake in the case of public debt, where a justified belief in the preparedness of governments to fulfil

the debt commitments of their predecessors seems to be necessary to explain sovereign debt at all. In a world of purely self-interested governments, it is hard to see how present governments can make credible undertakings about the preparedness of future governments to service and redeem the debt. In that sense, any story about public debt that ignores ethical constraints on government action seems hopelessly incomplete.

2. It is a mistake to infer facts about the trustworthiness of politicians from their electoral 'promises'. To be sure, there is some political cost in making undertakings that a government does not deliver on. But the electioneering setting is a special setting. To see the electioneering process as a matter of candidates offering competitive tenders to self-interested voters is at best a highly distorted picture. I think that policy undertakings are better seen as signals of candidates' priorities and dispositions; they are designed to persuade the voters that the candidate 'has her heart in the right place'. Candidates 'woo' voters; they do not 'buy' them. So viewed, the fact that candidates make somewhat extravagant gestures towards voters – and promise them much – is not to be taken entirely at face value. In other circumstances, and with contractual undertakings of a more formal kind, there is little reason to think that politicians are an especially untrustworthy bunch. In particular, undertakings to service and redeem public debt can be entirely credible even where electoral 'promises' are not (entirely credible).

3. The claim that the challenge that climate change associated with greenhouse gases poses is the greatest problem the world has ever faced seems to me to be right. The reason why it is such a problem lies primarily in the global public goods nature of carbon emission reduction – together with the fact that the locus of policy response is essentially national (sub-global). But one further aspect of the problem is that the benefits of current action lie some distance into the future (perhaps as much as a century or two). This latter feature requires a certain effort of imagination on the part of current decision-makers (including in particular current voters) and that effort of imagination is an additional aspect of the challenge. This aspect can, however, be ameliorated if governments have access to debt financing on a significant scale. So perhaps the biggest problem associated with current debt-to-GDP ratios across the globe is that such access is effectively denied. That problem cannot, however, be solved by large-scale debt default!

REFERENCES

Brennan, G. and G. Eusepi (2002), 'The Dubious Ethics of Debt Default', *Public Finance Review*, **30**: 546–56.
Brennan, G. and L. Lomasky (1993), *Democracy and Decision*, Cambridge: Cambridge University Press.
Broome, John (2012), *Climate Matters*, Oxford: Oxford University Press.
Buchanan, J. (1987), 'The Ethics of Debt Default', in J. Buchanan, C. Rowley and R. Tollison (eds), *Deficits*, New York: Basil Blackwell, pp. 361–73.
Buchanan, J. and R. Wagner (1977), *Democracy in Deficit*, New York: Academic Press.
Stern, N. (2006), *Stern Review: The Economics of Climate Change*, London: Her Majesty's Treasury.
Weitzman, M. (2009), 'On Modelling and Interpreting the Economics of Catastrophic Climate Change', *Review of Economics and Statistics*, **91**: 1–19.

4. Debt default and the limits of the contractual imagination: Pareto and Mosca meet Buchanan

Richard E. Wagner

4.1 INTRODUCTION

Nearly all promises create debtor–creditor relationships even though people rarely think in such formal terms. Whether a particular relationship is formalized or left informal, the essence of the relationship is a tying together of two or more people in some common activity over some interval of time. Only a small subset of those instances will entail financial indebtedness between or among the participants. The character of this tied relationship is summarized nicely by the title of Charles Fried (1981): *Contract as Promise: A Theory of Contractual Obligation.* That book is about private law and the sentiments that tie people together during the life of some contractual relationship. While personal indebtedness forms a good portion of the material of contractual obligation, contractual obligation reaches beyond usual notions about indebtedness.

Regardless of the range of that contractual reach, public debt enters into altogether different analytical and emotional material than personal debt does. In this difference in reaches, personal and public debt resemble the two parabolas, X^2 and $-X^2$, in that they share a common origin but point in opposing directions. All debt entails some relationship that extends over some duration of time. Personal debt, however, is mostly incurred through explicit agreement among the participants, though it is possible to imagine cases where one party has accepted a position of indebtedness under duress or even force. Where duress and force might be relatively rare in personal debt, it is common in public debt, especially with increases in the size of political units, as I shall explain below.

Vilfredo Pareto's (1916) distinction between logical and non-logical action has significant analytical work to do with respect to the distinction between personal and public debt. Personal debt falls within Pareto's category of logical action, as is typical of market choices. The choice between paying cash for something now and borrowing now and paying cash later leads readily and easily to Pareto's logico-scientific mode of thought. With public debt, however, the action is removed from the logico-scientific mode and shifted to the ideological mode because the individual cannot act directly on the object.[1] With personal debt, at any particular moment a person can pay the debt in part or in whole, and can form a judgment about the experience of being indebted. In contrast, no individual can undertake action with respect to public debt. One might embrace one of several ideological sentiments that political figures and associated interest groups advance, but that is all. How one might view public debt, along with the prospect for default, is more a matter of the strength of various ideological sentiments than of some logical calculation of individual costs and gains because no basis exists for logico-experimental calculation under most conditions of public indebtedness.

This chapter seeks to bring the analytical orientation toward public debt of James Buchanan (1958) onto the same analytical field as the analytical orientations of Gaetano Mosca (1896 [1939]) and Vilfredo Pareto (1916 [1935]) toward democratic oligarchy and ideological competition. Early in his career, Buchanan (1958) set forth the principle that public debt enabled current taxpayers to pass cost onto future taxpayers. Late in his career, Buchanan (1985, 1987) mused about the possibly positive moral value of debt default. Throughout his career, Buchanan advocated a contractarian orientation toward the material of political economy, with the exemplary reference being Buchanan (1975). Buchanan, though, had no truck with the ruling class theories that Gaetano Mosca and Vilfredo Pareto did so much to promote, though Wagner (2014) makes some modest effort to reconcile Buchanan with Mosca and Pareto. While Buchanan has surely done more than anyone to bring classical Italian ideas about public finance and political economy to an English-speaking audience, he never showed the same interest in the associated Italian fiscal sociology. Yet this line of Italianate thought can add much value to the theory of public debt and debt default, as I seek to show in this chapter.

---

[1] Pareto's category of non-logical action has often been described as a form of irrationality. This is a severe misunderstanding of Pareto's analytical scheme, as Patrick and Wagner (2015) explain. Pareto always has people acting to achieve objectives. It's only that what they can achieve and how they can achieve it differs between the logical settings of market action and the non-logical settings of political and religious action in particular. Pareto's distinction between alternative environments within which people act is similar to Gerd Gigerenzer's (2008) treatment of rationality as something that reflects interaction between environment and calculation, as opposed to being a matter of simple calculation.

4.2   TRANSFORMING PUBLIC DEBT INTO PERSONAL DEBT

Before exploring the logic of public debt default under conditions of non-logical action, it will be helpful to explore the logic of public debt under conditions of logical action. Whether individual appraisal of public debt is logical or non-logical depends on the institutional framework under which public debt is created and amortized. Under typical democratic frameworks, public debt belongs to the category of non-logical action because people cannot choose among and compare potential courses of action with and without public debt. It is, however, possible to imagine institutional circumstances under which public debt can be transformed into the category of logical action that pertains to personal debt.

Consider a town that has always financed its activities in balanced budget fashion, perhaps by a flat-rate tax on all income along the lines that Antonio de Viti de Marco (1936) set forth, and with Eusepi and Wagner (2013) exploring the contemporary relevance of De Viti's analytical scheme. This year, however, the town council has decided to replace a deteriorating earthen dam with a dam made of concrete. To finance this replacement will require a one-year doubling of the town's tax collections. The town could do this and let the individual residents decide how to finance their personal tax payments. Some people would make their added payment by drawing down their cash balances or selling off other assets. Other people would borrow the money to pay their tax. A set of debtor–creditor relationships would be created within the market, but there would be no public indebtedness. Public debt would not be created, but the town's action will increase the aggregate amount of indebtedness within the town all the same, even though the town itself is not indebted.

To simplify the exposition, suppose the debtor–creditor relationships that are established remain inside the town. Those town residents who borrow to pay their tax bill borrow from other town residents to obtain the proceeds with which to pay their tax bill. The town's construction of the dam creates a set of debtor–creditor relationships within the market, with some of the town's residents lending to other residents. The lenders will be compensated in future years by payment of principal and interest from the borrowers, and the entire operation will fall within the domain of logical action, given the doubling of each person's tax liability for the following year. Should individual borrowers move away from the town prior to discharging their liability to their creditor, that liability would remain in force until the debt was discharged. A lender might have some pragmatic difficulty in securing payment in some such cases, but this possibility is an element of any debtor–creditor relationship, as is conveyed by the presence of an allowance for bad debts within typical accounting schemes.

When faced with a temporary doubling of the tax bill, there is a good empirical basis for thinking that the immediate flow of cash-financed tax payments will be highly skewed, perhaps in Pareto-like fashion, as with 80 percent of the cash payments coming from 20 percent of the taxpayers. The majority of the residents would thus borrow to finance their extraordinary payments. While the resulting individual indebtedness could be accomplished through a set of personal loans, it is easy enough to understand how pragmatic political considerations might lead the town to borrow on behalf of those 80 percent of taxpayers. In this case, the town would bundle a large set of what would have been private loans into a single public loan, which the town would sell to that subset of the population willing to act as creditors. In this manner, what had been a set of personal loans is transformed into a public loan, and the debtor–creditor relationship is moved from the logical to the non-logical category.

It would, however, be a relatively simple matter to keep the relationship in the logical category. All that would be necessary would be for the town to assign liabilities for debt amortization to individual residents in proportion to their assigned extraordinary payments which they did not make at the time. In this case, the town council would organize the debt issue by distributing liability for that debt among those town's residents who did not make extraordinary tax payments. Those liabilities, moreover, would be permanent for those individual taxpayers, just as items like mortgage debt are permanent. Neither movement from the town nor death would erase a borrower's liability because that liability would remain to be settled as part of the decedent's estate. To be sure, lenders would face greater risk of default under this scheme than if the town were to service the debt or even just to guarantee it.

Perhaps the most notable feature of this institutional arrangement is that individual liabilities for debt amortization are established at the time the debt is created. The town itself, however, is not a participant in the credit market, but rather only establishes the pattern of liabilities that leads some residents of the town to become debtors and other residents to become creditors. Of central analytical significance for the rest of this chapter is the existence of a set of institutional circumstances under which public debt is indistinguishable from personal debt. Even though public debt is created by some governmental entity, it could operate in all relevant respects like personal debt. Among other things, allowances for bad debts would be part of the accounting scheme. Any person's nominal level of debt could not be increased in subsequent periods, regardless of whether some taxpayers had defaulted on their payments or because some taxpayer's income had declined, which normally would have increased tax liability on those whose incomes had not declined. Public debt would fall clearly within the rubric of the promise of contract even though the debt originated with a public entity. Public law would meld perfectly with private law and the principles of contractual obligation.

4.3 DEMOCRATIC GOVERNMENTS AS INDEBTED ENTITIES: A CATEGORICAL MISTAKE?

It was reasonable to describe the various feudal monarchs of times past as being indebted. Those monarchs would often borrow from subjects, and they also owned assets that might have given those subjects some modicum of hope of having their loans retired. Monarchs in feudal times operated inside a society's market economy, while also serving as a Big Player along the lines that Roger Koppl (2002) sets forth. There, Big Player status meant that monarchs were not subject to the ordinary principles of property and contract that held for ordinary market participants. Lending to a monarch was not identical to lending to other citizens. Still, it was meaningful to describe a monarch as being indebted, for indebtedness refers to a relationship between identifiably distinct entities, even if duress was sometimes involved when people lent to monarchs.

Democratic governments clearly accumulate debts in their name. This is a simple fact of direct observation. That fact, however, is a superficial fact that seems to dissolve on closer examination. To describe democratic governments as being indebted would seem to be a category mistake. Indebtedness entails a relationship between a debtor and a creditor. That relationship, moreover, is explicit. In feudal times a king might have been indebted to some nobles. In democratic regimes, however, that relationship vanishes and is replaced by a relationship of intermediation among people within the polity, and typically only a subset of the members of a polity and not everyone. This intermediary relationship can be seen most simply and clearly by assuming that public debt is held inside the indebted entity, though Buchanan (1958) extends his analysis to externally held debt. In any case, a democratic polity is not an entity within a society that can become indebted to other entities within that society, at least with respect to internally held debt.

With internally held public debt, a democratic government sells bonds to that subset of citizens willing to buy the bonds. Taxes are not increased presently, but rather are scheduled to be increased in future years to amortize the debt. As a first approximation, this public debt operation is an alternative to an explicit set of transactions on the credit market. As noted above, that first approximation could be converted into an exact copy by assigning liabilities for future payments at the time the debt is created. But democratic governments don't handle public debt in this manner, but rather leave the servicing of debt as something to be dealt with in future years.

Democratic governments are financial intermediaries when it comes to public debt. They mediate between people who want to save currently, which they can do by buying public debt, and the rest of society who are in an ambiguous position. It would be easy to describe these people as people who do not want to reduce their spending now, and so borrow to postpone paying taxes. But this would not necessarily be accurate. To put the matter this way is to presume that these people support the added spending but would prefer to pay for that spending at some later date. Perhaps some do, but it's also possible that some don't and would rather have less spending and less future taxation. For ordinary credit–market relationships, the debtor–creditor relationship is mutually agreeable to the participants. To be sure, there can be instances where borrowers borrow under some sense of duress, but this is mostly in consequence of the emergence of adverse circumstances for which borrowing subsequently is seen as superior to the alternative. Public debt, however, would be voluntary only within the framework of De Viti's cooperative state. Outside that limiting case, public debt is agreeable to some people but not to others.

Furthermore, public debt cannot be examined independently of the processes that generate the public spending that is provided through public debt. While public debt represents a substitution of future taxation for present taxation, any appraisal of that margin of taxation must take into account the political processes by which spending is increased, for without that increase in spending there would be no public debt. In the illustration at hand, it's the choice to replace the earthen dam with a concrete dam that brought about the public borrowing as an alternative to increased current taxation. Some people might support the new dam, but others might not. Moreover, the presence of a possible new dam on the public agenda does not simply emerge in mysterious fashion. Rather it is created through concerted entrepreneurial action from somewhere within the society. It is here where Buchanan's treatment of debt could gain much from integration with Mosca's and Pareto's recognition that rulership is always exercised by relatively small numbers of people, and proceeds through constructing and offering ideological images.

The offering of ideological images is the form that competition for rulership place takes in non-logical environments. The competitive challenge is to offer an ideological image that will resonate more strongly with desires held within the society than do other images. This situation is the reverse of the logico-experimental method that pertains to market settings where scientific-like tests can be performed. In Pareto's scheme, non-logical environments pertained particularly strongly to politics and religion. Pareto's distinction pertains to different approaches to the proof of God's existence. The logico-experimental method of rational action corresponds to Pascal's wager and to arguments based on original causation. The point of such arguments is to force belief through the power of logical reasoning. In sharp contrast resides Anselm's approach of *Fides Quaerens Intellectum* (faith seeking understanding) (Barth, 1931 [1960]), which starts from belief and explores the contours of belief. For Pareto, people choose among alternative articulations the one that resonates most strongly with their sentiments, which enables them to sound logical even though the logico-experimental method cannot be applied to credence goods.

Politicians compete for voter support by articulating images as points of attraction. We may be sure that a politician who wants to see a concrete dam built will support debt finance in place of a balanced budget, and the challenge is to offer an ideological image that secures more support than do images that would operate within the balanced budget framework. For instance, a belief in contractual obligation entails a presumption that people should pay their own way, which is roughly accomplished with a balanced budget. Someone who wanted the concrete dam would have to counteract that contractual image. One way to do that while supporting the contractual image is to invoke notions from capital budgeting. Hence, debt financing would be limited to the services the dam provides in future years, while tax financing would support current services. This competitive process, it should be noted, occurs within the non-logical and not the logical arena. Individuals have no ability to compare their experiences with alternative products or promises and to select what they judge to be superior. Such comparisons reside outside the pale of the logico-experimental method. If the capital budgeting rationalization resonates with a person's sentiments, public debt can be supported. If, instead, it is fiscal sobriety that resonates, one can support the balanced budget option.

Public debt is a form of promise, as is debt in general. With personal debt, however, it is generally quite clear who promises what to whom. With public debt, and hence with debt default, it is necessary to examine who promises what to whom. Such questions regarding public debt cannot be examined independently of the budgetary and political systems inside of which public debt emerges as an instrument to finance public expenditure. Antonio de Viti de Marco's (1936) contrasted cooperative and monopolistic states. Within De Viti's framework, promising would characterize a cooperative state, though De Viti recognized the cooperative state to be a limiting model and not a miniature replica of actual societies. Indeed, the essays collected in De Viti (1930) are dominated by the monopolistic orientation toward political action. Monopolistic states would operate with some variable admixture of promise and imposition. De Viti operated by making presumptions about the two types of democratic state and the relative mix of qualities. In contrast to De Viti, I do not advance assumptions regarding location along a cooperative–monopolistic spectrum. Rather I allow location along that spectrum to be determined through the institutional and organizational pressures at work within any particular scheme of governance. That scheme of governance, moreover, is characterized mostly in terms of different sizes of political units. In particular, I contrast small and large-scale democratic polities, seeking in particular to explore their possible scale-free qualities.

4.4   SCALABLE AND SCALE-FREE POLITIES

Many significant matters regarding both the creation of and the possible default on democratically created public debt depend on the extent to which democratic properties are scalable across size. As Barabási (2002) explains, some networks are scalable but others are not. All networks are constituted through connections among nodes or elements. In some cases those connections can be random, in which case a larger network will display the same pattern of connections as a smaller network. Such a network can be readily scaled from smallest to largest, with any new node equally likely to develop few or many connections in either sized network. In contrast, non-random networks are free of scale, with some nodes gaining in relative popularity as the size of the network expands. To claim that a government is scalable in some particular feature is to claim that variation in size has no effect on any essential feature of a government's operation. Democratic ideology, for instance, claims that everyone has equal access to political figures, which Bertrand de Jouvenel (1961) shows clearly to be wrong because of scale-free features of parliamentary assemblies. In a parliamentary assembly of five people it will be easy to have a full exchange and examination of views. With an assembly of 500 people, that will be impossible. An assembly of 500 people will necessarily have limits on the ability of people to address the assembly and it will operate in oligarchic fashion.

To illustrate with a simple numerical illustration, compare a town of 9000 residents, a city of 900 000 residents, and a nation of 90 000 000 residents. How, if at all, might there be systematic differences among the different sizes of government? The central question here is whether a claim about self-governance that might seem reasonable for a town might seem equally reasonable for a city or a nation. Democratic ideology holds that democracy is a system of self-governance. Is this attribute scalable across sizes of governments? Or might it be scale-free, in which case there is degradation in democratic qualities as size expands, much as De Jouvenel (1961) describes.

Suppose the town is divided into nine legislative districts of 1000 residents each. At this scale of governance, there will surely be a good deal of interaction among individual legislators and the citizens they represent. While there would doubtlessly be formal meetings, much relevant knowledge would be generated informally through encounters in shops, restaurants, theaters and the like. While the town council would surely follow some simple parliamentary procedure, a good deal of town business would operate under general principles of consensus as opposed to being subject to formal voting rules. To describe this town as being governed by consensus is not to say that it would operate with a strict voting rule of unanimity. Unanimity is a demonstrative rule; it is either satisfied or it isn't. Consensus is a principle of plausible reasoning (Polya, 1954). In significant degree, consensus is captured by the principle of going along to get along. One doesn't go along to get along if doing so brings harm. It's rather more like preferring to play soccer but being willing to play basketball since almost everyone else prefers to do that. Stated differently, the activities sponsored by towns are likely to be valued by most people. Towns can have cliques and coalitions, to be sure, but typically they wouldn't amount to more than the proverbial hill of beans.

A town's scale of governance is more likely to map into De Viti's (1936) notion of a cooperative state than is governance at the city or national scale, where the institutional arrangements are more likely to enable the emergence of monopolistic elements. For instance, the city of 900 000 people would require a city council of 900 people to maintain the same scale of governance as the town had. At this size of council, most members would know one another only as remote acquaintances. City business would be conducted in highly formal fashion with minutely divided agendas. The city council could be reduced to the nine members the town had, but this would mean that each council member represented 100 000 people. At this scale of representation, few people would have contact with legislators, as most of that contact would be filtered through interest groups. The remoteness of the relationship between citizens and political officials would intensify further at the national level. Where network patterns might be random at the level of towns and small cities, they would become non-random at the level of cities and nations.

4.5 CONTRACTUAL OBLIGATION AND DEFAULT WITH FORCED INDEBTEDNESS?

A theory of public debt within the spirit of De Viti's model of the cooperative state is straightforward. With respect to the preceding illustration
of replacing an earthen dam with a concrete dam, consensus would exist
within the relevant financing entity to make the change. The only issue
would be how to finance the replacement. To go further with the exposition, we may suppose that the polity sells bonds to some of its residents,
with the bonds to be amortized over ten years by a flat tax on income. In
this case, debt finance is agreeable to all taxpayers, and public debt fits
clearly within the sentiment of contractual obligation that accompanies
the making of promises (Fried, 1981). To be sure, De Viti's model was a
limiting model and, moreover, was not even his preferred model of collective action, judging from De Viti (1930), for he recognized numerous
margins along which non-cooperative collective action can occur. In real
democracies, and we should perhaps keep in mind that De Viti was a
member of the Italian parliament for some 20 years, collective action will
entail forced as well as voluntary indebtedness. What relevance might
forced indebtedness have for sentiments of contractual obligation and
debt default?

The easy answer is that forced indebtedness vitiates what otherwise
would have been a sense of contractual obligation. As is often the case with
easy answers, this one does not quite get the matter right by any reasonable
estimation, and for various reasons. One question that arises is how to
distinguish between forced and voluntary debtors when claiming to be a
forced debtor will secure tax relief. Obviously, self-determination in this
situation cannot be relied upon because incentives will exist for free-rider
types of activity. Yet if the possibility of being a forced debtor is recognized even though self-identification is not allowed, one is left wondering
how that distinction might be made.

The theory of statistical decision-making offers some clues. The central
feature of that theory is the impossibility of giving a definitive answer to
this type of question. Someone claims to be a forced debtor. That claim
could be granted even though it is actually false. It could also be rejected
even though it is actually true. Perfection is impossible within this analytical framework. All that is possible is to select a decision rule that minimizes
the cost of making the two types of error, presuming that such determinations can be made with reasonable plausibility.

As an explanatory matter, one can plausibly assert some positive
relationship between the extent of forced indebtedness and the degree
of support for debt default, though there is no reason to assume that

this relationship is linear and independent of the identities of those who support and oppose default. For instance, in the United States municipal pension funds are notoriously underfunded. These funds typically are of the defined benefit category, and actuarial soundness requires that they be pre-funded. But they typically are only partially funded, as Adrian Moore and Anthony Randazzo (2016) explain. While those funds operate with several rules and principles to keep them solvent, those rules have weak ability to withstand collusive action between labor unions and city councils or managers. Such coalitions of interest typically are able to exert more political force than ordinary people of the same aggregate size.

Ideological articulation operating on human sentimentality also is at work in this setting. One facet of that articulation is the claim that democracy entails an obligation to accept all democratically decided actions, as conveyed by the standard distinction between the rules of a game and the choice of strategies for playing the game. There is nothing in the logic of democratic governance that compels one to accept this claim under all circumstances. That claim is rather something that supporters of particular democratic practices advance through ideological articulation, with the hope that it becomes widely embraced within the population. It is reasonable to think that support for default will grow with increases in the share of the population that perceive themselves to be forced debtors, though I do not think there is any obvious linear relationship behind this proposition.

4.6   SOME CLOSING OBSERVATIONS

Contracts are promises, and it is understandable that public debt would be linked to personal debt to take hold of the promise-making character of personal debt. But public debt is not the same thing as personal debt, though the distance between personal and public debt is a variable and is not fixed. De Viti captured some of that variable quality in his distinction between cooperative and monopolistic states. There is surely nothing inherent in the nature of democratic regimes to provide a moral bar against supporting debt default because public debt is not *ipso facto* implicated in the same network of promises as is personal debt. It is easy enough to understand why supporters of expanded public spending financed by debt would support ideological formulations that wrap public debt inside the self-governing and promise-making and promise-keeping ideology that pertains to private ordering of human activity. But public ordering carries forward only some of those qualities. Indeed, the long-standing aphorism that 'eternal vigilance is the price of liberty' reminds us that such vigilance might well countenance episodes of default as a corrective measure for excessive drift into destructively collectivist territory.

REFERENCES

Barabási, A-L. 2002. *Linked: The New Science of Networks*. Cambridge: Perseus.
Barth, K. 1931 [1960]. *Anselm: Fides Quaerens Intellectum*. Richmond: John Knox Press.
Buchanan, J.M. 1958. *Public Principles of Public Debt*. Homewood: Richard D. Irwin.
Buchanan, J.M. 1975. *The Limits of Liberty*. Chicago: University of Chicago Press.
Buchanan, J.M. 1985. 'The Moral Dimension of Debt Financing'. *Economic Inquiry* **23**: 1–6.
Buchanan, J.M. 1987. 'The Ethics of Debt Default'. In J.M. Buchanan, C.K. Rowley and R.E. Tollison (eds) *Deficits*. Oxford: Basil Blackwell, pp. 361–73.
de Jouvenel, B. 1961. 'The Chairman's Problem'. *American Political Science Review* **55**: 368–72.
De Viti de Marco, A. 1930. *Un Trentennio di Lotte Politiche*. Rome: Collezione Meridionale Editrice.
De Viti de Marco, A. 1936. *First Principles of Public Finance*. London: Jonathan Cape.
Eusepi, G. and R.E. Wagner 2013. 'Tax Prices in a Democratic Polity: The Continuing Relevance of Antonio De Viti de Marco'. *History of Political Economy* **45**: 99–121.
Fried, C. 1981. *Contract as Promise: A Theory of Contractual Obligation*. Cambridge: Harvard University Press.
Gigerenzer, G. 2008. *Rationality for Mortals*. Oxford: Oxford University Press.
Koppl, R. 2002. *Big Players and the Economic Theory of Expectations*. New York: Palgrave Macmillan.
Moore, A. and A. Randazzo 2016. 'Causes and Cures of Public Pension Debt'. Paper presented at the 2016 meeting of the Public Choice Society, Fort Lauderdale, FL.
Mosca, G. 1896 [1939]. *The Ruling Class*. New York: McGraw-Hill.
Pareto, V. 1916 [1935]. *The Mind and Society: A Treatise on General Sociology*. New York: Harcourt Brace.
Patrick, M. and R.E. Wagner 2015. 'From Mixed Economy to Entangled Political Economy: A Paretian Social-theoretic Orientation'. *Public Choice* **164**: 103–16.
Polya, G. 1954. *Mathematics and Plausible Reasoning*, 2 vols. Princeton: Princeton University Press.
Wagner, R.E. 2014. 'James Buchanan's Public Debt Theory: A Rational Reconstruction'. *Constitutional Political Economy* **25**: 253–64.

PART II

Macro consequences and implications of
public debt

5. Political economy of government solvency: the institutional framework for stability and sustainability[1]

Andrea Rieck and Ludger Schuknecht

5.1 INTRODUCTION

The global financial crisis has left us with the highest public debt stock since the Second World War. It exceeds 100 per cent of GDP in many countries, including Italy, the US, Japan and Spain and it exceeds the EU Maastricht threshold of 60 per cent in almost all major industrialized countries. This limits governments' policy room for manoeuvre and makes us vulnerable to future crises. At the same time, private sector debt has been rising to historic highs, too. The problem is no longer limited to some – seemingly – distant parts of the world. It has become a global challenge affecting advanced, emerging and developing economies at the same time.

In addition, most advanced and many emerging economies are expected to encounter an unprecedented period of population ageing, with major increases in ageing-related expenditure over the coming decades. Finally, the experience and perception of governments as insurers of last resort at the national and international level for all kinds of calamities – including bank bail-outs, environmental problems, and international financial crises – has raised the scope of additional implicit or contingent liabilities of public sectors (Schuknecht, 2013).

Politicians, academics and market participants are holding heated debates on the right way forward. Many see an urgent need to reduce debt in order to raise the prospect of sustainable public (and private) finances in the long

---

[1] The ideas presented here have also been discussed in an earlier publication in CESifo DICE Report, Vol. 14, No. 4, Ifo Institute, Munich.

run and more resilience to crises and spillovers in the short run. Otherwise, we may risk a more serious and even systemic global fiscal crisis.

In this chapter we present an analysis of the existing debt overhang and look at ways to resolve it and prevent future over-borrowing. In section 5.2 we present some trends in public and private sector debt around the globe, which increasingly call sustainability into question. Section 5.3 describes different approaches to dealing with a debt overhang. Building on past experiences with these approaches, we discuss institutional settings needed to achieve and preserve debt sustainability in section 5.4. Section 5.5 concludes with a call for an institutional framework that aligns individual incentives with the common goal of stability.

5.2   UNHEALTHY DEBT LEVELS

Concerns about public debt levels are no longer only an issue for developing and emerging economies. Nor is the increasing private sector debt stock a source of vulnerability for advanced economies alone. Unhealthy debt levels have assumed a potentially systemic dimension. This was revealed rather starkly when the fiscal-financial crisis in Europe spread from Greece to Spain and Italy in 2011–12.

Since the 1970s public debt in advanced economies has been steadily increasing. A big increase has taken place since the outbreak of the international financial crisis in 2007. Public sectors have transferred large amounts of private sector debt onto their balance sheets, thereby further aggravating the already existing detrimental fiscal trends.

The aggregate debt ratio of G7 countries has reached its highest point since the Second World War (Figure 5.1). Following some consolidation efforts and the recent moderate economic recovery, public debt ratios are expected to peak in most advanced economies, but hardly any decline is discernible in the years ahead. Although starting at a much lower level, public debt in many emerging markets has also been on the rise, particularly in resource-rich countries suffering from low oil and gas prices (IMF, 2015b).

Private sector debt in several advanced and some emerging economies is at problematic levels, too (Figure 5.2). Australia, the Netherlands and Switzerland stand out in terms of household debt, while China, France and Sweden exhibit elevated levels of corporate debt. Looking at total non-financial private sector leverage, Canada, Australia and China have the highest levels among G20 countries, with more than 200 per cent of GDP, while a number of others have also reached levels well above the EU's indicative warning threshold of 133 per cent.

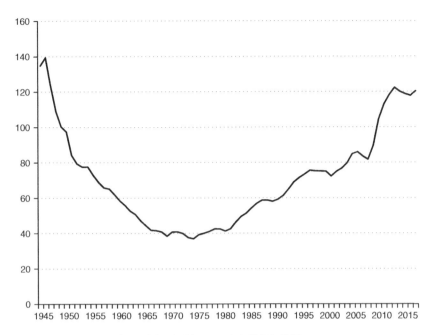

Note: Group aggregation weighted with countries' GDP in PPP terms.

Source: International Monetary Fund.

Figure 5.1   Public debt ratio of G7 countries in percentage of GDP

According to BIS data (Cecchetti et al., 2011), public and private non-financial sector debt taken together in 18 OECD countries almost doubled, from 167 per cent to 314 per cent of GDP, within three decades between 1980 and 2010. McKinsey Global Institute (2015) found a similar pattern when adding up public and private debt including the financial sector. The aggregate leverage of 47 advanced and emerging economies reached 286 per cent of GDP in 2014, an increase of US$112 trillion or 40 percentage points since 2000.

A growing number of economists and institutions are pointing to the risks of rising indebtedness. The political economy literature has been explaining public deficit and debt biases as a result of politicians' incentives to burden future generations with the costs of public programmes. The literature has also identified rules and institutions as a solution, for example balanced budget rules or quantitative debt limits (Buchanan and Wagner, 1977; Strauch and von Hagen, 2000; von Hagen, 2005; von Hagen and Harden, 1994).

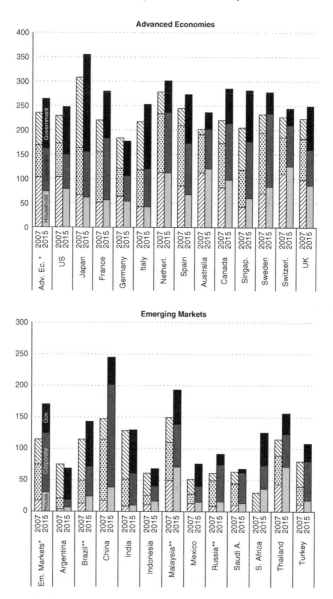

Notes: Credit to the government at nominal values except for Korea for which only market values are available. * Weighted averages of the economies listed are based on each year GDP and PPP exchange rates. **Breakdown of household debt and corporate debt is estimated based on bank credit data.

Source: Financial Stability Board (2015); Bank for International Settlements.

Figure 5.2   Total debt by sector (excl. financial sector) in percentage of GDP

High debt levels can place a drag on economic growth, limit the scope for policy action during acute crises, and increase financial market vulnerabilities (BIS, 2015). Declining trend growth in advanced economies and a succession of economic, fiscal and/or financial crises around the globe have exposed the limits of the debt-based global growth model. Financial boom–bust cycles may have contributed to the downward trend in potential growth observed over recent decades.[2] Apart from undermining growth and efficiency, credit-fuelled boom–bust cycles have also had disruptive distributional implications via the allocation of losses within and contagion across countries.

5.3   APPROACHES AND EXPERIENCES

There are five – actual or alleged – options for resolving a debt overhang, all of which have been pursued to a differing extent at various times.

5.3.1   'Organic' Debt Pay-down

The organic approach envisages a steady redemption of public debt through growth-friendly fiscal consolidation. Smaller deficits or even fiscal surpluses and higher economic growth bring public debt ratios down.

Successful consolidation means more than simple budgetary cuts. It includes a reprioritization of fiscal means towards growth-enhancing expenditures such as infrastructure and education, a streamlining of public sectors, and supply-side reforms of labour and product markets. In general, expenditure reforms are more likely to succeed than tax increases, which are usually accompanied by distortions to private sector activity (Alesina and Ardagna, 2012; Alesina and Perotti, 1996). The size of the public sector can be reduced by re-focusing on the provision of essential public goods, streamlining social welfare and privatizing business activities. Similarly, the government's role in stimulating the economy is most effective when limited to providing a functioning framework for the private sector to prosper, while automatic fiscal stabilizers reduce demand volatility over the cycle. Apart from sound public finances, such a framework also includes a reliable political, legal and judicial system, efficient labour markets and sensible regulation of product, service and financial markets.

Successful episodes of organic debt reduction can be found, for example, in Belgium and Sweden from the mid-1990s until the global financial

---

[2]   Borio et al. (2015) argue that credit boom-induced capital and labour misallocations undermine productivity growth during a boom as well as afterwards.

crisis. Belgium succeeded in reducing its public debt ratio from more than 130 per cent of GDP in 1995 to about 87 per cent in 2007. Sweden slashed public debt from over 70 per cent of GDP in 1996 to below 37 per cent in 2008, while also building up significant government pension assets. In both countries public deleveraging was accompanied by far-reaching expenditure reforms and drastic cuts in the size of the state, including the rationalization of welfare systems and improved fiscal governance (Hauptmeier et al., 2007; Tanzi and Schuknecht, 2000).[3] Such an approach has also been successfully applied in several European countries to halt adverse debt dynamics since the crisis (Hauptmeier et al., 2015).

While this strategy of debt reduction seems to be the least distortive and most lasting approach, it comes with an important challenge. Unfortunately for politicians, it requires a considerable adjustment, which is often unpopular with the domestic electorate. If it involves cuts to the privileges of special groups of the population who have a disproportionately large say in collective decision-making, such adjustment becomes even more difficult. The tangible fruits of necessary reforms are often reaped only by successor governments. Nevertheless, comprehensive reform is not necessarily detrimental to re-election (Alesina et al., 2011).

5.3.2 Monetization and Financial Repression

Monetization of public debt and financial repression redistribute wealth from creditors to debtors through an ultra-expansionary monetary policy that erodes the real value of debt via negative real interest rates.

The benign aim of expansionary monetary policy, including quantitative easing (QE) and extremely low interest rates, is to stimulate economic growth and prevent hysteresis directly after a crisis. Low interest rates also help debtors grow out of debt by limiting their debt service costs and by stimulating economic activity via the credit channel.

However, central banks can also monetize public debt by acquiring government bonds on the primary or secondary market, thereby steadily inflating their balance sheets. When money supply far exceeds the liquidity needs of the domestic banking sector, the central bank's role expands from 'lender of last resort' for commercial banks during a liquidity crisis to 'lender of last resort' for governments. In the past, this has frequently led to accelerating inflation via cash and credit creation, expectations, and contracting money demand.

---

[3]   The fiscal rule in Sweden requires a surplus in net lending of the public sector of 1 per cent of GDP on average over a business cycle. The rule was introduced in 1998 and, after a transition period, became fully effective in 2000 (Jonung, 2014).

But even without accelerating inflation, central banks' loose policies can reduce interest rates to negative real or even negative nominal territory. This gradually reduces the real value of the debt stock (financial repression or 'cold' monetization).

Other policy tools that can help put public debt at a funding advantage over other liabilities include preferential treatment of government bonds in bank regulation, political interference in bank governance bodies or moral suasion on domestic financial institutions (Reinhart and Sbrancia, 2011). Central banks can also 'monetize' debt held in the private sector, for example by buying mortgage-backed debt securities, by lending against very poor collateral, or through emergency liquidity assistance to commercial banks that are only notionally solvent. Such central bank subsidization of private debt may appear to politicians to be an easier alternative to the socialization of losses via public budgets or the risk of private agents bearing the costs of bankruptcies.

Experiences with monetization and financial repression over the last hundred years are mixed, at best, and the risk of losing control over inflation is always present. In Latin America the dramatic increase in the size of central banks' balance sheets led to hyperinflation in several countries in the late 1980s and early 1990s and to sovereign insolvency in Argentina in the early 2000s. This approach also proved to be a failure in Germany in 1923, when all government bonds ended up in the hands of the central bank and disastrous hyperinflation wrecked the economy. By contrast, after the two World Wars, a number of advanced economies managed to use financial repression for public debt reduction without losing monetary control. However, this typically required extensive government intervention in capital allocation.

Recently, experiences with central banks' zero-interest rate and asset purchase policy in advanced economies have proven relatively benign to date. Economic growth has returned, while inflation expectations in all advanced economies remain anchored at low levels. Institutional credibility has probably facilitated a situation whereby financial repression via balance sheet expansion can go much further than previously thought. Balance sheet expansion in the US, the UK, the euro area and Japan has nevertheless reached similar proportions to those in Latin America during the 1980s until 2002 (Figures 5.3 and 5.4). Moreover, the limit to balance sheet expansion in advanced economies before disorderly developments and 'hot' monetization and inflation set in is not yet known.

There are important risks to both monetization and financial repression. As mentioned, when central banks take on fiscal responsibilities, they may eventually lose control over monetary policy. Other negative side-effects are capital misallocation, the zombification of banks and corporations, and asset price bubbles as interest rates lose their signalling role. As

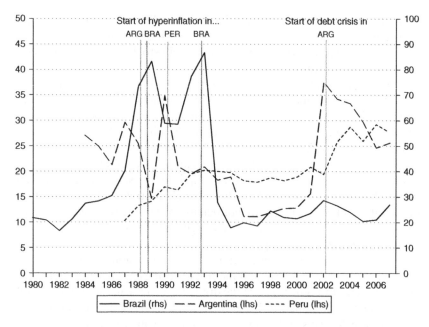

Source: IMF; Banco Central de la República Argentina; Banco Central do Brasil; Banco
Central de Reserva del Perú.

*Figure 5.3   Central banks' total assets in Latin American countries in
              percentage of GDP*

mentioned, subsequent inefficiencies in the real economy and possible
financial crashes could both cause a long-term drag on growth.

On the policy side, the ability to borrow cheaply creates moral hazard for
governments. The resulting lack of policy adjustment in turn increases the
need to continue the extraordinary monetary stimulus. The redistributional
effect from creditors to debtors not only affects the state and the financial
sector but also has an impact on society. Wealthy households with a diverse
portfolio can hedge against inflation more effectively and are better placed
to benefit from asset price increases, including shares and real estate, while
the middle class suffer from low returns on ordinary savings and old-age
provisioning (Schuknecht, 2013).

5.3.3   International Insurance

Countries may also seek international assistance or 'insurance' when
highly indebted. International insurance can work explicitly through
existing institutions such as the IMF and multilateral development banks,

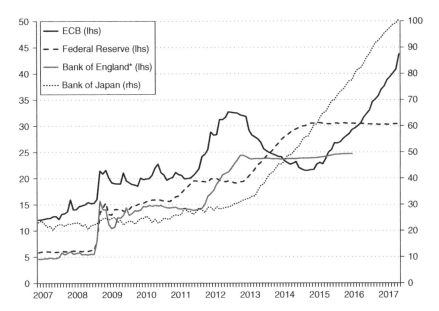

Note: *Bank of England discloses its 'consolidated balance sheet' with a lag of five quarters.

Source: European Central Bank; US Federal Reserve Bank; Bank of England; Bank of Japan; Eurostat.

Figure 5.4 *Central banks' total assets in advanced economies in percentage of GDP*

new institutions such as the European Stability Mechanism (ESM) and the Banking Union in Europe or implicitly through 'hidden' channels such as the European settlement system TARGET2.

Disorderly sovereign default would come at economic and political costs to the country concerned and, in an interconnected world, to others as well. Therefore, there is a collective interest in stabilizing an ailing economy and avoiding spillovers, especially if it is unclear whether the country is illiquid or insolvent. In order to prevent temporary (liquidity) assistance from becoming a bail-out, reform incentives that address the roots of a crisis need to be maintained. To this end, international financial assistance usually applies an adapted form of the Bagehot principle of lending to solvent parties at high rates against good collateral: in times of crisis, such international insurance provides temporary liquidity support in exchange for reform conditionality and assumes a preferred creditor status vis-à-vis pre-existing creditors (Bagehot, 1873).

Experiences with international insurance mechanisms have been mixed.

Several countries in Europe have used international financial assistance in return for domestic reforms. Ireland, Spain, Portugal and Cyprus successfully concluded the adjustment programmes set up during the European debt crisis. In Greece programme implementation has been more challenging as domestic ownership has been weak and uneven adjustment efforts have hindered the economic recovery. There are also several examples of IMF programmes outside Europe where successive financial assistance packages have ultimately failed, illustrating that international insurance is no panacea.

It is important to remember that the credibility of international insurance mechanisms is based on reliable and financially robust shareholders. Financial assistance by the IMF has essentially been based on loans being provided by strong member countries such as the US and other advanced economies. More recently an increasing share has also come from strong emerging markets.

For all insurance mechanisms, it is true that risks do not disappear by simply shifting them onto somebody else. Only risk reduction – through national fiscal adjustment and structural reforms, cleaning up banks' balance sheets and so on – allows debtors to regain stability and win back confidence. If, however, the necessary conditionality is softened to an extent that programme targets and debt sustainability can no longer be achieved, there is a risk of overburdening solvent sovereigns – or central banks. The world came close to the latter situation in 2011 when governments discussed (and eventually rejected) the idea of having the IMF print Special Drawing Rights in order to lend these monetary means on to crisis-stricken countries. International insurance can only work in a sustainable way if the anchor role of financially strong members is preserved and the number of insurance cases is kept limited.

5.3.4   Sovereign Debt Restructuring

An over-indebted country may choose default over monetization. The reduction of a government's debt can take place in the form of a write-off on the nominal value or a reduction in net present value terms through maturity extension, grace periods or lower coupon payments, for instance.

A sovereign default would entail high economic and political costs. However, a lack of debt sustainability cannot be addressed with the temporary liquidity assistance envisaged in international insurance schemes. If public debt is no longer sustainable, it is less detrimental to realize losses in a timely manner than risk a steady and long-lasting economic and political degradation (IMF, 2013).

Debt restructurings to date have tended to be ad hoc exercises. Evidence on whether they have been adequate in terms of volume, timing and management is inconclusive. In the early 1990s, Latin American states and a few other countries saw a restructuring of their debt through the Brady bond initiative. This usually implied debt forgiveness of 30–35 per cent, although individual arrangements differed in their terms, volume and participation (Cline, 1995). While the initiative was quite successful at the time, public debt in beneficiary countries has subsequently risen again. The default by Argentina in 2001 was not resolved until 15 years after the event.

In 2012 the private sector granted relief on Greek debt, which resulted in a cut in the face value of participating bonds of over 50 per cent and reduced Greece's public debt stock by about €107 billion, corresponding to 50 per cent of its GDP at the time (Zettelmeyer et al., 2013). The 2015 deal for Ukraine included a 20 per cent upfront haircut on the bonds held by private sector creditors, resulting in immediate relief of US$ 3.6 billion or 4.3 percentage points of the country's debt-to-GDP ratio. The global restructuring of low-income countries under the Heavily Indebted Poor Country (HIPC) Initiative led by the IMF and the World Bank entailed total costs to creditors of US$75 billion in end-2013 present value terms (IMF, 2014).

A significant challenge to public debt restructuring is its timing and legal framework. Market confidence is likely to take a hit and a disorderly procedure may prolong the period that a restructured country is shut off from international capital markets.

5.3.5 Reining in Private Sector Debt

While the above-mentioned approaches relate directly to public sector debt, instruments to rein in excessive private sector debt are an important complement. Otherwise, public budgets remain exposed to vulnerabilities arising from spillovers from over-indebted households, companies and the financial industry.

Individual actors behave most responsibly when they are held accountable for their actions and have to bear the consequences of their decisions. If they have reason to expect that someone else will foot the bill, they may take on excessive risks. Therefore, responsibility and decision-making power need to go hand in hand to avoid moral hazard. To protect this principle and keep incentives aligned, public bail-outs of private sector risks should generally be ruled out. A limited and conditional public bail-out should only be considered in exceptional cases of significant spillovers to other countries or segments of the economy that do not bear responsibility for the crisis.[4] In order for such cases to remain rare exceptions and limited in volume, private sector risks need to be kept in check so that they do not grow to become systemically important. In this respect, tax systems should be designed in a way that does not reward higher indebtedness. In addition, regulatory and macroprudential measures may be needed to avoid excessive debt and exaggerated asset prices.

Yet what we see in many countries is the opposite or deficient. Non-performing loans especially in some European countries still represent a heavy burden on the banking system and impede the overall economic recovery.[5] The transmission of monetary policy easing is hampered if banks cannot increase their lending due to legacy problems. To be fair, there has been some progress in individual cases, such as Spain and Ireland, which – helped by their financial assistance programmes – embarked on a deleveraging path involving the establishment of bad banks, the restructuring of viable banks, and improvements to their insolvency regimes.

As with the solutions to resolve the public debt overhang, reining in private sector debt is politically not easy. Governments can only influence private sector decisions indirectly by setting the right incentives. This includes vigilant supervision, appropriate regulation, macroprudential policies and the elimination of adverse fiscal/tax incentives. In a globalized world, regulation is most effective when it is internationally coordinated so as to minimize the side-stepping of rules or unfair competition.

5.4   THE NEED FOR INSTITUTIONAL REFORMS

The growing public debt burden over recent decades, the huge socialization of private debt in the context of the financial crisis, unsustainable social spending trends, and the limited ability of governments to undertake fiscal and structural reforms have raised the spectre of more outright or indirect government default in the future, even in advanced economies. Efforts to stabilize markets, banks and governments post-crisis has left our system with little resilience to further adverse developments, and we do not know how much scope for more debt there is before confidence caves in.

Moreover, the consensus to deal with the debt overhang via orderly pay-downs (in line with contracts and *ex ante* expectations of creditors and debtors) seems to have been replaced by the tacit expectation and desire on the part of many to get at least some help from financial repression, infla-

---

[4]   For the prerequisites of successful banking crisis resolution, see Lindgren et al. (1996).
[5]   According to IMF (2015a), gross non-performing loans as a percentage of total loans in 2014 stood at around 45 per cent in Cyprus, 35 per cent in Greece and 20 per cent in Italy.

tion or international risk shifting. With debt, moral hazard has increased as well. Central banks are also at risk of being compromised by so-called fiscal dominance, where fiscal (and/or financial) stability risks could hamper their ability to adjust interest rates in a timely fashion.

All this goes hand in hand with a serious and potentially destabilizing deterioration in institutional frameworks aimed at preserving hard budget constraints and fiscal solvency. Fiscal rules that aim to address government deficit and debt biases have eroded in line with a more cavalier view of deficits and debt. The European Stability and Growth Pact is a case in point. Private sectors have been given the impression that public balance sheets are readily available for debt shifting in the context of crisis-related bail-outs.

Nevertheless, it is important to carry out a conceptual and empirical analysis of what could work and what has worked in preventing and resolving over-indebtedness in the most market economy-friendly manner. Constitutional economics or the related concept of *Ordnungspolitik* in Germany emphasize the importance of rules and institutions to provide the right, time-consistent incentives for economic actors. Hard budget constraints with economic actors taking responsibility for gains as well as losses resulting from their actions constitute the appropriate macro- and micro-economic principles to guide the design of such institutions. Conditionality must continue to make financial assistance politically costly in cases where it cannot be avoided.

5.4.1 Public Debt: Achieving and Preserving Sustainability

As regards public debt, there are easy institutional solutions to this problem, the most simple of which is a balanced budget requirement. In principle, a balanced budget requirement is a guarantor of fiscal sustainability. The German and Swiss *Schuldenbremse* (debt brake), the Maastricht Treaty requirements, and balanced budget requirements for most US States are good examples of such institutional safeguards.

Balanced budget rules may not only be excellent preventive devices. Over time they may also contribute to resolving debt overhangs. As mentioned above, Sweden as of the mid-1990s is a prominent example in this regard.

However, such rules have proven difficult to implement in the past for reasons related to transparency, political economy and ideology. First, all fiscal responsibilities, including contingent and implicit ones, have to be included. Fiscal accounting and transparency, however, remains a major challenge in many countries. Government guarantees to the private sector or regional bodies and future social security obligations are often not provisioned for in annual budgets. Balanced budget rules may then not provide a full picture; they may even encourage liabilities to be moved off budget.

Perhaps even more importantly, the design of fiscal rules is crucial. Such rules should not allow too much leeway for interpretation. Incentives for strict implementation and provisions for enforcement need to be sufficiently strong. This is the only way that the political economy-related deficit bias can be broken. The European Stability and Growth Pact does not entirely live up to these requirements: rules are often complex (after two rounds of revisions that addressed symptoms rather than causes) and provide leeway for almost any possible interpretation. This leeway is prone to being taken advantage of in the course of politicized implementation, and there is a lack of enforcement provisions. German and Swiss rules are stricter. However, the *Schuldenbremse* has not yet been tested in bad times, at least in Germany. In any case, the more credibly a no-bail-out regime is communicated and implemented, the greater the efforts of a government to actually observe its fiscal rules are likely to be.

A third obstacle is the prevailing macroeconomic doctrine advocating fine tuning and deficit spending. Just as in the 1970s, 'naive' Keynesianism has provided the intellectual underpinning to deficit spending in bad times that never stopped in better times. Under the pretext of continued weak demand, fiscal consolidation has basically stopped throughout the industrialized world, although deficits in several countries continue to be very high.

5.4.2   Central Banks: Rebuilding Credibility

Developments relating to the quasi-fiscal role of central banks are possibly the most worrying. Zero interest rate policies coupled with massive QE programmes have reduced market monitoring and incentives for fiscal discipline. Once this has happened, it is hard to convey credibly to governments that it will not happen again. An eventual exit to normal size balance sheets and interest rates could well lead to major financial and economic upheaval.

Nevertheless, it is important to recall the 'old' principles of sound central banking and reflect on the implications for the future central banking order. Institutional and policy independence remains critical. But what should this imply for the future? Two ideas are to ensure that there is more accountability to the public rather than to politicians and markets, and to fill positions on central bank boards with end-career personalities rather than inept politicians or captured bankers.

The time-tested Bagehot principle for monetary operations needs to be re-established. The inability of a commercial bank to provide high-quality securities or to pay penalty rates to receive emergency liquidity should lead to the bank's restructuring or resolution. Monetary policy should not get involved in fiscal or quasi-fiscal policies. This is the role of national or international assistance programmes where conditionality limits moral hazard and fiscal dominance. A great deal of further thinking will be needed on this important challenge in the years ahead, as the debate on the future anchoring of monetary institutions and their credibility is only just beginning.

5.4.3 International Insurance: Preserving the IMF-based Order

Unfortunately, the possibility that government entities might get into financial trouble cannot be ruled out. If this happens to a city or a region, the federal government might provide conditional support or let the entity fail. But if whole nations are at risk of going bankrupt, the costs of economic and political destabilization in that country and via global interlinkages might be too high.

To prevent moral hazard the principle of lending against conditionality is essential. The political stigma of 'having to go to the IMF' (and the ESM in Europe) constitutes such a cost and should continue to work as a deterrence. In fact, the IMF is a strong institution in this regard and provides an important international stability anchor. IMF support should therefore remain a prerequisite for other international and regional safety-net lending. This also holds for Europe, where demands for ESM lending without IMF involvement seem motivated by a desire to benefit from solidarity without conditionality, thus violating the two principles specified above. But the IMF has also been subject to a number of demands to soften national budget constraints via unconditional international insurance. A lively debate on the future institutional design of global financial safety nets and the balance of incentives can also be expected in this area.

5.4.4 International Debt Restructuring: Strengthen Institutions via a Contractual Approach

Despite the above-mentioned international insurance, there are instances in which a country is unable to repay its legacy debt. Rather than resorting to indirect default via financial repression or inflation, debt restructuring may well be desirable for both debtors and creditors. Again, this should take place in an appropriate institutional context. Conditionality should ensure an adequate participation of debtor countries by making sure that domestic incomes and assets are taxed and state assets are liquidated.

Moreover, the process should be orderly. A contractual insolvency procedure could give the necessary clarity to a restructuring process, ensure efficient risk pricing beforehand, and keep incentives aligned. Such a restructuring regime would serve as a tool for crisis resolution and, perhaps more importantly, crisis prevention, as it would strengthen market discipline on the part of both creditors and debtors. To this end, debt relief should mainly be at the expense of private creditors so as to ensure future market monitoring as a deterrent against renewed indebtedness. Restructuring should be commensurate with the solvency problem and ensure that the country can make a fresh start.

Timing is a challenge. When restructuring is done too early, it imposes undue costs on the creditor, while the debtor government could avoid necessary adjustment efforts. When done too late, many private sector creditors can exit prior to the event and thus shirk responsibility. This further aggravates the financial situation and unnecessarily raises the costs for the country in question, the remaining bond-holders and global taxpayers. The other challenge is collective action. Without appropriate aggregation clauses, there is a risk that holdout creditors seek preferential treatment via litigation – at the expense of those creditors negotiating in good faith. The better the timing, the more orderly the process, and the better the policy programme accompanying a debt deal is, the better the prospects for a swift return of trust and credibility, low losses and, ultimately, market access.

Recent initiatives in this regard have been quite promising. Euro area members and a number of other governments have included collective action clauses in all new central government bonds. This is the basis for an orderly negotiation process. In order to prevent the socialization of private losses via international financial assistance, an IMF-supported programme should include the prolongation of bonds held by the private sector. Such prolongations could apply in cases where a country applying for financial assistance has lost market access, exhibits public debt or financing needs above a certain threshold, and its debt sustainability is in doubt. In some cases mandatory debt restructuring may also be required. Changes in IMF procedures have been moving in this direction.

The euro area crisis and notably the Greek experience have shown that avoiding adverse feedback loops between banks and governments is essential. An excessive exposure of banks to certain governments could undermine required private sector bail-in if there is a risk of spreading financial instability. It is therefore essential to break the bank–government loop by removing regulatory privileges for government bonds on banks' balance sheets, notably their exemption from risk-weighted capital requirements and from large exposure limits.

Apart from addressing the debt overhang, the mere existence of an orderly debt restructuring option would already work as a crisis prevention tool as it would enhance market discipline and thereby reduce governments' debt bias.

5.4.5 Private Debt: Promoting Private Sector Responsibility

Finally, institutional solutions could reduce public sector risks arising from private sector exposures. The real economy and the financial sector have an inherent incentive to socialize private debt. It is therefore important to have strong property rights underpinned by a well-functioning legal and judicial system that make market transactions and enforcement of contracts cheap and reliable. This deters debtors *ex ante* from opportunistic debt accumulation. While this suggestion is almost embarrassingly commonplace, things often look different in reality and there is a great need for action, not least in Europe, as many indicators and anecdotal evidence show.

Moreover, capital and ownership structures, notably in the financial sector, have been deficient in the past, meaning that governments could all too easily be blackmailed into expensive bail-outs. There has been significant progress in this area. The global community has embarked on an ambitious financial regulation agenda under the auspices of the Financial Stability Board (FSB), while Europe has made progress towards a level playing field and coherent application of rules through the Banking Union's single supervision and bank resolution framework. Notable enhancements are global requirements for more capital (core and contingent) and bank resolution plans, especially for systemic players. Bail-in requirements have been enshrined in (European) law, thus protecting taxpayers from private losses migrating onto public balance sheets. It is now crucial to implement these agreements.

5.5 CONCLUSION

Global over-indebtedness poses systemic risks to economic growth and stability. There has recently been some progress in deficit reduction and the stabilization of the debt stock. However, little, if any, progress has been made in deleveraging in the public and private sectors.

There is also good news and bad news in Europe. EU members found an appropriate response to the financial and subsequent debt crisis; but once immediate stability risks abated, complacency set in. This is all the more worrisome as systemic risks from global debt trends loom large.

In this chapter we argued that the debt crisis was the result of an institutional crisis. To preserve solvency, we called for an institutional framework that aligns individual and political incentives with the global interests of stability and sustainability. Hard budget constraints for public and private sector debt are one side of the coin. The other side are transparent, effective rules and de-politicized enforcement procedures that ensure compliance. Discipline can only be re-established when all actors (politicians, investors, corporations and the financial industry) are held accountable for their decisions.

Picking up on Buchanan's ethical debate on public debt (Buchanan, 1987), we do not see default as a solution to remedy a possible 'immoral' use of money borrowed by the government in the past. Instead, we agree with Brennan and Eusepi (2002) that spent money, whether it has been used efficiently or not, cannot be recouped by reshuffling claims and liabilities between present bond-holders and taxpayers. Similarly, we do not see inflation and financial repression as an acceptable way out of debt. The people who are likely to bear the costs of such implicit default are the middle classes. Let's not prove Marx right after all in his view that capitalism, market economies and democracies destroy themselves. Instead, we need to strengthen national and international institutional underpinnings to ensure that contracting parties are able and willing to serve their obligations. This would seem to be the best way to prevent and resolve over-indebtedness.

REFERENCES

Alesina, A. and S. Ardagna (2012), 'The Design of Fiscal Adjustments', *NBER Working Paper*, 18423.
Alesina, A. and R. Perotti (1996), 'Fiscal Adjustments in OECD Countries: Composition and Macroeconomic Effects', *NBER Working Paper*, 5730.
Alesina, A., D. Carloni and G. Lecce (2011), 'The Electoral Consequences of Large Fiscal Adjustments', *NBER Working Paper*, 17655.
Bagehot, W. (1873), *Lombard Street: A Description of the Money Market*, London: Henry S. King & Co., published at Online Library of Liberty, accessed 19 April 2016 at http://oll.libertyfund.org/titles/128.
Bank for International Settlements (2015), *85th Annual Report*, Basel: BIS.
Borio, C., E. Kharroubi, C. Upper and F. Zampolli (2015), 'Labour Reallocation and Productivity Dynamics: Financial Causes, Real Consequences', *BIS Working Papers*, 534.
Brennan, G. and G. Eusepi (2002), 'The Dubious Ethics of Debt Default', *Public Finance Review*, **30** (6), pp. 546–61.
Buchanan, J. (1987), 'The Ethics of Debt Default', in M. Buchanan, C. Rowley and R. Tollison (eds), *Deficits*, Oxford: Basil Blackwell, pp. 361–73.
Buchanan, J. and R. Wagner (1977), *Democracy in Deficit: The Political Legacy of Lord Keynes*, Indianapolis: Liberty Fund, Inc.
Cecchetti, S., M. Mohanty and F. Zampolli (2011), 'The Real Effects of Debt', *BIS Working Papers*, 352.

Cline, W. (1995), *International Debt Reexamined*, Washington, DC: Institute for International Economics.

Financial Stability Board (2015), *Corporate Funding Structures and Incentives: Final Report*, Basel: FSB.

Hauptmeier, S., M. Heipertz and L. Schuknecht (2007), 'Expenditure Reform in Industrialised Countries: A Case-Study Approach', *Fiscal Studies – The Journal of Applied Public Economics*, **28** (3), pp. 293–342.

Hauptmeier, S., J. Sánchez-Fuentes and L. Schuknecht (2015), 'Spending Dynamics in Euro Area Countries: Composition and Determinants', *Hacienda Pública Española Review of Public Economics*, **215**, pp. 119–38.

International Monetary Fund (2013), *Sovereign Debt Restructuring: Recent Developments and Implications for the Fund's Legal and Policy Framework*, Washington, DC: IMF.

International Monetary Fund (2014), *Heavily Indebted Poor Countries (HIPC) Initiative and Multilateral Debt Relief Initiative (MDRI)*, Washington, DC: IMF.

International Monetary Fund (2015a), *A Strategy for Resolving Europe's Problem Loans*, Washington, DC: IMF.

International Monetary Fund (2015b), *Fiscal Monitor – The Commodities Roller Coaster*, Washington, DC: IMF.

Jonung, L. (2014), 'Reforming the Fiscal Framework: The Case of Sweden 1973–2013', *Department of Economics School of Economics and Management Working Paper*, 2014:26, Lund University.

Lindgren, C., G. Garcia and M. Saal (1996), *Bank Soundness and Macroeconomic Policy*, Washington, DC: International Monetary Fund.

McKinsey Global Institute (2015), *Debt and (not much) Deleveraging*, McKinsey & Company, accessed 19 April 2016 at http://www.mckinsey.com/global-themes/employment-and-growth/debt-and-not-much-deleveraging.

Reinhart, C. and B. Sbrancia (2011), 'The Liquidation of Government Debt', *NBER Working Paper*, 16893.

Schuknecht, L. (2013), 'Has Public Insurance Gone Too Far?', *CESifo Working Paper*, 4217.

Strauch, R. and J. von Hagen (eds) (2000), *Institutions, Politics and Fiscal Policy*, Dordrecht: Kluwer Academic Publishers.

Tanzi, V. and L. Schuknecht (2000), *Public Spending in the 20th Century: A Global Perspective*, Cambridge: Cambridge University Press.

von Hagen, J. (2005), 'Political Economy of Fiscal Institutions', *GESY University of Mannheim Discussion Paper*, 149.

von Hagen, J. and I. Harden (1994), 'National Budget Processes and Fiscal Performance', *European Economy Reports and Studies*, **3**, pp. 311–418.

Zettelmeyer, J., C. Trebesch and M. Gulati (2013), 'The Greek Debt Restructuring: An Autopsy', *Peterson Institute for International Economics Working Paper*, 13-8.

6. On some recent proposals of public debt restructuring in the Eurozone

Ernesto Longobardi and Antonio Pedone*

6.1 INTRODUCTION

This chapter has the limited purpose of introducing a discussion on some recent proposals for restructuring the sovereign debts in the Eurozone (EZ).

It may be worthwhile recalling the reasons why the issue of sovereign debts' reduction has become central, although public debts were not among the causes of the disruptive economic and financial crisis, which has been long lasting and cannot yet be considered completely over.

Actually the fast, large and disordered growth of leverage in the private sector is unanimously considered as the origin of the US financial crisis in 2007. A number of factors contributed, to a different extent and in different times: a lax monetary policy, which fuelled the exuberance of the markets; the changing orientation of the banking activity from "originate and hold" to "originate to distribute", also favoured by financial innovation directed to a widespread diffusion of risks in a very complex and opaque fashion; the lack of adequate information on the quality of the different assets and on the actual final distribution of the associated risks; an often uninformed and complaisant behaviour of regulators, supervisors and rating agencies; the uncontrolled expansion of banking and financial systems.[1]

The initial underestimation of the severity of the crisis by influential observers, the hesitations and indecision on the part of the authorities

---

* The authors wish to thank the participants at the conference *Inside Public Debt: Ethical Arguments Against Default*, for their comments. The authors also acknowledge helpful insights and suggestions from Massimo Bordignon, Carlo Cottarelli, Claudio Gnesutta, Andrea Ventura and Annalisa Vinella.

[1] The influence of these different factors was foreseen and clearly enlightened by Spaventa (2008) in his pioneering analysis, which emphasized the need for an orderly reduction of private leverage. Among the most recent contributions on the theme of excessive private debt, the obstacles that have been encountered in the attempts to reduce it, the small results obtained and the developments of the debate, see Buttiglione et al. (2015).

responsible for economic policy, the liquidity shortages, the collapse in the value of assets and the breakdown of the credit circuit have contributed to the rapid and tumultuous international spread of the financial and banking crisis and to its heavy extension to real economies.

In the EZ, governments' measures directed to tackle the crisis have resulted in a quick and large deterioration of the public finances, even in the most virtuous member countries. Between 2007 and 2010, in Ireland the general government overall balance changed from a small surplus to a deficit of more than 32 per cent of GDP; in Spain from a surplus of 2 per cent to a deficit of more than 11 per cent (2009); at the same time, in the former country the public gross debt/GDP ratio jumped from a reassuring 27.3 per cent to almost 90 per cent (a level that was later largely overtaken) and, in the latter, from a quiet 36 per cent to over the fateful level of 60 per cent. In the same time span, in Germany the general government overall balance turned from a surplus of 0.2 per cent to a deficit of 4.2 per cent, while the debt/GDP ratio increased from 63.5 per cent to 81 per cent (IMF, 2016).

Overall, soaring public deficits and debts have mainly been the effect and not the cause of the financial and economic crisis. They can be attributed to the rescue of the banking systems with public funds and to the operating of the automatic stabilizers, notably taxes and transfers. Only at a later time, especially in countries with a high legacy debt, was the deterioration of public accounts worsened by a crisis of confidence in sovereign debts.[2]

The sovereign debts were no longer considered risk-free. This markets' belief was reinforced by the delays and hesitation with which the Greek crisis was addressed. It was particularly detrimental that the procedures eventually adopted failed both to comply with the no bail-out clause and to avoid the private sector involvement (PSI).

At the basis of the perception that the sovereign debts in the EZ are no longer risk-free is the absence of a lender of last resort for government bonds' markets, an aspect that has long been stressed by De Grauwe (see, most recently, De Grauwe, 2014, 2015).

The lack of this implicit guarantee, which is instead available to countries that have maintained their central banks and national currencies, in which government bonds are issued, exposes the states of the EZ to sudden liquidity crises (difficulties of access to markets) and to upsurges in the costs of the debt (spread). They are thus forced to adopt austerity policies, which, in turn, tend to aggravate the recession.

---

[2]   In a number of cases the crisis of public finances was accentuated by the poor reliability of fiscal data, highlighted by continued substantial revisions of time series. Among the several accounting deficiencies, the difficulty of assessing implicit guarantees and liabilities was particularly detrimental.

Moreover, the perception of sovereign risk has strengthened the "diabolical loop" (Corsetti et al., 2015) between banks and sovereigns. The issues of how to evaluate government bonds in the portfolios of banks and insurance companies, and of establishing capital requirements, have been raised.[3]

In such circumstances, in order to ensure financial stability and to face emergency situations in the markets, which were particularly severe in 2011 and 2012, the European Central Bank (ECB) has gradually extended the scope and intensity of unconventional measures. This choice was necessary and useful: the ECB succeeded in stabilizing the markets and preventing dangerous contagions. However, if unconventional measures can ease the symptoms, they cannot remove the causes of economic and financial problems in the EZ.

Moreover, a persistent and large recourse to unconventional tools is a source of criticism and concern for a number of reasons. First, it can encourage opportunistic behaviour (moral hazard) by highly indebted countries. Second, it can give rise to inflationary flames and bubbles in asset prices, whose resolution may be very costly for the real economy. Finally, in the case of insolvency of a member state, the losses incurred by the ECB may fall on the taxpayers of other states.

The drawbacks of a long-lasting policy of low interest rates must also be accounted for. Resources are driven towards more risky assets and capital-intensive investments, to the detriment of labour employment. The real income of older people, whose main source is the return of assets accumulated during their working lives, is shrunk, with a negative impact on demand and economic activity and with undesirable equity implications. These effects are particularly severe in rapidly aging regions and countries.

It must be also mentioned that, when a change in the stance of monetary policy occurs and the time of unconventional measures and low interest rates comes to an end, the effects on the stability of financial markets and on economic activity will be unpredictable and difficult to tackle.

Finally, while the ECB's monetary policy has proved essential to avoid the disintegration of the euro and to shield the prospects of recovery for the EZ, it is not sufficient to boost growth if it is not accompanied by effective measures of fiscal and structural policies in the member states. In particular, it is unlikely that a process of sustained and lasting growth can restart without overcoming the obstacle of the overhang of private and public debt.

---

[3] As is known, this problem has also blocked the completion of the Banking Union, preventing the construction of the third pillar, the *Common Deposit Guarantee Scheme*, while the other two pillars – the *Single Supervisory Mechanism* and the *Single Resolution Mechanism* – have started to operate.

This chapter deals only with the issue of sovereign debt, even if the two aspects – private and public leverages – are closely intertwined. It is organized as follows. The next section summarizes the main causes of the financial crisis and describes its effect on public accounts. In section 6.3 the reasons for reducing sovereigns' debts in the EMU countries are briefly discussed. High public debt can hamper economic growth; it exposes national countries to the risk of liquidity crises, as opposed to insolvency; it restrains both the room for national fiscal policies and the freedom of the ECB to pursue its own monetary policy's goals, being the central bank's choices constrained by the need of preventing debt crises. A high public debt may have relevant social costs, because high interest payments are detrimental to welfare expenditure and limit the possibility of reducing taxation. Moreover, the links between public debts and banking system represent a main obstacle to the completion of the Banking Union. Finally, high public debts may not be sustainable in the long run, in the presence of both growing implicit liabilities due to demographic factors and phenomena of tax bases' erosion caused by international tax competition.

In section 6.4 the different possible strategies to reduce the debt/GDP ratio while avoiding any form of debt restructuring are dealt with. A number of measures, which have often been adopted in the past, are not available at present. In the first place, the most frequently used – and probably most effective – way for burning debt, that is, a sudden (unexpected) upsurge of inflation, accompanied by a heavy "financial repression" and a strict control on capital movements, is unworkable and probably undesirable today in Europe.

A number of extraordinary finance instruments for cutting the debt of a sovereign – such as wealth taxes, privatization of public companies, sale of public assets – are, instead, viable at least in principle. Their possibilities and limits are briefly considered.

The theme of debt restructuring is dealt with in sections 6.5 and 6.6. The issue of a once-and-for-all reduction of outstanding debt (legacy debt) is addressed separately from that of designing a permanent mechanism to deal with insolvency of sovereigns in the EZ. Section 6.5 is dedicated to the former aspect. The German Council of Economic Experts (GCEE, 2011) triggered a stream of research on the ways to cut down existing debt. Two main proposals followed on the same lines: the Politically Acceptable Debt Restructuring in the Eurozone Politically Acceptable Debt Restructuring in the Eurozone (PADRE) programme, due to Pâris and Wyplosz (2014) and the plan designed by a group of CEPR's economists (Corsetti et al., 2015). The effectiveness of the two projects in actually achieving the benefits that are expected from debt reduction is questioned. Section 6.6

deals, instead, with the group of proposals concerning the institution of an ordered procedure of insolvency for sovereigns. Four main plans are considered: the Bruegel proposal of a European Crisis Resolution Mechanism (Gianviti et al., 2010); the resolution mechanism designed by the European Economic Advisory Group of CESifo (EEAG, 2011); the European Sovereign Debt Restructuring Regime (ESDRR) proposed by the Committee on International Economic Policy and Reform (CIEPR, 2013) and the proposal of a viable insolvency procedure for sovereigns (VIPS), advanced by Fuest et al. (2014). All these plans are meant to make effective the no bail-out principle, whose compliance has proved very difficult so far: the question is raised if this perspective is really realizable in the absence of any element of fiscal union.

Section 6.7 concludes, arguing that instead of relying exclusively on bail-in, as opposed to bail-out, an equilibrium should be looked for between these two perspectives which could effectively address the moral hazard problem.

6.2   PRIVATE DEBT AND PUBLIC FINANCES OVER THE CRISIS

The main cause of the financial crisis was an exceptional growth of private debt, while public debt increased only as a consequence of the crisis. The global debt of the non-financial sector – which includes households, non-financial firms and general government – began to expand rapidly long before the crisis: it more than doubled in nominal terms after the beginning of the 2000s, reaching the historic peak of $152 trillion in 2015, which amounts to 225 per cent of world GDP. However, about two-thirds of the total (100 trillion) was made up of private debts, which grew by 35 GDP points in the six years preceding the crisis in advanced economies.[4] The overhang of private debt was not limited to the subprime mortgage market, but concerned the total indebtedness of households and businesses; nor it was a phenomenon limited to the United States, because it pervaded many other countries.

Among the main causes of the exceptional accumulation of private debt were: the intensity and persistence of major macroeconomic imbalances within and among the major economies; the expansive sign of monetary policies – justified, *inter alia*, by a low inflation environment – which produced a plentiful supply of liquidity and credit; the uncontrolled

---

[4]   The source of all the figures presented in this section is IMF (2016).

acceleration of financial innovation in forms that made the distribution of risk opaque; the transition of banks from the "originate and hold" model to that one of "originate to distribute"; and the deregulation of financial markets, favoured by the prevailing ideological climate and by a somewhat drowsy vigilance. In such a scenario, the worsening of the mortality rate on the subprime mortgages in the United States was the spark of a colossal fire, which rapidly extended to the credit system (with the bankruptcy of many banks until the liquidation of Lehman Brothers in September 2008) and then to the entire international financial system and the global economy.

Faced with the explosion and the expansion of the crisis, many governments intervened massively for the rescue of financial institutions, causing a sharp and rapid increase in public deficits and debts. The automatic effects of the crisis on tax revenues and on some items of public expenditure contributed to worsen the public accounts.

The deterioration of public finances was very different in the single countries. Tables 6.1 and 6.2 show the data on debt and budget balances respectively, for the major countries and geo-political areas (EZ, G7, G20), since the eve of the crisis until today (2007–16). It can be noticed that each case represents a single story: very different relationships link the initial situations in terms of balance/GDP and debt/GDP ratios and their evolution during the acute phase of the crisis (2007–13) and the ensuing slow recovery (2013–16).

Between before and after the crisis (2007–13), the gross debt/GDP ratio was increasing in all countries: from 13.6 points in Germany to 95.6 in Ireland. The average for EZ was 28.4, noticeably lower than the increase of 38.5 GDP points in the G7 countries and of 35.8 in the G20. The evolution of the debt/GDP ratio in the next phase (2013–16) is also much differentiated: it is striking that, in this case too, the EZ countries, with a slight reduction in the ratio, do better than those of the G7 and G20, where the ratio continued to grow.

The change over time of the overall and of the primary balance is also very heterogeneous among the different countries. Countries which appeared mostly virtuous until the outbreak of the crisis show the highest deterioration during the crisis: Ireland moves from a slight overall budgetary surplus in the year preceding the crisis (2007) to a deficit of over 32 per cent of GDP (2010), Spain from a surplus of 2 per cent to a deficit of 11 per cent (2009); throughout the crisis (2007–13), the two countries accumulate a total deficit of 78.9 and 49.7 points respectively, while in Italy the cumulated overall deficit during the crisis was 23 GDP points.

The cumulated primary balance over the entire period (2007–16) is positive only in Germany and Italy, near to zero in Belgium, negative in all

Table 6.1 *General government gross and net debt in some advanced economies: 2007–16*

	2007	2008	2009	2010	2011	2012	2013	2014	2015	2016	2013–07	2016–13	2016–07
Germany	**63.5**	**64.9**	**72.4**	**81.0**	**78.3**	**79.4**	**77.1**	**74.5**	**71.0**	**68.2**	**13.6**	**−8.9**	**4.7**
	47.9	47.8	54.4	57.1	55.2	54.4	53.4	50.1	47.5	45.4	5.5	−8.0	−2.5
France	**64.4**	**68.1**	**79.0**	**81.7**	**85.2**	**89.6**	**92.4**	**95.3**	**96.1**	**97.1**	**28.0**	**4.7**	**32.7**
	57.7	60.3	70.1	73.7	76.4	81.6	84.4	87.4	88.2	89.2	26.7	4.8	31.5
Italy	**99.8**	**102.4**	**112.5**	**115.4**	**116.5**	**123.3**	**129.0**	**132.5**	**132.7**	**133.2**	**29.2**	**4.2**	**33.4**
	85.9	87.9	96.3	98.3	100.4	105.0	109.9	112.5	113.3	113.8	24.0	3.9	27.9
Spain	**35.5**	**39.4**	**52.7**	**60.1**	**69.5**	**85.4**	**93.7**	**99.3**	**99.3**	**100.1**	**58.2**	**6.4**	**64.6**
	19.2	22.3	32.8	42.3	51.5	65.8	73.8	78.6	79.7	81.4	54.6	7.6	62.2
Portugal	**68.4**	**71.7**	**83.6**	**96.2**	**111.4**	**126.2**	**129.0**	**130.2**	**129.0**	**128.4**	**60.6**	**−0.6**	**60.0**
	61.4	67.2	79.3	91.6	100.8	115.7	118.4	120.0	121.6	121.9	57.0	3.5	60.5
Ireland	**23.9**	**42.4**	**61.7**	**86.3**	**109.6**	**119.5**	**119.5**	**105.2**	**78.7**	**74.6**	**95.6**	**−44.9**	**50.7**
	14.2	22.5	36.5	66.2	77.7	86.1	89.2	86.2	67.0	63.8	75.0	−25.4	49.6
Greece	**103.1**	**109.4**	**126.7**	**146.2**	**172.1**	**159.6**	**177.7**	**180.1**	**176.9**	**183.4**	**74.6**	**5.7**	**80.3**
	–	–	–	–	–	–	–	–	–	–	–	–	–
Belgium	**87.0**	**92.5**	**99.6**	**99.7**	**102.3**	**104.1**	**105.2**	**106.6**	**106.1**	**105.8**	**18.2**	**0.6**	**18.8**
	54.3	55.1	61.0	59.6	60.8	62.5	63.6	62.8	61.0	62.0	9.3	−1.6	7.7
United Kingdom	**42.2**	**50.3**	**64.2**	**75.7**	**81.3**	**84.8**	**86.0**	**87.9**	**89.0**	**89.0**	**43.8**	**3.0**	**46.8**
	37.1	44.4	57.4	68.5	72.9	76.2	77.6	79.5	80.4	80.5	40.5	2.9	43.4

United States	**64.0**	**72.8**	**86.0**	**94.7**	**99.0**	**102.5**	**104.6**	**104.6**	**105.2**	**108.2**	**40.6**	**3.6**	**44.2**
	44.5	50.5	62.0	69.4	75.9	79.4	80.8	80.3	79.8	82.2	36.3	1.4	37.7
Japan	**183.0**	**191.8**	**210.2**	**215.8**	**231.6**	**238.0**	**244.5**	**249.1**	**248.0**	**250.4**	**61.5**	**5.9**	**67.4**
	80.5	95.3	106.2	113.1	127.2	129.0	124.2	126.2	125.3	127.9	43.7	3.7	47.4
Canada	**66.8**	**67.8**	**79.3**	**81.1**	**81.5**	**84.8**	**86.1**	**86.2**	**91.5**	**92.1**	**19.3**	**6.0**	**25.3**
	22.1	18.4	24.4	26.8	27.1	28.2	29.4	28.1	26.3	26.9	7.3	-2.5	4.8
Eurozone	**64.9**	**68.5**	**78.3**	**84.1**	**86.7**	**91.3**	**93.3**	**94.3**	**92.5**	**91.7**	**28.4**	**-1.6**	**26.8**
	44.9	46.5	53.9	57.8	60.2	65.7	67.8	68.3	67.6	67.4	22.9	-0.4	22.5
G7	**80.9**	**88.9**	**103.7**	**111.9**	**117.1**	**121.3**	**119.4**	**118.6**	**117.9**	**121.7**	**38.5**	**2.3**	**40.8**
	52.0	58.3	69.3	75.5	81.3	84.1	83.1	82.8	82.1	84.3	31.1	1.2	32.3
G20	**77.1**	**84.8**	**99.2**	**106.1**	**110.6**	**114.5**	**112.9**	**112.4**	**112.2**	**116.0**	**35.8**	**3.1**	**38.9**
	49.5	55.5	66.1	71.5	76.7	79.3	78.5	78.5	78.2	80.4	29.0	1.9	30.9

Note: Gross debt figures in the first row, net debt in the second one.

Source: IMF (2016, tab. A7 and A8).

Table 6.2 General government overall and primary balance in some advanced economies: 2007–16

	2007	2008	2009	2010	2011	2012	2013	2014	2015	2016	2013–07 (*)	2016–14 (*)	2016–07 (*)
Germany	**0.2**	**−0.2**	**−3.2**	**−4.2**	**−1.0**	**0.0**	**−0.2**	**0.3**	**0.7**	**0.1**	**−8.6**	**1.1**	**−7.5**
	2.6	2.2	−0.8	−2.1	1.1	1.8	1.4	1.7	2.0	1.2	6.2	4.9	11.1
France	**−2.5**	**−3.2**	**−7.2**	**−6.8**	**−5.1**	**−4.8**	**−4.0**	**−4.0**	**−3.5**	**−3.3**	**−33.6**	**−10.8**	**−44.4**
	−0.1	−0.5	−4.9	−4.5	−2.6	−2.4	−1.9	−1.9	−1.6	−1.5	−16.9	−5.0	−21.9
Italy	**−1.5**	**−2.7**	**−5.3**	**−4.2**	**−3.5**	**−2.9**	**−2.9**	**−3.0**	**−2.6**	**−2.5**	**−23.0**	**−8.1**	**−31.1**
	3.0	2.0	−1.0	−0.1	1.0	2.1	1.7	1.4	1.4	1.3	8.7	4.1	12.8
Spain	**2.0**	**−4.4**	**−11.0**	**−9.4**	**−9.6**	**−10.4**	**−6.9**	**−5.9**	**−5.1**	**−4.5**	**−49.7**	**−15.5**	**−65.2**
	3.1	−3.4	−9.6	−7.8	−7.6	−7.9	−4.0	−2.9	−2.4	−2.0	−37.2	−7.3	−44.5
Portugal	**−3.0**	**−3.8**	**−9.8**	**−11.2**	**−7.4**	**−5.7**	**−4.8**	**−7.2**	**−4.4**	**−3.0**	**−45.7**	**−14.6**	**−60.3**
	−0.4	−1.1	−7.1	−8.5	−3.6	−1.4	−0.6	−2.8	−0.2	1.3	−22.7	−1.7	−24.4
Ireland	**0.3**	**−7.0**	**−13.8**	**−32.1**	**−12.6**	**−8.0**	**−5.7**	**−3.7**	**−1.9**	**−0.7**	**−78.9**	**−6.3**	**−85.2**
	0.9	−6.3	−12.4	−29.7	−9.7	−4.4	−2.0	−0.3	0.3	1.3	−63.6	1.3	−62.3
Greece	**−6.7**	**−10.2**	**−15.2**	**−11.2**	**−10.2**	**−6.5**	**−3.5**	**−4.1**	**−3.1**	**−3.4**	**−63.5**	**−10.6**	**−74.1**
	−2.2	−5.4	−10.1	−5.4	−3.0	−1.4	0.5	0.0	0.7	0.1	−27.0	0.8	−26.2
Belgium	**0.1**	**−1.1**	**−5.4**	**−4.0**	**−4.1**	**−4.2**	**−3.0**	**−3.1**	**−2.6**	**−2.7**	**−21.7**	**−8.4**	**−30.1**
	3.6	2.4	−2.0	−0.7	−0.9	−1.0	−0.1	−0.3	−0.1	−0.5	1.3	−0.9	0.4

United Kingdom	**-2.9**	**-4.9**	**-10.5**	**-9.5**	**-7.6**	**-7.7**	**-5.7**	**-5.6**	**-4.2**	**-3.3**	**-48.8**	**-13.1**	**-61.9**
	-1.3	-3.4	-9.1	-7.1	-4.9	-5.4	-4.3	-3.8	-2.8	-1.6	-35.5	-8.2	-43.7
United States	**-2.9**	**-6.7**	**-13.1**	**-10.9**	**-9.6**	**-7.9**	**-4.4**	**-4.2**	**-3.5**	**-4.1**	**-55.5**	**-11.8**	**-67.3**
	-0.8	-4.6	-11.2	-8.9	-7.3	-5.7	-2.4	-2.2	-1.5	-2.1	-40.9	-5.8	-46.7
Japan	**-2.1**	**-4.1**	**-10.4**	**-9.3**	**-9.8**	**-8.8**	**-8.6**	**-6.2**	**-5.2**	**-5.2**	**-53.1**	**-16.6**	**-69.7**
	-2.1	-3.8	-9.9	-8.6	-9.0	-7.9	-7.8	-5.6	-4.9	-5.2	-49.1	-15.7	-64.8
Canada	**1.8**	**0.2**	**-3.9**	**-4.7**	**-3.3**	**-2.5**	**-1.9**	**-0.5**	**-1.3**	**-2.5**	**-14.3**	**-4.3**	**-18.6**
	2.4	0.5	-2.8	-3.9	-2.7	-1.8	-1.2	0.0	-0.6	-2.0	-9.5	-2.6	-12.1
Eurozone	**-0.6**	**-2.2**	**-6.3**	**-6.2**	**-4.2**	**-3.7**	**-3.0**	**-2.6**	**-2.1**	**-2.0**	**-26.2**	**-6.7**	**-32.9**
	1.9	0.4	-3.8	-3.7	-1.6	-1.0	-0.5	-0.2	0.1	-0.1	-8.3	-0.2	-8.5
G7	**-2.1**	**-4.5**	**-10.0**	**-8.8**	**-7.4**	**-6.4**	**-4.4**	**-3.8**	**-3.2**	**-3.6**	**-43.6**	**-10.6**	**-54.2**
	-0.2	-2.6	-8.1	-6.8	-5.3	-4.4	-2.5	-2.0	-1.5	-1.9	-29.9	-5.4	-35.3
G20	**-1.8**	**-4.2**	**-9.5**	**-8.3**	**-7.0**	**-6.0**	**-4.1**	**-3.6**	**-3.0**	**-3.4**	**-40.9**	**-10.0**	**-50.9**
	-0.1	-2.4	-7.8	-6.5	-5.1	-4.1	-2.4	-1.9	-1.5	-1.9	-28.4	-5.3	-33.7

Notes: (*) Cumulated. Overall balance figures in the first row, primary balance in the second one.

Source: IMF (2016, Tab. A1, A2).

other countries. Between Germany and Italy, the latter does better, both in the acute phase of the crisis (8.7 vs. 6.2) and throughout the whole period considered (12.8 vs. 11.1). The diverging trend in debt/GDP ratio in the two countries was therefore the effect of other factors (growth rate, interest rates, initial stock) rather than less stringent budgetary policies.

The heterogeneity of the single countries' situations and their evolution over time would appear even greater – and they could be better explained – if the differences were analysed considering the multidirectional relationships among all the factors that influence the short- and long-term dynamics of the debt/GDP ratio: the initial stock of debt and its average cost; the inflation rate and the GDP rate of growth; the primary balance and its structure (the different components of public expenditure and tax revenue). Just as an in-depth analysis of the factors affecting the perverse loop between banking system and sovereign debt would help: it should consider the composition and characteristics of the bank assets, in particular non-performing loans, derivatives and sovereigns' bonds; the level and structure of banks' capital and the incidence on it of the Basel rules; the forms and the conditions of direct intervention and guarantees provided by the state.

6.3   THE MAIN REASONS FOR REDUCING SOVEREIGN DEBTS

The main reasons that are usually put forward in favour of a significant reduction of sovereign debts, when they have reached a level that may be considered "excessive", are the following.

1. The persistence of a high, and possibly growing, public debt can hamper economic growth, for a number of reasons. We can mention just two of them. The first is that domestic demand can be restrained by expectations that, because of the debt, future tax payments will overcome the flow of benefits from public expenditure. The second reason is that public debt can crowd out private investments. It is worth noticing that, while most empirical studies find evidence of significant negative long-run effects of public debt on output growth, they instead do not confirm the hypothesis of a universally applicable threshold effect, that is, a tipping point for public indebtedness, beyond which economic growth drops off significantly.[5]

---

[5]   Reinhart and Rogoff (2010) estimate a threshold effect at a 90 per cent debt/GDP ratio, using a panel of advanced economies. Among the following collection of literature, which is large and still growing, we limit ourselves to referring to Chudik et al. (2015), who do not

2. High-debt countries are exposed to heavy risks of liquidity crisis, even when they may be considered solvent, in a context where financial markets swing between periods of risk on and risk off (Corsetti et al., 2015). This tendency is heightened in the EZ by the uncertain prospects of the monetary union and the confused and wavering way in which the recent events in Greece (and, to some extent, Ireland and Portugal) have been addressed.

3. A high public debt may have relevant social costs, because high interest payments are detrimental to welfare expenditure and limit the possibility of reducing taxation on low and middle incomes.

4. A high stock of public debt restricts the room for an active fiscal policy, which could boost domestic demand and investment spending and thus counteract the fall in growth potential, induced by the prolonged and deep recession of the last years. It must be emphasized that the space for a greater flexibility in fiscal rules, recently introduced in the EZ system, has to some extent contributed to increase, rather than reduce, the degree of uncertainty about fiscal policies perceived by markets, because of a number of issues concerning the interpretation and application of the norms.

5. The reduction of sovereign debts would allow a greater and effective autonomy of monetary policy to be restored, freeing it from the need to make more and more use of unconventional tools. The continuous extensions of quantitative easing are progressively reducing its effectiveness because the expectation of such measures, in the presence of high and rising sovereign debts, prevents other factors from contributing to reverse deflationary expectations.

6. A diabolic loop links the possibility of banking crisis to one of sovereign debt crisis. In normal conditions the creation of the Banking Union – however incomplete in the third pillar (common deposit-insurance scheme) and still uncertain and questionable in the application of the first two pillars (common supervisory authority and common resolution fund and mechanism) – would significantly reduce the risk of contagion. In the present exceptional circumstances, however, it may end up being insufficient for that purpose.

7. A significant reduction in the stock of sovereign debt would also permit the credibility of the policy commitments of national governments to be enhanced. Their credibility is presently weakened by two very important phenomena, although difficult to quantify. The first is the looming implicit liabilities, mainly related on the one hand to

---

find a statistically significant threshold effect, while stressing the importance of the debt trajectory.

the effects of aging (social security and health expenditure) and on the other hand to the guarantees provided to banks. The second phenomenon is the intensification of different forms of international tax competition (see the OECD BEPS project) that undermine the taxing power of the national countries, which is the only real safeguard of the ability to honour the debt service.

These various reasons for reducing sovereign debts assume a different importance in each individual country according to a variety of economic, social and political circumstances. The concrete importance attributed to each of them, in different cases and times, conditions the choice of the instruments that can be employed in order to cut the debt/GDP ratio.

6.4   CUTTING PUBLIC DEBTS: LESSONS FROM PAST EXPERIENCES

Historical experience shows that, apart from measures of restructuring (haircuts), two other main ways have been followed in order to achieve a large reduction of the debt/GDP ratio. On the one hand, a violent upsurge of inflation, on the other, a prolonged period of economic growth and adequate (but tolerable) primary surpluses. They are, in certain respects, two polar solutions. Inflation is a form of debt repudiation and allows the debt stock to be cut very rapidly. With the accumulation of primary surpluses, instead, the initial contractual terms are honoured, but the reduction of debt is necessarily slow and gradual. Beyond these two main ways, other instruments, which will be considered below, have been used, but they can assure only limited reductions of the debt/GDP ratio.

The inflationary solution is not feasible today. It is certainly not possible for the EZ countries. In the words of the European Economic Advisory Group at CESifo: "Under the euro . . . a country cannot inflate its debt away because its bonds are denominated in a common currency whose value cannot be manipulated by national policymakers" (EEAG, 2011, p. 80). Probably, however, nowadays the inflationary option is neither available for countries which still have a national currency, or, let's say, for those countries of the EMU which would decide to return to a national currency by exiting the euro. The reason is that cutting the debt by means of a very high inflationary process requires a number of further conditions: a very tight control of currency and capital movements, strong measures of "financial repression", such as the obligation for the Central Bank to provide cash advances to the Treasury and to purchase whatever quantity of public bonds were not placed in the market, and the introduction of portfolio constraints on the assets of the banks and so on (Pedone, 2011). At present, to a large extent, these measures, whose desirability is debatable, are outside the realm of possibility for the majority of countries opened to the worldwide integrated capital market.

Thus, when the inflationary choice is discarded, the other way to reduce the public debt remains, that is, to comply with the conditions of sustainability, highlighted by the simple dynamic model of public debt. A rate of growth persistently higher than the interest rate, along with a moderate rate of inflation and a certain level of primary surplus, can ensure a gradual reduction of the debt/GDP ratio to a comfortable level within a reasonable time span. However, fiscal consolidation, that is, a series of primary surpluses, should be carried out in periods of expansion, which is what Keynes suggested and what, among others, the United Kingdom from 1815 and the Kingdom of Italy from 1894 managed to achieve (Toniolo, 2011).

Instead, when the rate of growth is low or negative, in any case less than the interest rate, when there is no inflation, and when such a situation lasts for a long time, the size of the primary surplus required to stabilize or reduce the debt/GDP ratio may be so high as to be economically counterproductive and socially intolerable. Thus, the austerity policy of the EMU to meet the crisis was, in many cases, ineffective in ensuring the reduction of the debt/GDP ratio and socially costly. Some high-debt countries were tied into a vicious spiral of high debt/GDP ratio, restrictive budget rules, their negative impact on growth, and further increases in the debt/GDP ratio.

At the origin of this approach, beyond the basic principles of the Maastricht Treaty, the influence of the German ordoliberalism and of the idea of a "social market economy", requiring a balanced budget as an element of economic order, may be envisaged (Di Maio, 2015).

The later developments of the rule-based system established with the Stability and Growth Pact (GSP) were, however, also influenced by the theory of expansionary austerity.[6] According to this approach, in the presence of a perfect Ricardian equivalence between debt and taxes, a policy of fiscal consolidation would not dampen private demand, because the expansionary effects due to the expectation of lower future taxes would offset the potential deflationary impact deriving from the measures of fiscal consolidation. In addition, cuts in public spending would reduce the crowding out of private investment. The expansive result of restrictive fiscal policy would be accentuated by a permissive monetary policy, by a

---

[6] A description of the rise and fall of the expansionary austerity myth is in Nuti (2013) and Daniele (2015); a critical analysis is provided in the review article by Krugman (2013).

weakening of the exchange rate and an improvement in expectations and confidence.

The basic assumptions of the theory of expansionary austerity, however, have proved unrealistic and the values of fiscal multipliers higher than estimated, especially in economies in recession. Nuti (2013) shows that:

> if the fiscal multiplier is greater than the inverse of the Public Debt/GDP ratio, fiscal consolidation necessarily raises instead of lowering the Public Debt/GDP ratio with respect to what it would have been without consolidation. Fiscal consolidation reduces the PD/PIL ratio only in the least indebted countries that do not need such a reduction.

In countries with a high debt/GDP ratio it is very likely that a policy of fiscal consolidation brings about the vicious circle mentioned above.

In general, it should be noted that the quantitative assessment of the sustainability conditions is based on very uncertain long-term forecasts and equally uncertain estimates of the complex relationships between the different variables that determine the dynamics of the debt/GDP ratio (stock of debt, interest rates, growth rates, inflation rates, primary balances and their composition). The results of the econometric analysis are, as often happens, ambiguous.[7]

The relationship between the stance of fiscal policy (proxied by the cyclically adjusted primary balance) and the evolution of the debt/GDP ratio is not very tight and unique, because the effects of any given fiscal stance on the debt ratio depend on a very large number of factors and circumstances: the rate of growth and inflation; the monetary policy stance; the foreign exchange regime and capital movements; the functioning and the degree of turbulence in the domestic and international financial markets; the breakdown of the general government debt by subsectors (central government, local governments, other public entities); the structure of debt maturities; the distribution of government bonds between residents and non-residents; the prospects for political stability in the country and the degree of confidence.

A favourable combination of these different elements can certainly start a process of significant reduction, albeit gradual, of the debt/GDP ratio. As well as the effective implementation of reforms that increase the economy's competitiveness and growth potential in the medium term, along with a rise in inflation up to the ECB target, a vigorous expansion of exports, a tolerable level of primary surplus and the continuation of an

---

[7] For the relationship between the stance of fiscal policy, measured by the cyclically adjusted primary balance, and economic growth, see Mauro and Zilinsky (2015).

expansionary monetary policy could trigger a virtuous spiral: higher economic growth – improvements in primary and overall general government balance – reduction of the public debt/GDP ratio.

However, even supposing such a favourable environment, the reduction in the debt/GDP ratio will be gradual and slow. Thus, both in the presence of a virtuous spiral, and obviously even more so in the presence of the vicious one, the reasons of concern about the effects of high public indebtedness, mentioned in the previous section, may justify considering the possibility of cutting the stock of public debt by means of extraordinary measures.

As a matter of fact, there are a number of historical experiences of the recourse to extraordinary finance tools in order to cut the debt stock more rapidly than what is implied by the accumulation of primary surpluses.

This was primarily the case in particular in periods of profound social upheaval, linked to wartime events, when various forms of wealth taxation were used, including compulsory loans, which are an indirect way of taxing wealth.[8] This solution is still sometimes proposed nowadays in high-debt countries like Italy. The obstacles and difficulties that would be encountered with this method, are not, however, negligible. An extraordinary wealth tax, able to bring down the stock of public debt significantly, should provide adequate revenues and therefore have a very wide base. Then the problems of definition, evaluation and assessment of the various wealth components become central and hard to deal with, on technical as well as on social and political grounds. Let us just mention that, for equity considerations, a set of exemption thresholds, differentiated on the basis of the characteristics of the tax unit, should be established. It should also be necessary to take appropriate measures to address the liquidity problems that can arise with a wealth tax, especially when extraordinary. The issue is particularly complex because the probability and the relevance of liquidity problems vary with the magnitude and the composition of wealth. Beyond all these difficulties, there is a strong risk that a heavy wealth tax can hamper demand and distort the allocation of capital and savings. In the Italian case, in addition, real estate, which for a number of reasons is the most advisable tax base, is by now already heavily taxed. The taxation of movable wealth, on the other hand, as is well known, encounters

---

[8]   The discussion of the different forms of amortization, repudiation and conversion of public loans contained in the Public Finance treaty of Einaudi (1948, chapters 7, 8 and 9) is of extraordinary interest, also for the numerous references to historical experiences in different times and countries. For an analysis of the long-run evolution of the Italian public debt and, in particular, of its early formation in the first fifteen years of the unitary state, see Pedone (2011).

strong limitations in the present scenario of lack of any control on capital movements.

The demise (or the valorization) of public properties is another kind of extraordinary measure that has also been frequently proposed and used in the recent past. It can take on different characteristics, depending on the type of asset to be demised, the channels and methods of the sale, the procedures and the organizational and institutional arrangements involved. Let us just mention that in Italy – but a number of countries are likely to face similar problems – such a perspective has encountered numerous obstacles: the complex and overabundant legislation and regulation; the length of the procedures and the size of the bureaucracy; the overlapping of competences between different levels of government; the difficulty of establishing a correct and fruitful partnership between public and private.[9]

If it is true that the feasibility of extraordinary measures and their efficacy in reducing the stock of debt are limited and if the issues of concern for very high sovereign debts, outlined in section 6.3, are considered valid and working in practice, then the various recently advanced proposals for restructuring sovereign debts should be considered and discussed.

The valid objections that such operations imply serious risks – on the one hand, to produce contagion, especially through the banking systems; on the other, to induce opportunistic behaviour on the part of national governments – must be weighed against the high cost of the uncertainty produced by the confused, partial and delayed use that has been made of debt restructuring during the recent crisis of some Eurozone countries.

6.5 THE "SWAP" APPROACH TO THE EXCESSIVE LEGACY DEBT ISSUE

6.5.1 At the Origin of the Discussion on Eurozone's Debt Restructuring: the Deauville Meeting

On 19 October 2010, after a walk on the beach of Deauville, Chancellor Merkel and President Sarkozy agreed that, after 2013, financial assistance to sovereigns from the European Stability Mechanism would require that losses be imposed on their private creditors. Their statement sparked a scandal and it was considered a contributory cause of the worsening of the

---

[9] Astrid (2012) presented a detailed proposal for the reduction of the Italian public debt of 180 billion euros in five years. It would be interesting to investigate the main obstacles that have prevented its realization.

sovereign debt crisis.[10] Since then, the mere mention, even in an academic seminar, of a default option in the proper sense, that is with capital losses borne by the private holders of government bonds, was long viewed as unforgivable recklessness. Yet the possibility of losses is part of the contractual relationship between the lender and the borrower and, in the case of insolvency, renouncing part of the capital can be the most efficient solution for the creditors. On the other hand, avoiding inflicting losses on private creditors is in stark contrast to the prohibition to intervene in support of the insolvent states, a principle that in the Union has a constitutional basis. If sovereigns are not to be bailed out, then creditors should be bailed in, including private people and entities. It is precisely what, in the philosophy behind the architecture of the single currency, should trigger a strict market discipline, designed to contain the natural tendency of states to borrow excessively.

The bail-in should thus have the same constitutional importance of the no bail-out. It is, instead, excluded from the realm of possibility because it is considered extremely dangerous for the endurance of the monetary union. In particular, it is feared that the recourse to bail-in in the case of insolvency of a member state could induce a double contagion, with the banking system on one side, and the other high-debt countries on the other, undermining financial stability in the whole EZ.

In the bottleneck of two contrasting clauses, "no bail-out" and "no bail-in", the only way out has so far been envisaged in a slow process of debt reduction through the accumulation of primary surpluses. The cost of debt reduction is made to fall on the citizen-taxpayers, who should receive less in the way of public services and pay more taxes for a long period of time. This way would be practicable to some extent in the presence of reasonable growth rates that are higher than the interest rates. It becomes prohibitive in the absence of growth or with very slow growth. But the absence of growth depends, in turn, on such a fiscal policy stance.

However, despite official outrage, the Deauville meeting triggered a stream of research on sovereign debt restructuring, which has now produced a consistent body of literature. Two different issues have been addressed. The first concerns a once-and-for-all reduction of excessive legacy debt; the second deals with the design of permanent insolvency procedures for sovereigns. The two perspectives should be kept quite separate, because they answer to different needs and have different institutional implications.

---

[10]   The blame was not justified. Mody (2014) discusses a number of papers on market reactions to policy initiatives and shows that, with the exception of Greece, the increase in sovereign spreads following the Deauville announcement was within the range of variability of the previous 20 days.

The rest of this section considers the proposals mainly addressed to the former issue, even if they do not ignore the longer run's requirements, while the next section is devoted to papers that are focused on the design of an insolvency mechanism for sovereigns.

6.5.2   A European Redemption Pact: The German Council of Economic Experts Proposal

The line of research on the ways to eliminate the existing excess of debt was opened by the German Council of Economic Experts (GCEE, 2011; Bofinger et al., 2011; Doluca et al., 2012). About a year after the Deauville meeting, the GCEE presented a plan to reduce to 60 per cent the debt/GDP ratio in all the EZ countries within two decades.[11] The proposal of a European Redemption Pact (ERP), associated with a European Redemption Fund (ERF), aimed to establish a scheme of joint liability in the EZ without weakening the incentives of the member countries to consolidate their public finances. The joint debt mechanism envisaged was intended, unlike Eurobonds, to be temporary, for a period of about 25 years (including a 5-year roll-in phase). According to the authors of the plan, the aim of demonstrating to the markets "that solidarity will prevail" could "only be reached by strong countries lending their reputation, i.e. their low risk premia in the bonds market, to member countries facing a liquidity crisis" (Bofinger et al., 2011).

The central idea was to separate the part of the legacy debt of each EZ country corresponding to 60 per cent of GDP from the quota exceeding the threshold. In the roll-in phase of the scheme (2012–16) the EZ countries would have renewed the maturing debt through the ERF, until the fund had completely absorbed the part exceeding 60 per cent in each country. Each participant should henceforth service its own debt posted into the fund, until it was completely redeemed and the fund expires. However, given the joint liability, countries with a bad reputation would have benefited from the better reputation of the most reliable countries through a relevant reduction of the cost of servicing the debt.

A "serious commitment" was required to guarantee that the debt not included in the fund would not rise again above the 60 per cent threshold. According to the German experts, this need could be satisfied by the introduction of "debt brakes" into the participants' national constitutions.[12]

---

[11]   The proposal was initially contained in the Council's annual report 2011–12, released on 9 November 2011.

[12]   "Debt brake" is the literal translation of the German "*Schuldenbremse*", introduced in article 109, paragraph 3 of the Basic Law in 2009.

Two further guarantees were called for. The first was to assign part of the revenue of a major tax (VAT and/or the income tax) to the redemption of the debt ("special tax provisions"). The second was a deposit of part of the national currency reserves: it was estimated that these latter provisions could amount to 20 per cent of the fund. Whenever a participant failed to honour its commitments, it would forfeit the collateral deposited into the fund.

The authors of the plan were fully aware that the redemption would have required "tremendous efforts" (Bofinger et al., 2011) from countries starting the process with a higher debt ratio. The example of Italy was revealing. The required annual primary surplus for Italy to redeem its debt in the fund in a time span of 20 years (2016–35) would be 4.2 per cent of GDP, assuming a nominal GDP rate of growth of 3 per cent, a cost of the debt in the fund of 4 per cent and an interest rate on the remaining debt of 5 per cent. However, according to the authors, the scheme should still be attractive to Italy because the primary surplus required to achieve the same reduction in debt without the ERF scheme (assuming an interest rate of 7 per cent) would initially be more than 8 per cent of GDP (GCEE, 2011, Table 13).

Conversely, participating in the fund would have been a disadvantage for Germany. However, it was emphasized, the participation would have been worthwhile even for Germany if the alternative had been "the worst-case scenario of unlimited refinancing of EZ members through the European Central Bank" (Bofinger et al., 2011).

In rereading the GCEE proposals today, it is striking to notice how the "worst-case scenario" dreaded by the German experts began to material- ize just in the aftermath of the presentation of the report. The plan was announced on 9 November 2011: shortly after, on 22 December, the first LTRO (long-term refinancing operation) auction opened the season of unconventional monetary measures of the ECB. The ensuing story – through Mario Draghi's announcement of "whatever it takes to preserve the euro" on 26 July 2012 up to the launch of quantitative easing in March 2015 – is well known. The reduction in the cost of debt, that is, the benefit that German experts envisaged for high-debt countries from their project, was instead the result of the monetary policy implemented by the ECB: the Italy–Germany 10-year bond spread collapsed from the maximum of 505.63 reached on 2 August 2012 to the minimum of 87.51 on 12 March 2015.

On the other hand, in the meantime, the idea of a 20-year time span to reduce the debt/GDP ratio to 60 per cent, which was advanced with the plan, has been transposed into the weaker form of a yearly 1/20 reduction of the excess of the ratio over 60 per cent, as a fundamental rule of the SGP both in six-pack and fiscal compact.

Thus the GCEE redemption plan proposal seems to have been quickly overcome, on one side by the encroachment of monetary policy in territories where the plan would have liked to foreclose and, on the other one, by the reception of a strict rule for a quick reduction of the debt/GDP ratio towards the goal of 60 per cent within the framework of budgetary rules.

Nevertheless the philosophy underlying the plan of the German experts did not die. Instead, the way opened by the GCEE report has been followed by a number of authors. The remainder of this section considers two major projects of sovereign debts restructuring in the EZ: the PADRE project (Pâris and Wyplosz, 2014) and the plan recently developed by a group of economists from different countries under the auspices of the CEPR (Corsetti et al., 2015).

These two proposals are particularly representative of the main terms of the current discussion. Both of them move from the conviction that a substantial restructuring of EZ public debt is an inescapable condition to restart growth and to get out of the austerity–debt trap. It is, however, recognized that, in the present state of things, the restructuring must be designed in compliance with two main political constraints, even if the possibility of their loosening is taken into account in both plans. The first constraint is to exclude transfers between states, deemed inadmissible in the current state of development of European integration, given the absence of a common fiscal policy; an aspect, that of sharing fiscal policy, which instead characterizes federal countries, where the redistribution between different member states is a foundational element of togetherness. The second constraint is not to inflict losses on private creditors, that is, to avoid bail-in, which, as we have seen, is considered too risky for the stability of the financial markets at this stage.

6.5.3 The PADRE Plan

According to the PADRE project (Pâris and Wyplosz, 2014) the EZ countries should ask the ECB to buy in the secondary market government securities of each country at their face value. The purchases are to be divided between the different member states according to the ECB's capital keys. Governments, not the ECB, must take the decision because the action belongs to the realm of fiscal policy and therefore is outside the mandate of the ECB. In principle the ECB could even reject the request, being an independent institution.

The ECB purchases the governments' bonds in the market, but does not hold them among its assets; if that were the case, it would result in transfers between states, given the differences in interest rates on the various national debts and the different degrees of risk. It also would create an incentive not to honour the debt, because the loss would be shared between the different countries according to their capital shares.

The envisaged solution to both problems is to change the sovereign bonds acquired by the ECB into other bonds with a zero interest rate. The ECB, then, transforms (swaps) the sovereign bonds acquired into irredeemable zero coupon securities (perpetuities). These securities are recorded at face value on the asset side of the ECB's balance sheet. The ECB finances its purchases by issuing its own bonds (ECB Notes), which are interest bearing, choosing the most appropriate maturity structure. These notes are posted on the liability side of the ECB balance sheet. Therefore the ECB, having bought non-interest-bearing securities and financing itself by issuing interest-bearing securities, will suffer annual losses indefinitely. The present value of the infinite series of annual losses corresponds to the debt that is cancelled out with the swap operation. These losses reduce the seigniorage income of the ECB, so that each country bears a loss in proportion to its share in the ECB capital, which is also its share of debt cancelled out. There is therefore no transfer between countries; the cost of the operation falls fully on the present and future generations of taxpayers in each country.

The authors of the PADRE plan note that in theory these losses could cause the ECB to fail, but they argue that central banks cannot fail, because the seigniorage always allow them to recapitalize. The claim is in principle acceptable, but its concrete application to the ECB case would deserve further scrutiny, because the ability of the ECB to generate seigniorage is constrained by statutory limits and may result in being severely limited by operational difficulties.

For the aftermath of the restructuring, the PADRE project requires that the member states subscribe a binding covenant that avoids the accumulation of new debt. An upper limit to the debt/GDP ratio should be fixed, above which a debt containment mechanism would take effect that should be simple and automatic. The upper limit on the debt can be made to coincide with the level reached following the restructuring, increased by a margin (for example 10 per cent) to allow for some flexibility. If a country exceeds the limit, the ECB will exercise a put option on perpetuities, for an amount equal to the share of debt of the country concerned, which would have the obligation to repurchase them. The government of the defaulting country would have to issue debt to finance the purchase. There would therefore be a swap with an opposite sign to the one initially put in place with the operation of restructuring, the perpetuities being transformed back into interest-bearing debt. If the non-complying country refuses to repurchase the perpetuities, it would be considered in default. A number of measures are envisaged in order to deter deviant behaviour and to force the state concerned to acquire the perpetuities: it is contemplated, for example, that its debtors be allowed to settle their obligations (for example taxes) with perpetuities.

It is not surprising, in the light of the simplest arithmetic of the debt/GDP ratio, that the feasibility of the PADRE project depends on the relationship between the rate of growth and the interest rate. The authors show that, assuming a restructuring of half of the public debt of all EZ countries, an inflation rate of 2 per cent, a rate of growth in real terms of 1.5 per cent and an interest rate of 3.5 per cent (that is, an interest rate equal to the nominal rate of growth), the present value of the infinite series of income from seigniorage would largely exceed the present value of the infinite series of losses due to the restructuring. For 50 years, however, the annual losses would exceed the annual income from seigniorage. Already with an interest rate of 4 per cent, the other assumptions being the same, the present value of the income would be less than the losses and the restructuring would not be feasible. Instead, with a nominal growth rate higher than the interest rate, the present value of the seigniorage is infinite. That is the case, for example, if, keeping inflation at 2 per cent and the interest rate to 3.5 per cent, the real growth was 2 per cent.

The sustainability of the PADRE project depends, therefore, crucially on the ability of the one-off cut in sovereign debts to stimulate growth in the EZ and to contain nominal interest rates, provided that the ECB is successful in achieving its objective of an inflation rate close to 2 per cent.

Two possible variants of the plan are evaluated in case it proves unsustainable. The first possibility is to reduce significantly the amount of debt cancelled; the second one is to allow for some transfers between states. In the first perspective, the study simulates the effects of a debt reduction of outstanding debt equal to half of that provided for in the basic exercise, that is to say a 25 per cent reduction instead of 50 per cent. The conclusion is that the effects in terms of reduction of debt in the highly indebted countries would be too small, of a size that would not justify the political and technical costs of the operation. Instead, removing the constraint of absence of transfers, although very complicated from a political point of view, would be more promising. The study simulates the possibility of reducing the stock of debt of each country for a share equal to that of the ECB's capital, corrected by the difference between the debt/GDP ratio and the average for the EZ. It is shown that, in this case, a reduction of the debt/GDP ratio of 25 per cent would allow results to be achieved, in terms of reduction of the debt/GDP ratio, very close to those obtained in the basic assumption. Distributional effects, however, would be particularly heavy for the small and low-debt countries. The possibility is then discussed, as a further alternative, of allowing countries not to join the plan.

Finally, the possibility of limiting the debt restructuring to the most indebted countries is considered. The study simulates, for example, the effects of applying the scheme only to countries with more than 80 per cent debt/GDP ratio, reducing the share of debt required to bring to 80 per cent the most indebted country (Greece).

6.5.4   The CEPR Proposals

The CEPR plan (Corsetti et al., 2015) moves along similar lines. Each country of the EZ participating in the scheme would commit a certain amount of future budget revenue to redeem (buy back) a large fraction of its outstanding debt. The expected flow of such revenue, over a very long time span (50 years), would be capitalized into a stability fund. The revenue, which governments should constrain for this purpose in a credible way, would result from one or more additional taxes and from seigniorage. In particular, among the taxes which could possibly be used for the purpose, a VAT increase and a tax on wealth transfers are discussed. Like the project PADRE, the stability fund, which could act under the supervision of the ESM, would convert the debt into non-interest-bearing perpetuities, in order to rule out any transfer among countries. The fund would be financed by issuing interest-bearing securities, whose interest would be covered by the current fiscal revenue stream entered into the fund from participating countries, while the future revenue capitalized would represent the collateral.

So far the main difference with the PADRE project is that the latter relies exclusively on seigniorage. The group of economists who worked on the CEPR project believe, instead, that seigniorage, if distributed to the participating countries according to the ECB keys, in order to avoid transfers between states, would be far below what is necessary to bring all countries to a debt/GDP ratio not exceeding 95 per cent, which is the goal of the project. The amount of seigniorage available for the scheme should, in fact, be quantified very prudently, giving the assurance that the operation would not affect the possibility for the ECB to cover potential temporary budget losses and avoiding interference with the Bank's mandate of ensuring price stability.

In the overall architecture of the design, however, the CEPR project gives more space than the PADRE project to the possibility that the debt restructuring could lead to both transfers across states and the involvement of the private sector.

A first possibility of transfers is that of pooling the seigniorage, which in this case would be sufficient to finance a debt ratio cut for all states to the target level of 95 per cent, without the need to resort to taxes. A second possibility that is discussed is that of a "solidarity levy", such as that applied at the time in Germany to finance the unification. In particular an increase in VAT in each country, which ensures an increase in the revenue corresponding to a percentage point of GDP, is considered. The revenue would then be redistributed between the states on a per capita basis.

On the second aspect, that of involving the private sector, imposing on bondholders some of the cost of the debt reduction, the CEPR report envisages a debt–equity swap. In all EZ countries, a given share of government bonds would be converted to GDP-indexed bonds, that is, bonds in which principal and/or interest payments depend on the rate of growth of GDP. Within the swap operation a haircut could also be imposed on debt holders. The haircuts could vary across countries. Countries with ample fiscal space could choose the characteristics of the GDP indexed bonds so as to avoid haircuts. Instead, in high-debt countries, the debt–equity swap would imply significant haircuts on investors, "provided, of course, that the banking system can absorb the corresponding losses" (Corsetti et al., 2015, p. 31).[13]

The CEPR report also contains a series of recommendations relating to the issue of how to prevent, after the restructuring, the accumulation of new debt by the states. The restructuring has, in fact, the purpose of allowing a restart, by pressing the reset button, but the problem remains of how to remove the causes that have brought debt excesses. The report emphasizes the need to build a new institutional framework and rules that prevent the moral hazard problem, making fully credible the commitment not to resort to bail-out. The conditions should be envisaged so that, in the case of insolvency, it would be possible to proceed in an orderly way to debt restructuring involving private creditors (private sector involvement).

The issue will be more extensively dealt with in the next section. On this topic, the CEPR report moves along the lines designed by the IMF with regard to new contract rules that prevent the problem of holdouts in the case of debt restructuring, the reform of the ESM lending framework and so on.

With reference to a key issue – how to break the loop between sovereign debt crisis and banking crisis – the report proposes the creation of a synthetic bond representative of a number of national debts. The bond

---

[13]   It may be recalled that the hypothesis of a new type of sovereign bonds with characteristics similar to those of equities has been widely considered in the literature. Barkbu et al. (2012) and Mody (2013) envisage, for example, the use of "coco" (contingent convertible) bonds, built on the model of banks' contingent bonds, convertible into equity when their equity ratios fall below a given threshold. Similarly, with the sovereign cocos, the contract should provide for the capital repayment and interest payments to be contingent on certain economic and financial developments.

should be risk-free and could therefore be held by banks without being involved in a possible insolvency crisis of sovereigns. It should be noted that, conversely, within a revision of the Basel Accords, a greater degree of risk should be attached to the remaining sovereign bonds and to those newly issued, with negative consequences for the banks' capacity to meet the capital requirements at any given volume of risk-weighted assets.

6.5.5 Some Doubts about the Effectiveness of the "Swap Proposals" for the Legacy Debt Reduction

The main features of the three proposals for a one-off reduction of the existing stock of sovereign debt, which have been considered, are summarized in Table 6.3.

All these proposals are built under the constraint of avoiding any loss for both the official sector (no bail-out) and the private bondholders (no bail-in). The cost of debt restructuring is thus charged to present and future taxpayers of the involved countries.

Then the question can be raised as to whether this strategy is truly different from the one which is pursued today of accumulating primary surpluses over time. In fact the difference appears very weak: it concerns the temporal distribution of flows and costs, while the two approaches are equivalent in terms of present values. In this perspective it may be even doubtful whether the "swap" proposals entail any actual debt restructuring.

The possibility that these operations produce some advantage compared to the current scenario rests on their ability to reverse expectations. The challenge is that removing from the market a significant portion of debt

Table 6.3   The proposals for outstanding debt restructuring: the main features

Plan	Gov. Revenue bound for debt redemption	Time span	Amount of debt cancelled
GCEE (2011)	"Special tax provisions" (VAT and/or PIT)	5+20 years	Quota exceeding 60% of GDP for each country
PADRE (2014)	Seigniorage	Infinity	50% of the total EZ debt
CEPR (2015)	Additional taxes (VAT increase and tax on wealth transfers) and Seigniorage	50 years	Amount necessary to bring the most indebted countries (excluding Greece) to 95%

would reduce the perceived risk and thus stimulate private demand, especially for investment. The boost to growth would in turn open new fiscal spaces.

The belief that the securitization in a stabilization fund of a flow of fiscal resources would change the spending decisions, in particular for investment, compared to the current situation in which the same amounts of resources are in fact bound because of fiscal rules, can be questioned. In the early perspective of the GCEE report of 2011, the greatest benefit for high-debt countries was the expected reduction in the spread resulting from "the loan" of the stronger countries' higher reputation to the weakest countries. As already stated, in the meantime the lowering of interest rates to unusually low levels has been the product of the unconventional monetary policy adopted by the ECB. However, such a policy has not yet produced the desired effects in terms of growth and inflation. The proposed swap operations of sovereign debts can be seen, at best, as a way to restore freedom of manoeuvre for monetary policy and bring it back within conventional territories. It is difficult, instead, to believe that they would actually open new significant spaces for fiscal policy and alleviate the social hardship of reducing the stock of debt by means of huge primary surpluses.

The scenario would be quite different if the possibility of transfers among states were accepted, even to a limited extent. The CEPR report is illuminating in this respect, where it shows how, in this case, the distribution of seigniorage, even calculated in a conservative way, would be sufficient to reduce to 95 per cent the debt ratio in all the EZ countries. However, within the Union, the appetite – as is commonly said these days – for federal redistribution seems by now entirely lacking, even more than it was, not only at the time of the GCEE report (2011), but also of the CEPR report (2015).

6.6 A GLOBAL INSOLVENCY PROCEDURE FOR THE EUROZONE?

In this section some contributions to the ongoing debate on establishing a permanent insolvency regime for sovereign states in the Eurozone are briefly considered. These projects, as already mentioned, must be distinguished from those considered in the previous section, which address the issue of restructuring outstanding debts and design transitional mechanisms in order to bring the debt/GDP ratio in all EZ countries below a level deemed acceptable in a given span of time. Three main differences between the two groups of projects may be outlined.

The first difference is straightforward: the latter group of designs refer to the past (legacy debt), while the former refer to the future (newly issued bonds). This is because resolution mechanisms for cases of sovereign insolvency are considered viable only with reference to government bonds issued after the entry into force of the new insolvency regime and not to pre-existing debt. An insolvency procedure for outstanding debt is seen as an unacceptable change in the initial contractual terms, whereas, for bonds to be issued, the contract will contain clauses relating to the insolvency procedure.

A second difference is that the problem of a cut in legacy debts can be addressed within the current legal and institutional framework of EMU, while the establishment of a permanent mechanism to deal with situations of sovereign crises requires amending the Treaties, with all the procedural, institutional and political consequences that this entails.

A third difference, finally, is that the projects relating to the existing debt waive private sector involvement (PSI), although, as we have seen, eventually such a possibility is sometimes considered, but quite marginally. The PSI is, instead, the primary goal of the other group of projects.

The reasons for excluding the PSI when restructuring outstanding debts may be found, in the first place, on ethical grounds, as already mentioned with reference to the first difference.[14] In the case of legacy debt, the PSI would not be ethically acceptable, because the possibility of a debt restructuring is not covered by the initial contracts. The problem would not arise, instead, for new issues, whose contracts would include rules to deal with such contingencies. A PSI when restructuring legacy debts is also considered very risky. The problem mainly concerns banks and other financial intermediaries. Limiting their exposure to sovereigns is both a condition and a goal of establishing resolution mechanisms for sovereigns. It is a condition, because, if the link between banks and sovereign debts is not preliminarily loosened, it is feared that the involvement of the former in the insolvency procedures of the latter can jeopardise the stability of financial markets and, ultimately, the endurance of the euro. It is also a goal, because the establishment of specific rules to deal with sovereign insolvency is meant to increase the awareness of financial operators about the risks inherent in the loans to sovereigns: their propensity to lend to them would be constrained. Such a design is closely connected to the bank resolution mechanism, approved under the Banking Union and already operative. The bail-in of the subjects exposed with banks (shareholders, bondholders and depositors) would submit the latter to a stricter market discipline. In turn, the bail-in of the banks in the sovereign insolvency

---

[14]   On the ethical implications of sovereigns' default, see Buchanan (1987) and Brennan and Eusepi (2002).

procedures should exercise the same effect with regard to sovereigns. A number of issues and concerns about such connections will be raised in the last paragraph of this section.

6.6.1   The Debate and the Proposals for the Eurozone: the Bruegel Report (2010)

The theme of insolvency rules for sovereigns, which has been addressed only recently in Europe, is not at all new in the wider international community.[15] The issue was alive at least as long ago as the 1980s (the Brady plan was in 1989), with reference to a number of countries, largely but not only South Americans, who had heavily borrowed in the previous decade. It came back on the agenda with the Mexican crisis of 1994–95. In the early 2000s the International Monetary Fund (IMF, 2002, 2003; Krueger, 2002) proposed a Sovereign Debt Restructuring Mechanism (SDRM). The proposal aimed to neutralize the problem of holdouts in the event of negotiations for restructuring a sovereign debt. It provided, in particular, for the redefinition of collective action clauses (CACs) allowing for the aggregation of the voting procedures across groups of bond issues, in order to limit the power of minority veto. It also planned to make the outcome of the vote binding for all bondholders in order to prevent hold-outs from claiming for a full refund. The proposal aroused much debate, but in the end it produced nothing, especially because of the strenuous opposition of some private finance sectors.[16]

The debate in Europe was triggered, as we have seen, by the declaration of Deauville. A few days later (28–29 October), the European Council (2010) stated:

> Heads of State or Government agree on the need for Member States to establish a permanent crisis mechanism to safeguard the financial stability of the Eurozone as a whole ... not modifying article 125 TFEU ("no bail-out" clause). The European Council welcomes the intention of the Commission to undertake ... preparatory work on the general features of a future new mechanism, i.e. the role of the private sector, the role of the IMF and the very strong conditionality under which such programmes should operate.

A number of proposals for establishing a permanent mechanism for the resolution of sovereign debt crisis followed.

---

[15]   Comprehensive reviews of the proposals and the actual experiences of sovereigns' default are contained in Gianviti et al. (2010), CIEPR (2013), Fuest et al. (2014), Dolls et al. (2016).

[16]   This line of action has been recently re-proposed by the Fund, following the experience of litigation between the holdouts and the Government of Argentina started in 2013 (IMF, 2014).

These proposals move from the acknowledgement that, on the one hand, the fiscal rules are not sufficient to avoid crises of sovereign debts and, on the other, when these crises occur there are no rules to cope with them. It is noted that, without rules, the no bail-out clause is not credible: the issue of soft budget constraint arises, and the Greek case was there to confirm it.

At first an important report was released by Bruegel towards the end of the same year (Gianviti et al., 2010). It proposed a European Crisis Resolution Mechanism (ECRM) based on two pillars. The first consisted of a procedure to start and carry on negotiations between a state in conditions of insolvency and its creditors, which would lead to a binding agreement for all creditors on the amount and manner of restructuring, in order to restore the sustainability of its public finances. The procedure must be dealt with by a special court, which could be identified in the Court of Justice of the European Union or in a special chamber of its own. The second pillar consisted of a set of rules for granting adequate financial support to the state concerned, as an integral part of the crisis resolution mechanism. Financial assistance would be subject to reaching an agreement between the sovereign debtor and its creditors.

6.6.2 The Proposal of the European Economic Advisory Group (2011)

Shortly after the Bruegel report, the European Economic Advisory Group (EEAG) of CESifo (Munich) presented, as part of the 2011 European Economy Report, its own proposal for a crisis mechanism in the EZ (EEAG, 2011).

The document starts with the distinction between illiquidity, impending insolvency and actual insolvency. A liquidity crisis is when a sovereign has temporary difficulties of access to the markets despite being solvent, in which case no restructuring is necessary, but only financial assistance strictly limited in time. Impending insolvency, instead, denotes a condition in which the sovereign state has serious difficulties in meeting the payment of debts as they come due at maturity, but this situation can be overcome with a restructuring of a limited extent and with the help of substitutive securities (replacement bonds) issued by the ESM and partially guaranteed (80 per cent). Actual insolvency, finally, occurs when the state has very serious problems of sustainability and the difficulty is not limited to the renewal of maturing debt, but the entire debt on the market is at risk.

It is established that all new debt contracts include a collective action clause ("CAC bond") that contemplates the possibility of an agreement about restructuring between the sovereign debtor and a qualified majority (that is, 75 per cent) of creditors holding bonds with the same maturity. The agreement is binding for all the holders of that class of bond.

Creditors accept the rule when they subscribe to the contract. Importantly enough, the majority rule should apply only to that group of creditors and only within that group, should the agreement be binding over all. Holders of bonds with later maturities must remain non-parties. To negotiate the refund of their bonds, they have to wait for the moment when their bonds mature.

It is thus a multi-step mechanism (piecemeal solution), deemed indispensable to face gradually a situation of impending insolvency and preventing it from degenerating into a real default. The CAC bonds make the risk of a haircut explicit and structured, and the mechanism is designed to prevent panic attacks near or during the negotiations.

The sequence is designed as follows. In the event of a debt crisis of a state, it is assumed at first that it is a liquidity crisis. The ESM intervenes with loans of a limited extent and for a short period. If, on the expiry of the period, the situation remains difficult, the diagnosis will be of impending insolvency. The state must then negotiate the haircut with creditors that hold bonds at maturity. After the agreement, the residual value of securities is convertible into the ESM replacement bonds, guaranteed at 80 per cent. The holders of bonds with longer maturities are not involved; they have to wait their turn at the maturity of their bonds. The amount of the haircut should be determined by the market: it will be equal to the reduction in the value of bonds during the three months preceding the announcement of the negotiations, within a minimum (20 per cent) and a maximum (50 per cent). It follows that the greatest possible loss is 60 per cent (50 per cent of haircut plus another possible maximum of 20 per cent on ESM securities). If the country cannot sustain the service of replacement bonds, a situation of actual insolvency of the entire outstanding debt should be declared.

6.6.3 Other Proposals: the European Sovereign Debt Restructuring Regime (ESDRR) and the Viable Insolvency Procedure for Sovereigns (VIPS)

In 2013 the Committee on International Economic Policy and Reform (CIEPR, 2013) proposed the creation of a European Sovereign Debt Restructuring Regime (ESDRR).

The scheme was to be implemented by amending the ESM Treaty. The Treaty change should authorize the ESM to lend only conditionally to debt restructuring and should establish the guidelines for determining the minimum amount of haircut. The modification of the Treaty would also have to make the assets and payments of the restructuring state immune from attacks by holdouts. The restructuring scheme was to be embedded into the framework of existing European fiscal rules, by using the 60 per cent debt level as a threshold for conditioning official lending. At debt levels below 60 per cent, the ESM loans would have been unconditional. Above 60 per cent to an upper threshold, tentatively set at 90 per cent, the assistance from the ESM should be conditional on the fiscal consolidation measures and structural reforms. Above the upper limit of the ESM, loans would be subject to debt restructuring.

Two rules were foreseen to govern the amount and forms of restructuring. The minimum haircut should bring the debt level below the upper threshold and the shorter maturity debt would be subject to a heavier cut.

This proposal wanted to reconcile the goal of limiting the range within which states can gamble for bail-out, and the consequent moral hazard problems, with the need for some flexibility in dealing with crises.

The proposal of a viable insolvency procedure for sovereigns (VIPS), advanced by Fuest et al. (2014), moves along partially similar lines. Under the proposal, the ESM financial assistance should be strictly limited to a "shelter period" of three years. After that, the debtor country must choose between either returning to the market or starting the insolvency procedure. If the country does not consider the market conditions acceptable for new issues, the only option that is left is to open the procedure in order to restructure its debt.

The negotiations between the debtor country and the representatives of the creditors are moderated by the ESM. The start of negotiations triggers an immediate moratorium on the debtor country's debt service. Providing privileges to certain groups of creditors must be kept to a minimum in order to protect the interests of the creditors as a whole. During the phase of negotiation, the ESM provides the necessary liquidity to ensure basic public functions. The maximum duration of this liquidity assistance is twelve months, which, consequently, is also the maximum time for the negotiation.

It is considered not appropriate, nor theoretically justified, to predetermine the extent of the haircut. The insolvency procedure should only include a rule to determine the maximum loss. However, under no circumstances should the debt settlement push the debt/GDP ratio below the Maastricht reference value of 60 per cent. Instead, a haircut which leaves the debt level above 60 per cent should be possible if the debtor country is deemed solvent also with a higher debt level, for example because of favourable growth prospects or the presence of large public assets.

A key difference with the previous proposals is that during the shelter period the ESM loans should be included in the debt restructuring. A taxpayer exposure to risk is therefore considered inevitable. The recognition of a privileged status to the loans granted by the ESM in the shelter period is deemed to reduce the stabilizing properties of the mechanism.

In the case of seniority of ESM loans, the quality of private loans to the country in crisis would worsen progressively as the share of ESM increases. Thus the shelter period could not fulfil its diagnostic and stabilizing function. However, the potential losses for the ESM (and, therefore, taxpayers) should be limited by specific rules on the maturity structure of government bonds, which limits the liquidity requirements during the period of protection.

Like the other projects, the VIPS plan tackles the issue of minimizing the risks and uncertainties arising from the possibility of long disputes with holdout creditors. Two main precautions are suggested. First, the CACs as currently prescribed by the ESM treaty should be revised through a stronger aggregation principle. The quorums for single bond issues are to be eliminated completely, an aggregate quorum being a necessary and sufficient condition for creditors' decisions binding on all. The aggregate quorum should be reduced to two-thirds of the invested capital. Second, a new rule should be introduced in the Treaty to allow the Eurozone countries involved in the programme through the ESM immunity from creditors' attacks.

6.6.4   Major Issues

The main features of the proposals for a permanent insolvency procedure for sovereigns are summarized in Table 6.4.

Table 6.4   The proposals of a permanent insolvency procedure for sovereigns: the main features

Plan	CAC Voting majority	Institutions involved	Amount of the haircut
Bruegel (2010)	Tentatively 2/3 (aggregate)	Court of Justice, EC and ECB, EFSF (now ESM)	Not specified (determined by negotiations)
EEAG (2011)	75% (bonds of the same maturity)	ESM	Determined by the market min 20% max 60%
CIEPR (2013)	Not specified	ESM	Minimum: the amount necessary to bring the debt/GDP ratio below 90%
Fuest et al. (2014)	2/3 (aggregate)	ESM (possibly assisted by the Troika)	Not predetermined (but a rule should be established by ESM)

These designs respond to the objective of integrating and partially replacing the current rule-based system, whose limits are by now much evident, with mechanisms relying more on market discipline. That is, the principle of no bail-out must become fully operational in the event of a crisis of sovereign states, and this implies adopting bail-in. When the prospect of losses is fully embedded in the expectations of people and entities buying government bonds, then the no risk assumption will fall definitively and, as a result, sovereigns will find it more difficult to borrow. This new scenario presumes that the diabolic loop between banking systems and sovereign states is loosened, because at present such a loop limits, as we have seen, the possibility of imposing a real burden on the private sector by means of an insolvency procedure for sovereigns. This is one of the main reasons why, with the banking union, a resolution mechanism for banks has been adopted that relies on the bail-in. The change from bail-out to bail-in moves the burden of losses from taxpayers to shareholders and creditors of the banks, with the aim of reducing opportunistic behaviour (moral hazard) and exposing the banking system to market discipline. The next step is meant to do the same with sovereigns, adopting a resolution mechanism of the kinds that have been briefly reviewed in this section implying PSI.

However, there are sound reasons to believe that, in the current circumstances, the bank resolution mechanism, on the one hand, can not completely avoid risks of contagion and, on the other, it can induce pro-cyclical behaviour by banks and lead to a high litigation.

The objective of reducing moral hazard cannot be fully achieved, especially for banks with a diversified shareholder base, because, for a number of reasons, shareholders cannot control managers fully, while the creditors (bondholders and depositors above a certain level) do not even have an institutional space for trying to discipline the managers. They can only do so indirectly by shifting their resources outside the banking system towards other investment sectors, which, however, at present have little prospect of profitability. All the more so in the absence of the banking union's third pillar, the European Deposit Guarantee Scheme, for which the actual size and the ways of funding are still uncertain (as are those related to the resolution fund of the second pillar). Moreover, pro-cyclical behaviours of banks derive from the difficulties of capitalization.

Thus, in order to avoid consequences on economic activity, in some recent experiences governments have resorted to various indirect forms of intervention. These experiences seem to prove that, in addition to market discipline, some form of insurance (adopting all the measures tested in the insurance industry to reduce the moral hazard) may contribute to financial stability and that the contrast between savers and taxpayers, as recipients of the losses, should be used with caution in order to avoid high costs for both.

A similar issue arises with regard to the relationships between the states in the Eurozone. As we have seen, both the plans for the reduction of outstanding debts and those concerning the establishment of a permanent mechanism to address sovereign insolvency are difficult to implement in the absence of some forms of even partial risk sharing.

A fiscal or budgetary union would represent the main form of insurance (risk sharing) and would also imply an overall reduction of risks. The numerous proposals for fiscal union (FU) for the EZ, so far formulated, have very different forms and content. They range from the establishment of a genuine federal state to the appointment of an EZ Finance Minister responsible for monitoring and ensuring compliance with the fiscal rules. The details of such proposals and the timing of their implementation cannot be examined here, even if such details and timing deserved great attention, because they are crucial for the practicability and effectiveness of the designs.

Only a few issues that should be addressed and resolved and which are decisive in determining the actual content of the FU can be mentioned. A FU implies a transfer of budgetary decision-making powers – both on the expenditure side and on the revenue side – to the Parliament and the Federal Government. This requires individual member countries renouncing national sovereignty to some extent. What may be taken for sure is that, without attributing to the Union an – albeit limited – autonomous power to tax, the EU would remain an aggregation of fragile and unstable countries, as demonstrated by Einaudi (1945) with reference to the two constitutions of the United States (1781–87 and 1787).

The assignment to the Centre of the Union of a more or less extensive independent power to tax would also allow a federal debt (authentic Eurobonds), whose repayment and interest would be precisely guaranteed by the power to tax. In the end, as happens in the federal states, only bonds issued by the Federal Government could be purchased by the central bank, while bonds issued by Member States would lose their sovereign debt characteristics. Then, the debt of states could be restructured and renegotiated much more easily than in the present circumstances. Moreover, as happens in the federations, the no bail-out clause referred to the states could be complied with much more easily, at least in principle.

The FU would also allow a better stabilization of the EZ economy and in particular deal with asymmetric shocks, for example recessions in single countries, without implying permanent and unconditional transfers among states. Of course, its implementation would require the settlements of very sensitive issues related to the choice of the indicators and of the policy instruments.

The transfer of sovereignty and the sharing of the risks, required by a FU, may be realized to different extents and with different timing. It is, however, unlikely they can take place in an atmosphere of mutual distrust and if the various aspects of the FU are not dealt with in a unitary framework. For sure, starting a path towards a FU without in-depth analysis and an extensive public discussion, and bypassing the democratic procedures for setting economic policy and budgetary decisions established by the constitutions of the individual countries, would increase the feeling, on the part of the peripheral countries, that expensive and ineffective austerity policies are imposed to them from outside, and, by central countries, that permanent transfers will be paid by their citizens.

6.7 CONCLUSIONS

In recent years the economic policy debate in the EZ focused on how to reduce sovereign debt, particularly in the most indebted countries, rather than on how to boost growth and employment. It seems that we are going towards a state of substantial preclusion of the possibility to resort to debt by EU Member States. At the same time such a possibility is not assigned to the Centre of the Union by establishing a Fiscal Union, as occurs in the context of federal states. Thus the debt is banned both at the Centre of the Union and in the Periphery. Instead, in other advanced countries (such as Japan, UK, USA) and also in many emerging economies, the use of debt is allowed and is extensive.

Many of the reasons for significantly reducing the debt/GDP ratio in the most indebted countries, which have been mentioned briefly in section 6.2, are common to all countries.

The greater emphasis and urgency with which this issue is addressed in the EZ are due to a number of factors:

1. The influence of the principles of the "ordoliberalism" and of the "social market economy" – among which a government-balanced budget assumes an absolute centrality – on setting the Maastricht Treaty and later on, together with the theory of expansionary austerity, on the establishment and development of the GSP.[17]

---

[17] The ordoliberalism, also when assuming the form of "social market economy", requires a balanced budget, because it denotes a correct functioning of the "State Order", while a deficit would undermine other "orders" of the society (Di Maio, 2015, p. 32).

2. The impact on public budgets of the financial and economic crisis, because of the measures taken to save the banks and the effects of automatic stabilizers. The deterioration of public finances, in turn, has produced a crisis of confidence for a number of EZ countries characterized by high debt and low growth, relative to others with a lower debt and higher growth.
3. This dichotomization between groups of countries has been accentuated by the unavailability, for single EMU members, of the currency and monetary policies as instruments for pursuing economic adjustment. It was made clear that a number of countries could possibly fail in guaranteeing the payment of interest and the repayment of a debt denominated in a currency outside their control.

The Treaty (TFEU) precludes the possibility of bail-out in the event of a crisis of a member state. This should imply that creditors should be "bailed in", if they are part of both the official sector and the private sector. A PSI is not, however, for the moment, thought possible, because it would endanger the stability of financial markets and the endurance of the euro. The debate is therefore developing along two main streams. On the one hand, mechanisms for the resolution of sovereign debt crises are designed on the assumption of imposing the full cost of restructuring over bondholders. These mechanisms should come into force in the longer term, when the link between banking systems and sovereign states will be dissolved. Moreover, in compliance with some ethical principle, they are deemed to apply only to newly issued debt. On the other side, solutions to break down the outstanding sovereign debts without imposing any cost to the private sector have been studied. These solutions, which are based on complex mechanisms of securitization of future revenues of the member states (seigniorage and taxes), are of doubtful effectiveness and difficult to apply.

Meanwhile, in the bottleneck "no bail-out" and "no bail-in", the only viable exit has been seen in a slow process of debt reduction through the accumulation of primary surpluses. The cost of debt reduction is made to fall on the citizen-taxpayers, who suffer from lower public spending and pay more taxes for a long period of time.

As a matter of fact, however, things did not go, and do not go, exactly like that. In recent years, after the onset of the global financial crisis, more than once, in order to cope with situations of difficulty of individual EZ members, a combination of "a bit of a bail-out" and "a bit of bail-in" has been used, sometimes in indirect ways, and sometimes more explicitly. This was done in a confused and disordered way, launching ambiguous signals, which have a high cost in terms of expectations.

The issue of sovereign states' debt in Europe is inextricably linked to that of growth. If a significant and continuous economic growth can restart, it will be possible to avoid both bail-out and bail-in: in conditions of vigorous and persistent growth, which once would have been considered "normal", public debt is not a problem. Instead, in the absence of (or with very small) growth, it is hard to believe that the problem of public debt can be addressed relying fully on bail-in and excluding bail-out, as is now called for. It will probably be necessary, instead, as it was in these years, to resort to a mix of both. In order to avoid doing this in the messy way used so far, this perspective should be considered explicitly and regulated within the framework of an overall review of the fiscal rules in Europe.

REFERENCES

Astrid (2012), 'Le proposte per la riduzione dello stock del debito pubblico: Pregi e difetti', 1 August, available at: http://www.astrid-online.it. Accessed 23 March 2018.
Barkbu, B., B. Eichengreen and A. Mody (2012), 'Financial crises and the multilateral response: What the historical record shows', *Journal of International Economics*, **88**(2): 422–35.
Bofinger, P., L.P. Feld, W. Franz, C.M. Schmidt B. Weder di Mauro (2011), 'A European Redemption Pact', *VOX-EU online*, 9 November.
Brennan, G. and G. Eusepi (2002), 'The dubious ethics of debt default', *Public Finance Review*, **30**(6): 546–61. Available at: https://voxeu.org/article/european-redemption-pact. Accessed 23 March 2018.
Buchanan, J.M. (1987), 'The ethics of debt default', in J.M. Buchanan, C.K. Rowley and R.D. Tollison (eds), *Deficits*, Oxford: Basil Blackwell, pp. 361–73.
Buttiglione, L., P.R. Lane, L. Reichlin and V. Reinhart (2015), 'Deleveraging? What Deleveraging?', ICMB and CEPR, *Geneva Report on the World Economy* No. 16.
Chudik, A., K. Mohaddes, M.H. Pesaran and M. Raissi (2015), 'Is there a debt-threshold effect on output growth?', IMF Working Paper15/197, IMF Asia and Pacific Department.
Committee on International Economic Policy and Reform (CIEPR) (2013), *Revisiting Sovereign Bankruptcy* (lead authors: Lee C. Buchheit, Anna Gelpern, Mitu Gulati, Ugo Panizza, Beatrice Weder di Mauro and Jeromin Zettelmeyer), Brookings, October.
Corsetti, G., L.P. Feld, P.R. Lane, L. Reichlin, H. Rey, D. Vayanos and B. Weder di Mauro (2015), *A New Start for the Eurozone: Dealing with Debt*, Monitoring the Eurozone 1, Centre for Economic Policy Research, March, CEPR Press, London.
Daniele, V. (2015), 'L'austerità espansiva. Breve storia di un mito economico', in A. Di Maio and U. Marani (eds), *Economia e Luoghi Comuni*, Rome: L'Asino d'Oro, pp. 39–68.
De Grauwe, P. (2014), 'The European Central Bank: Lender of last resort in the government bond markets?', in P. Catte, C.M. Fenu and S. Nicoletti Altimari (eds), *Conference in Memory of Tommaso Padoa-Schioppa*, Rome: Bank of Italy, pp. 133–50.

De Grauwe, P. (2015), 'Legacy of the Eurocrisis and the Future of the Euro', Federico Caffè Lecture, Rome, 10–11 December.

Di Maio, A. (2015), 'I compiti a casa. I riferimenti teorici della disciplina fiscale in Europa', in A. di Maio and U. Marani (eds), *Economia e Luoghi Comuni*, Rome: L'Asino d'Oro, pp. 15–38.

Dolls, M., C. Fuest, F. Heinemann and A. Peichl (2016), 'Reconciling insurance with market discipline: A blueprint for a European Fiscal Union', CESifo Working Paper No. 5767.

Doluca, H., M. Hübner, D. Rumpf and B. Weigert (2012), 'The European Redemption Pact: An illustrative guide', German Council of Economic Experts Working Paper 02/2012, February.

EEAG (2011), *The EEAG Report on the European Economy*, 'A new crisis mechanism for the Euro Area', CESifo, Munich, pp. 71–96.

Einaudi, L. (1945), 'Il mito dello Stato sovrano', *Il Risorgimento liberale*, 3 January, reprinted in *Riflessioni di un liberale sulla democrazia 1943–1947*, Florence, Leo S. Olschki Ed., pp. 96–100; English trans. 'The myth of the sovereign state', in D. da Empoli, C. Malandrino and V. Zanone (eds), *Selected Political Essays*, London: Palgrave Macmillan, 2014, vol. 3, pp. 169–73.

Einaudi, L. (1948), *Principi di Scienza delle Finanze*, 4th rev. edn, Turin: Giulio Einaudi Editore.

European Council (2010), Conclusions 28–29 October, EUCO 25/1/10 REV 1, CO EUR 18, CONCL 4, Brussels, 30 November.

Fuest, C., F. Heinemann and C. Schröder (2014), 'A Viable Insolvency Procedure for Sovereigns (VIPS) in the Euro Area', ZEW Discussion Paper No. 14-053, Mannheim, August.

German Council of Economic Experts (2011), 'European redemption pact', *Annual Report 2011/12*, Third Chapter, 106–114, available at: http://www.sach verstaendigenrat wirtschaft.de/index.html (transl. of the German version, 'Ein Schuldentilgungspakt für Europa', Verantwortung für Europa wahrnehmen, *Jahresgutachten* 2011/12, 109–18). Accessed 15 April 2016.

Gianviti, F., A.D. Krueger, J. Pisani-Ferry, A. Sapir and J. von Hagen (2010), 'A European mechanism for sovereign debt crisis resolution: A proposal', Bruegel Blueprint Series, vol. X.

International Monetary Fund (2002), 'The design of the sovereign debt restructuring mechanism – Further considerations', prepared by the Legal and Policy Development and Review Departments (in consultation with the International Capital Markets and Research Departments), approved by François Gianviti and Timothy Geithner, 27 November.

International Monetary Fund (2003), 'Report of the Managing Director to the International Monetary and Financial Committee on the IMF's Policy Agenda', Washington, DC, 11 April.

International Monetary Fund (2014), 'Strengthening the contractual framework to address collective action problems in sovereign debt restructuring', Washington, DC, October.

International Monetary Fund (2016), 'Debt: Use it wisely', *Fiscal Monitor*, October.

Krueger, A.O. (2002), 'A new approach to sovereign debt restructuring', April, Washington, DC: International Monetary Fund.

Krugman, P. (2013), 'How the case for austerity has crumbled', *The New York Review of Books*, 6 June.

Mauro, P. and J. Zilinsky (2015), *Fiscal Tightening and Economic Growth: Exploring Cross-Country Correlations*, Washington, DC: Peterson Institute for International Economics Policy Brief 15-15.

Mody, A. (2013), 'Sovereign debt and its restructuring framework in the euro area', Bruegel Working Paper No. 2013/05, Brussels.

Mody, A. (2014), 'The ghost of Deauville', *VOX CEPR's Policy Portal*, 7 January.

Nuti, D.M. (2013), 'Austerity versus development', Conference Paper, Kozminski University, Warsaw.

Pâris, P. and C. Wyplosz (2014), 'PADRE: Politically Acceptable Debt Restructuring in the Eurozone', Geneva Reports on the World Economy Special Report 3, ICMB and CEPR.

Pedone, A. (2011), 'Alle origini del persistente alto livello del debito pubblico italiano', paper presented at the Intermediate Siep Conference, Bank of Italy, Rome, 2 March.

Reinhart, C.M. and K.S. Rogoff (2010), 'Growth in a time of debt', *American Economic Review*, **100**(2): 573–8.

Spaventa, L. (2008), 'Avoiding disorderly deleveraging', CEPR Policy insight No. 22.

Toniolo, G. (2011), 'Episodi di crescita e rientro dei debiti sovrani', paper presented at the Intermediate Siep Conference, Bank of Italy, Rome, 2 March.

7. Economic governance in the euro area: balancing risk reduction and risk sharing

Fabrizio Balassone, Sara Cecchetti, Martina Cecioni, Marika Cioffi, Wanda Cornacchia, Flavia Corneli and Gabriele Semeraro*

INTRODUCTION

The consensus narrative of the euro area (EA) crisis identifies as its proximate cause the rapid unwinding of large intra-EA lending imbalances, which built up largely unchecked during the 2000s. The lack of institutions capable of dealing with this 'sudden stop' turned it into Europe's worst economic crisis since WWII.[1]

The sovereigns–banks nexus was one of the main amplifying factors of financial distress during the crisis. On the one hand, the difficulties encountered by banks affected the sovereigns directly, through the bailout of troubled intermediaries, and indirectly, through the impact of reduced lending on the economy. On the other hand, sovereigns' weaknesses affected banks' balance sheets, their ratings and their cost of funding, while the economic recession worsened the quality of their lending portfolios.

In Greece the dire conditions of the public finances ignited the crisis and the problems of the sovereign rapidly spread to the banking system, opening the door to second-round effects. Europe's hesitation in dealing with Greece's difficulty, up to the announcement of 'private sector involvement' in the summer of 2011, sparked contagion in countries suffering from macroeconomic imbalances of diverse natures as financial markets began to fear the break-up of the EA and quickly priced in the risk of large outstanding government debts being redenominated in the national currency.[2]

---

* The usual disclaimer applies. Based on information available as of June 2016.
[1] Baldwin et al. (2015); Baldwin and Giavazzi (2016).
[2] This is consistent with the idea of 'wake-up call contagion' (Giordano et al., 2013). Sovereign risk premiums rose rapidly after the agreement between German Chancellor

The first to be hit were Ireland and Portugal. The former was suffering from a systemic banking crisis, which impaired the sovereigns' resilience in the face of financial turmoil (because of the bailout of the banking sector, Irish public debt increased by 21 percentage points in 2010), the latter from a mix of excessive private lending and weak public finances. Spain and Italy followed suit, with large losses in the banking sector and a high public debt being their respective weaknesses.[3] In some cases, most notably in Cyprus, the contagion also made its effects felt through large losses on domestic banks' holdings of crisis-hit foreign sovereign bonds.

In response to the crisis, European authorities embarked on a thorough process of reforming the economic governance of the EU and the EA. It aimed to strengthen the resilience first of sovereigns, then banks to shocks by both reducing their individual risk potential and increasing risk sharing. Although some have criticized the process for being lengthy and failing to keep pace with the quick reaction of financial markets, in six years – and in an extremely difficult economic environment – the institutional and regulatory landscape of Europe has been overhauled.

Significant progress was achieved, but risk reduction was favoured over risk sharing. More efforts are needed. This chapter reviews the measures taken concerning sovereigns and banks and discusses possible ways forward on both fronts. After a double recession and financial crisis, the EA has entered an environment of weak and uncertain growth, marked by deflationary pressures. Only further risk sharing can avoid harm-ful pro-cyclical excesses. Common financial backstops introduced (or planned for introduction) during the crisis must be strengthened, guarding against asymmetries in the way European decisions enter national laws, which sometimes risk undoing the progress achieved. A currency union cannot survive repeated shocks without adequate policy instruments:

Merkel and French President Sarkozy, at a summit in Deauville in October 2010, on having distressed sovereigns restructure their debts to private creditors. Although some challenge the causal link (for example Mody, 2015), others point out that 'even as late as April 2010, after the first sampling indicated the scale of the [Irish] banking losses, sovereign spreads were little more than 1%. By November of that year (just a few weeks after the Deauville statement [. . .]) large banking outflows and spreads exceeding 5% made recourse to official assistance inevitable' (Hohonan, 2013, p. 12). Di Cesare et al. (2012) present evidence that, for several countries, risk premiums reached levels well above what could be justified on the basis of fundamentals. Among the possible reasons for this, they focus on the perceived risk of a break-up of the EA. See also Ignazio Visco's interview with *Corriere della Sera* on 8 July 2012 and Visco (2012 and 2013).

[3]   Spanish banks needed recapitalization amounting to €61.5 billion, €41.3 billion of which was provided by the European Stability Mechanism to the FROB (the bank recapi-talization fund of the Spanish government) and then channelled to the financial institutions concerned. After declining by about 20 percentage points over 1994–2007, Italy's debt-to-GDP ratio rose sharply in 2008–09, from 102 to 112, mainly because of the recession.

countercyclical fiscal policy is a necessity; either the EA moves swiftly towards fiscal union and a federal budget or member states must be in a position to run their own fiscal stabilization in the face of exceptional circumstances.

STRENGTHENING THE SOVEREIGNS

Risk Reduction

To reduce the risks from sovereigns, macroeconomic surveillance was reinforced. The so-called 'six-pack', 'two pack' and 'fiscal compact' introduced deep changes.[4] The debt rule became operational (almost twenty years after the Maastricht Treaty)[5] and an expenditure benchmark flanked the structural balance in assessing countries' fiscal positions. Independent institutions ('fiscal councils') were set up at the national level to assess compliance with the rules, and sanctions applicable in both the preventive and the corrective arms of the Stability and Growth Pact (SGP) were strengthened.[6] A common timeline was defined to synchronize key steps in the preparation of national budgets, promote peer review and multilateral coordination, and allow the assessment of national draft budget laws by the European Commission (with a view to their consistency with European fiscal rules). In addition, a procedure was introduced to allow the timely

---

[4]   The six-pack came into force at the end of 2011, it includes: (1) four regulations on the prevention and correction of excessive fiscal and macroeconomic imbalances (n. 1175 and n. 1177 on budgetary deficits and regulations; n. 1174 and n. 1776 on macroeconomic imbalances); (2) one regulation on the effective enforcement of budgetary surveillance (n. 1173); and (3) one directive on national fiscal frameworks (n. 85). The two-pack entered into force in 2013; it includes one regulation on common provisions for monitoring and assessing budgetary plans (n. 473) and one regulation on strengthening the surveillance over member states in difficulty (n. 472). The fiscal compact is part of the Treaty on Stability, Coordination and Governance in the EMU, which also entered into force in 2013.

[5]   The Treaty and the annexed protocols require countries to avoid excessive deficit and debt and specify that national debt should not exceed 60 per cent of GDP or, if above the threshold, it should be 'sufficiently diminishing and approaching the reference value at a satisfactory pace'. Failure to comply with this rule was intended to trigger the excessive deficit procedure, the same way as trespassing the 3 per cent of GDP threshold for deficit. However, since the words 'sufficiently' and 'satisfactory' were not given a quantitative counterpart, the debt rule played no role in practice.

[6]   Specifically, the obligation to lodge an interest-bearing deposit has been introduced if the member state does not comply with the recommendation of the Council within the preventive arm. Such a deposit is converted into a non-interest-bearing one in the case of serious non-compliance or when an Excessive Deficit Procedure is opened, and finally into a fine if the country fails to take effective action to correct its excessive deficit. Also, in order to strengthen the automaticity of the enforcement a reverse majority voting system has been included.

detection and correction of macroeconomic imbalances in individual member states, with a focus on the potential for negative externalities for other countries.

The poor pre-crisis compliance record warranted a tightening of fiscal rules. Over 1998–2007 countries in the EA (including Greece, which joined in 2001, and excluding later members) recorded deficits in excess of 3 per cent of GDP 18 times. Germany violated the threshold four times, followed by France, Greece, Italy and Portugal with three violations each. Although weak market pressure contributed,[7] this was clearly the result of flaws in monitoring and enforcement of fiscal rules.

However, European fiscal rules (or their prevailing interpretation) lack the necessary flexibility in the face of exceptional circumstances. Buti et al. (1997), in an exercise of retrospective application of the SGP, consider the effect of automatic stabilizers on government budgets in cases of negative growth over 1961–96 for the then 15 members of the Union. They conclude:

> the risk of incurring an excessive deficit is relatively high for countries involved in lengthy recessions which result in significant negative output gaps and make it extremely difficult to re-absorb the deficit within the first year of recovery. [. . .] in 9 out of the 24 recession episodes considered, GDP declines for two or three years. In 5 of these 9 events, even starting with a balanced budget, the deficit exceeds the 3.5 per cent level in the recession period and remains above the 3 per cent level during the following year. (p. 20)

The authors also point out that:

> in case of recessions, the margins for implementing large-scale discretionary countercyclical policies are rather limited, unless budgets move into surplus. [. . .] In the event of a severe recession during the early years of EMU, since several countries will still have deficits in the 2 per cent to 3 per cent of GDP range, they risk moving into excessive deficit, unless they take a pro-cyclical budgetary stance. [. . .] Long recessions may pose serious threats even to countries with sound pre-recession budgetary positions (p. 30).

This is especially problematic in a context where institutional and economic rigidities hamper other sources of macroeconomic stabilization. In a currency union, monetary policy cannot react to the economic

---

[7] Prior to the crisis, markets neglected cross-country differences in economic fundamentals and fiscal discipline. Sovereign spreads were nil. It was a confirmation of the 1989 Delors Report warning that 'rather than leading to a gradual adaptation of borrowing costs . . . the constraints imposed by market forces might either be too slow and weak or too sudden and disruptive' (Committee for the Study of Economic and Monetary Union, 1989, p. 20).

conditions of individual countries, nor can member states rely on exchange rate movements to cushion them against shocks. In addition, labour mobility is far from perfect and rigidities in product and service markets remain significant in the EA. Last, but not least, the EA does not possess a 'federal budget' to provide fiscal stabilization.

The experience with the recent crisis exemplifies the risks involved in this set-up. Without a lender of last resort, shocks to the perception of fiscal sustainability can be (and were) unboundedly amplified. To reign in escalating risk premiums, most EA member states had no other choice than to undertake pro-cyclical fiscal policies to regain market confidence and avoid a financial disaster. The extent of the needed consolidation was amplified by (the excessively restrictive interpretation of) European fiscal rule, which tended to leave little space, if any, even for the operation of automatic stabilizers. This resulted in a strongly pro-cyclical fiscal stance at the height of the crisis in many member states and, absent the counterbalance of a federal budget, in the EA as a whole.

Though outweighed by the benefits from the avoided financial meltdown, the macroeconomic costs of this strategy have been significant. In Italy, for instance, it is estimated that 'the measures to consolidate the public finances adopted in the second half of 2011 with the aim of preventing an uncontrolled deterioration in the conditions on the financial markets had an adverse effect on demand equivalent to 1 percentage point of annual GDP growth' (Banca d'Italia, 2013, p. 38).

In some cases the need for fiscal consolidation originated from insufficient fiscal prudence before the crisis, but more flexible rules could have made it less costly. A concerted European strategy could have credibly phased in the implementation of the needed fiscal effort and attuned it to the prevailing cyclical conditions. Within a more flexible, though rules-based, fiscal framework, the EA might have led the markets rather than follow them in the effort to ease tensions and regain stability in the face of an exceptional shock. The macroeconomic costs of the adjustment would have been reduced.

The 2015 communication by the Commission on the flexibility within the existing rules of the SGP is a step in the right direction. The communication clarifies how cyclical conditions should be taken into account in the implementation of the SGP. It operationalizes the provisions dealing with the modulation of fiscal effort over the economic cycle under the preventive arm of the SGP. It also stresses that the Commission will continue to assess effective action under the corrective arm of the Pact based on a measurement of structural fiscal effort, excluding budgetary developments that are outside the control of governments. Finally, it affirms the Commission's willingness to use the provisions allowing deviations from the fiscal adjustment required under both the preventive and the corrective arm of the SGP in the face of 'a severe economic downturn in the EA or in the EU as a whole' (European Commission, 2015a, p. 17).[8]

But the recognition is still missing that, lacking a federal budget, exceptional circumstances may call for exceptional measures. First, even under exceptional circumstances a fiscal expansion (that is, a worsening of the structural balance) is not explicitly allowed; at best a neutral fiscal stance is conceded. Second, if a severe economic downturn were to push a country's nominal deficit well above the 3 per cent of GDP threshold (for example over 3.5 per cent), the Treaty on the Functioning of EU (TFEU, Art. 126) would still trigger an excessive deficit procedure (with the annexed stigma effect). Third, the interaction between the adjustments towards the medium term objective (MTO) prescribed under the preventive arm and the debt rule can give rise to conflicts whereby a fiscal stance allowed under the former would not be in line with the latter, and vice versa.

Risk Sharing

When public finances in some EA member states started deteriorating in 2008–09, the EU lacked a common and agreed framework for dealing with sovereign debt crises. The urgency to intervene in order to help EU partners and limit financial contagion resulted in ad hoc and targeted actions with bilateral loans and loans granted directly by the EU budget (through the European Financial Stability Mechanism, EFSM) of limited amounts (€80 billion and €60 billion respectively). Meanwhile instruments for dealing with current and future sovereign debt crises were defined:

1. The European Financial Stability Facility (EFSF) was set up in 2010 as a temporary institution. Designed under paramount pressure, it was far from being optimal. The funding of its lending operations was treated as public debt of the guarantor countries, adding to the tensions affecting the public finances of some member states. Its financial capacity was limited (€255 billion at inception), insufficient to contain the risk of contagion in the area.
2. To address these limitations, the European Stability Mechanism (ESM) was set up to gradually replace the EFSF from 2013 as a permanent firewall, thus flagging the commitment of member states to the single currency. Its implementation represented a significant improvement over its predecessor. Its lending capacity was much higher (€500

---

[8] European Commission (2015a). The communication also clarifies margins allowed with respect to the financing of investment and the implementation of structural reforms.

billion at inception) and its lending operations did not influence
member states' public finances.[9] Moreover, its legitimacy was secured
by an amendment to EU treaties (Art. 136, TFEU) authorizing EA
countries to establish a stability mechanism to protect the common
currency.[10]

Although the financial commitment of the member states is considerable in absolute terms, it is small relative to the size of government debt
in the area. The ESM residual lending capacity currently stands at about
€370 billion against a total of government debt in the area amounting
to €9.5 trillion, about 90 per cent of the area's GDP. It would have been
barely enough to cope with the financial assistance programmes launched
over 2010–12. While adequate as a first line of defence against the loss of
market access for a small or mid-size EA country, it would barely cover one
year of refinancing needs for a large country.

Moreover, the procedure for and the number of actors involved in the
approval of an assistance or precautionary ESM programme may hamper
its timeliness and create significant uncertainty. The complexity of the
procedure also reflects the unwillingness of EA member states to delegate
decisions on matters concerning financial assistance. The ESM Board
of Governors is currently composed of the 19 Ministers of Finance of
the EA and is chaired by the President of the Eurogroup. Decisions on
financial support require unanimity. An emergency procedure is foreseen
for cases in which both the European Commission and the ECB deem that
there is a risk to the financial stability of the EA as a whole, but this still
requires a qualified majority of 85 per cent. The European Commission
and the ECB are involved first in the preliminary assessment that follows a
request of assistance and then in the definition of the programme's details.
The ESM Treaty mandates that, whenever possible, the involvement of
the IMF should also be sought. The final programme agreement needs the

---

[9]   Only the paid-in capital (€80 billion over a total of €700 billion) accrued to the
guarantor countries' public debt. Additional capital can be called to avoid ESM default on its
obligation to its creditor and in this case it would weigh on the guarantor countries' public
finance. However, the likelihood of this scenario is minimized by the prudent funding strategy
by the ESM.
[10]   This was necessary to avoid potential conflict with the 'no bail-out' clause in Art. 125
of the TFUE: 'The Union shall not be liable for or assume the commitments of central governments, regional, local or other public authorities, other bodies governed by public law, or
public undertakings of any Member State, without prejudice to mutual financial guarantees
for the joint execution of a specific project. A Member State shall not be liable for or assume
the commitments of central governments, regional, local or other public authorities, other
bodies governed by public law, or public undertakings of another Member State, without
prejudice to mutual financial guarantees for the joint execution of a specific project'.

approval of the 19 members of the Board of Directors (one for each EA member state) by a qualified majority of 80 per cent, while all subsequent reviews need approval by unanimity. The complexity of the approval process is reflected in the length of the procedure, estimated by the ESM to be about three to four weeks for loan agreements. In practice, the agreement over programmes during the crisis (most of them took place before the ESM was operational) has generally taken less, with the exception of the programme for Cyprus.[11]

A positive note is the ESM flexibility with respect to debt restructuring. The Treaty establishing the ESM does not make private sector involvement a mandatory companion to ESM financial assistance. An analysis of debt sustainability must be conducted before deciding on granting a loan, but there is no automatic link between the result of such analysis and debt restructuring. The preamble to the Treaty does, however, foresee that 'in accordance with IMF practice, in exceptional cases an adequate and proportionate form of private sector involvement shall be considered in cases where stability support is provided accompanied by conditionality in the form of a macro-economic adjustment programme.'

Overall, the degree of risk sharing has significantly increased but remains limited. Compared to the pre-crisis situation, a lot of ground has been covered. A strict interpretation of the no bail-out clause as impeding any form of financial assistance has been overcome. Not only were financial facilities set up, but also their nature and the nature of their operations has gradually evolved. EFSF loans were backed by guarantees individually provided by member states, while the ESM has its own capital. Early loans were granted at a premium over the funding cost, while the financial terms of later ones only allow cost recovery.[12] In addition, in the context of the Greek programme, the maturity of outstanding loans was significantly extended ('reprofiling', a soft form of debt relief). However, as noted above, the financial capacity of the ESM is relatively small and ESM bonds are not backed by the unlimited joint guarantees of its shareholders in addition to their participation in the ESM capital.[13]

---

[11] A proposal by the EU-IMF-ECB was ready by the end of July 2012 but the Cypriot authorities requested further negotiations, mostly on measures for the financial sector. Elections held at the beginning of 2013 also delayed the agreement.

[12] The interest rate charged on the first Greek programme was based on three-month Euribor plus a margin (300 basis points for three years and 400 subsequently). For Ireland, the effective cost of lending was set to 5.9 per cent, while for Portugal it was between 5 and 6 per cent, depending on maturity and lender (EFSM or EFSF). In July 2011, the European Council agreed to a common 3.5 per cent interest rate for the three countries under programme and a longer maturity (15 years).

[13] This implies that, in order for the ESM bonds to retain a high rating, their lending capacity must be lower than the total capital subscription.

The birth of the ESM made it institutionally possible for the ECB to define appropriate rules of engagement for monetary policy in the face of 'unjustified' runs on sovereign bonds. After the introduction of the ESM, the Governing Council of the ECB decided on the modalities for government bonds purchases in secondary markets (outright monetary transactions, OMT) with the purpose of safeguarding monetary policy transmission and the singleness of monetary policy. Tensions in EA sovereign markets eased significantly right after the announcement, which was interpreted as a clear sign of the Governing Council resolve to address distortions related to fears of euro reversibility. The fact that the ECB did not have to buy a single bond to achieve this result suggests that the problem was one of multiple equilibria. Markets were converging to a 'bad' equilibrium in which concerns over the sustainability of public finances in some member states were pushing rates up, thus providing the conditions for defaults. The announcement of the ECB's possible intervention was sufficient to guide markets towards the 'good' equilibrium. Altavilla et al. (2014) find that the OMT announcement decreased the Italian and Spanish 2-year government bond yields by 2 percentage points, leaving unchanged the bond yields of the same maturity in Germany and France.

OMT filled a gap in the economic governance of the EA. That is why their announcement was so effective. However, they remain untested and there are concerns as to whether they allow timely intervention. The activation of OMT is subject to the agreement on an ESM assistance programme or an Enhanced Conditions Credit line, including the possibility of ESM primary market purchases. Both forms of assistance come with macroeconomic conditionality attached. Precautionary assistance without an adjustment programme (which the ESM can also grant) or assistance for financial institutions are not sufficient for OMT, nor is the mere application for a programme by the country concerned. We have noted above how long ESM programme approval can take. Moreover, the introduction of OMT met with significant opposition in some countries. Most notably, the German Constitutional Court considered that the OMT exceed the competences given to the ECB by the Treaties and forwarded the case to the European Court of Justice (ECJ) for a legal opinion. Although the ECJ ruled in favour of OMT as a monetary policy instrument, the actual use of OMT remains likely to be accompanied by controversy, which could further delay intervention.

The link with ESM programmes and the attached macroeconomic conditionality, while useful to prevent moral hazard, can also determine unwanted outcomes. OMT can be terminated either when the monetary policy transmission mechanism and/or the singleness of monetary policy are no longer in danger, or when there is non-compliance with the conditionality established in the ESM programme. These two perspectives can be in contrast. Halting OMT because of non-compliance with conditionality may result in the implosion of the market for the concerned country's debt. In its ruling on OMT the ECJ clearly distinguished between the monetary policy concern of the ECB and the economic policy concern of the ESM.[14] The ECJ judgment suggests that the role of the ECB in future programme reviews should be limited. Others have also argued that the ECB should interpret its formal role in future ESM programmes as narrowly as possible (for example Gros, 2015). Consistently, compliance with conditionality should only be sought by the ESM, not by the ECB. For this, however, an amendment to the ESM treaty is likely to be necessary, which would require unanimous ratification and in some countries, possibly, a referendum.

STRENGTHENING THE BANKS

Risk Reduction

The project of a banking union was rapidly defined and announced in June 2012. It involved both risk reduction and risk sharing. The international operating scale of major European banks required a centralized supervisory responsibility, so that fragmented information would no longer risk allowing growing imbalances to go undetected. Moreover, the definition and application of common rules for banks in the EA (and any non-euro member states that would want to join) was deemed necessary to reassure the markets of the comparability of information on banks based in different countries. At the same time, the responsibility for the management of banking crisis and for deposit insurance was to be moved at the European level to help sever the link between banks and sovereigns, including by use of a common public financial backstop.

The implementation of the banking union has so far privileged risk reduction over risk sharing. The project consisted of three complementary pillars: a Single Supervisory Mechanism (SSM); a Single Resolution Mechanism (SRM); and a European Deposit Insurance Scheme (EDIS). However, only the SSM is fully operational (since November 2014). The

---

[14]   The ECJ in its judgment of 16 June 2015 argued that OMT are part of monetary policy, not economic policy ('The OMT programme, in view of its objectives and the instruments provided for achieving them, falls within monetary policy and therefore within the power of ESCB'). It further pointed out that OMT contribute to price stability, the primary objective of the European System of Central Banks (ESCB), and that OMT do not infringe the prohibition of monetary financing of member states.

SRM has been defined but it lacks a common public financial backstop. Only the first two loss-absorption lines foreseen in the Bank Recovery and Resolution Directive (BRRD) are active: private sector involvement through the bail-in of creditors and a resolution fund financed by the banking industry. The EDIS remains at the stage of proposal.

The SSM was set up in record time. It comprises the ECB and national supervisory authorities, and monitors all credit institutions – with systemic banks directly supervised by the ECB. Its:

> rapid implementation was possible thanks to a provision in the Treaty expressly assigning the ECB prudential supervision functions. The SSM could right from the beginning rely on a whole set of common prudential rules (single rulebook), contained in the package of regulations CRR/CRD4 which had already transposed Basel III agreements in Europe. (Rossi, 2016, p. 4)

In order for the ECB to have a clear view of the situation of the banks it supervises from the outset, a comprehensive assessment of banks' financial health was also carried out. From an operational viewpoint, the launch of the SSM has certainly been successful, in light of the complexity of the project and of the very short time frame available. In addition, the establishment of the SSM has been a fundamental step in the process of restoring investors' confidence in European banks. With the SSM banks should be stronger and less exposed to shocks; common supervision should ensure effective enforcement of stronger prudential requirements for banks, requiring them to keep sufficient capital reserves and liquidity. This should make EU banks more solid, strengthen their capacity to manage risks linked to their activities adequately, and absorb losses they may incur.

The BRRD is now implemented in national legislation in almost all member states. The deadline was 31 December 2014.[15] According to ISDA BRRD Implementation Monitor,[16] as of 2 June 2016 only Poland, among EU countries, has not yet implemented the BRRD, while Slovenia has only partially implemented it.[17]

The success of the SSM will depend on its ability to perform effectively a difficult balancing act between micro- and macro-prudential considera-

---

[15] The BRRD entered into force on 2 July 2014. EU member states were required under Article 130 of the BRRD to adopt and publish the laws, regulations and administrative provisions necessary to comply with the BRRD by 31 December 2014 and to apply those with effect from 1 January 2015, except in relation to the bail-in provisions, which are to apply from 1 January 2016 at the latest.

[16] Available at http://www2.isda.org/isda-brrd-implementation-monitor/. Accessed 2 December 2016.

[17] Belgium, Croatia, France and Latvia have implemented most of the provisions in the BRRD; all other EU countries have fully implemented it.

tions. Regulatory changes that tighten capital ratios are particularly challenging after a financial crisis when banks are already deleveraging. The conflict with an accommodating expansionary monetary policy stance may help smooth the transition towards higher capital ratios by providing accommodative financing conditions (for example, the TLTRO2, announced last March by the ECB Governing Council, guarantees to banks certainty on funding availability at exceptionally low costs, thus potentially shielding credit supply from financial market volatility). However, the monetary policy stimulus is weaker when the private sector is deleveraging as a consequence of the financial crisis and the bank transmission channel is broken.

The SRM faces similar challenges. The BRRD contains some legal exemptions from the bail-in rule, aimed to balance the different objectives of a 'resolution' procedure (that is, protection of taxpayers, of systemic stability, depositors' protection, continuity in the supply of essential financial services). First, not all debt is subject to the bail-in (exempted categories include covered deposits, secured liabilities derivatives and inter-institution liabilities with maturities of less than seven days). Second, national resolution authorities can decide to 'exclude, or partially exclude, liabilities on a discretionary basis if they cannot be bailed-in within a reasonable time; to ensure continuity of critical functions; to avoid contagion or to avoid value destruction that would raise losses borne by other creditors.' The careful management of these exemptions will be key. Risks to legal certainty in the EU will have to be taken into account (the same liability could be subject to two different treatments depending on whether the bank is directly supervised by the ECB, in which case the Single Resolution Board (SRB) will decide on the exemptions, or not).[18]

The abrupt introduction of the new standards set in the BRRD (and before that by the Commission communication on state aid) gave prominence to the need to reduce investors' moral hazard over the risks for financial stability.

> During the technical negotiations on BRRD held in 2013 the Italian authorities had formally argued in favour of applying the bail-in tool only to newly issued bonds expressly containing a contract term entrusting the authorities with the power to write-down or convert them upon the occurrence of the conditions for resolution. In addition, to allow time for investors to become aware of the new rules and for banks to provide an adequate buffer of bail-inable liabilities, it was stressed the need to defer the entry into force of the new rules to 2018. The objections raised in technical contexts, by both the Bank of Italy and the

[18]   See Visco (2016a) for a detailed discussion.

Ministry of Finance, were not taken into account. The political pressure coming from the Northern European countries prevailed. (Rossi, 2016, p. 7)

The first applications of burden sharing in Portugal and in Italy have shown limitations and risks. The concerns of Italian authorities were confirmed: the retroactive application of new rules to instruments issued prior to the introduction of both burden sharing and the bail-in and the little time given to investors to adapt their choices to the new rules resulted in significant litigation and political pressure to reimburse the households involved. Contagion effects from the troubles of even small intermediaries impacted the public's confidence in the resilience of the banking system. More in general, since the summer of 2015, there has been evidence of variations in the performance of individual banks' share prices mainly ascribable to fears over asset quality and transparency. As underlined in Banca d'Italia (2016a), the recent increased attention of investors to the characteristics of bank assets is likely to be partly due to uncertainty among operators as to the direction bank regulation is taking in the EA and to the as yet incomplete banking union. The resulting uncertainty in the banking sector is confirmed by the high levels of volatility reached by the aggregate banking indices.

Risk Sharing

On the side of risk sharing, as already noted, the banking union largely remains unfinished business. The size of the Single Resolution Fund (SRF) seems very low compared with the magnitude of State aids and guarantees during the peak of the global financial crisis and with the size of large European banks. Moreover, it is building up slowly, with full funding expected to be achieved only by 2024. The creation of common public financial backstops to the SRF has been postponed to an indefinite future. Finally, the common deposit insurance scheme is still at the stage of proposals.

The SRF has a target size of at least 1 per cent of covered deposits of banks in the Banking Union. It has become operational since January 2016 and its funding will build up gradually with the contributions by banks by means of annual deposits. The Single Resolution Board determines the size of contributions year by year (upon consultation of the ECB or the national competent authority and in strict cooperation with national resolution authorities).[19] De Groen and Gros (2015a) estimate that, even

---

[19] See Banca d'Italia (2016b).

if SRF contribution is estimated at only about a quarter of the total losses incurred by banks during the recent financial crises, it should be capable of dealing with major crises, even of similar proportions as the last one.[20] Even if some limited bridge funding might be needed in the event of an early crisis, De Groen and Gros (2015b) argue that this could be mobilized at short notice.

However, under a systemic crisis, the losses expected to be absorbed by the private sector may well exceed its resilience: in this case the SRF would need a public financial backstop. The absence of such a backstop has often been taken to mean that the SRF is useless (Schoenmaker, 2014). Member states have agreed that the banking union requires access to an effective common fiscal backstop to be used as a last resort:

> Such a backstop would imply a temporary mutualisation of possible fiscal risk related to bank resolutions across the banking union. However, use of the backstop would be fiscally neutral in the medium term, as any public funds used would be reimbursed over time by the banks (via ex-post contributions from the banking sector). (European Commission, 2015b, p. 6)

Moreover, the design of a temporary public backstop would be needed:

> for cases where the application of the bail-in might exacerbate, rather than alleviate, the risks of systemic instability. It would be fully consistent with the provisions of the Key Attributes of Effective Resolution Regimes of the Financial Stability Board, that are the global standards for the resolution of large financial intermediaries crises (Rossi, 2016, p. 8)

A proposal to use the ESM as a financial backstop for crisis management has been put on hold.

Equally important, a Single Deposit Insurance Scheme is missing. Deposit insurance is currently implemented at the national level based on the 1994 Directive on Deposit Guarantee Schemes (DGS) as amended in 2010 with the aim to harmonize the coverage and funding arrangements of national DGS and clarify responsibilities. The amended Directive aims to guarantee that deposits up to a limit of €100 000 in any European bank will be reimbursed to depositors in the event of bank failure, without any haircut. Its requirements should be fully phased in by 2024. Today, almost all European countries have an explicit deposit insurance (the only two exceptions are Israel and San Marino).[21] The system is structured in such

---

[20]   This reflects the provisions allowing its intervention only after a bail-in of 8 per cent (of liabilities) has taken place and limiting its funding to 5 per cent (of liabilities including own funds).
[21]   See Demirgüç-Kunt et al. (2014) for details.

a way that it can absorb isolated bank failures, not a systemic banking crisis.

The EU Commission has recently proposed an EA-wide deposit insurance scheme (EDIS) for bank deposits, supplementing national DGS. The rationale of the proposal is to increase the resilience of the Banking Union against future financial crises by reducing the vulnerability of national deposit guarantee schemes to large local shocks and further reducing the link between banks and their home sovereign. The EDIS is intended to establish a mutual system of private deposit insurance based on a Deposit Insurance Fund (DIF), to which the already existing national funds would gradually transfer the resources collected by the participating banks. The scheme would guarantee the same protection in all countries participating in the SSM. EDIS would be built on the existing system and developed over time: it would fully insure national DGS as of 2024.[22]

Negotiations are proceeding slowly and there are heated discussions about the design of the single deposit guarantee scheme. Notwithstanding the scheme does not envisage any public backstop, and has a very long transition, a climate of mistrust still prevails along national borders:

> [The] proposal has faced firm opposition from some countries . . .. They call for the harmonization of major national regulations – bankruptcy laws, collateral framework, tax rules, company law and consumer protection – before mutual guarantee schemes are even discussed; and, above all, they call for the preliminary introduction of prudential requirements for banks' sovereign exposure. (Rossi, 2016, p. 10)

Among the opponents, the German Council of Economic Experts (2015) takes a critical view of a common European deposit insurance scheme warning of the risks involved in a premature introduction. In particular they point to the need to first sever the financial sovereign–bank nexus with the aid of regulatory reforms as necessary preconditions to prevent the danger of risks in one member state being transferred to the others. A similar position has been taken recently by the EU Dutch Presidency and by the President of the Bundesbank.[23]

---

[22] See European Commission (2015c) and (2015d) for details of the proposal.

[23] See: 'Strengthening the banking union and the regulatory treatment of banks' sovereign exposures', Presidency note, Informal ECOFIN, 22 April 2016; 'Solidità e solidarietà nell'Union e monetaria', speech at the German Embassy in Rome, 26 April 2016, available at: http://www.bundesbank.de/Redaktion/EN/Reden/2016/it_2016_04_26_weidmann.html. Accessed 30 April 2016.

FURTHER REFORMS OF THE FISCAL GOVERNANCE

In the medium to long run fiscal stabilization should become a 'federal function'. This is consistent with the theory of fiscal federalism, which emphasizes the trade leakages impairing the effectiveness of 'local' stabilization policies (Musgrave and Musgrave, 1984), as well as with prevailing international practice. No federation works with a share of 'local' to total expenditure as high as the EU's (98 per cent).

In monetary unions, a centralized fiscal policy is indispensable. Monetary policy cannot react to the economic conditions of individual countries, nor can member states rely on exchange rate movements to cushion them against shocks. As early as 1969, Kenen argued that a 'central' fiscal policy would limit the 'local' adjustments in price and wages necessary to cater for an idiosyncratic shock. A 'federal budget' would be particularly desirable in the EA as its member states display less cross-country labour mobility compared to the US and other established federations (Obstfeld and Peri, 1999), have less integrated financial markets and appear relatively more likely to be hit by asymmetric shocks (Bayoumi and Eichengreen, 1992). In federations like Canada, Germany and the US, around 80 per cent of income shocks to sub-national components are smoothed, either via private credit and capital markets – smoothing about 50–70 per cent of shocks – or public transfers from the centre to sub-national components – between 10 and 30 per cent (Bluedorn et al., 2013).[24] By contrast, income shocks to Eurozone countries are only about 40 per cent smoothed, with fiscal risk sharing found to be nearly zero.

The necessity to complement a monetary union with a fiscal union has been knowingly side-stepped by European policy makers for a long time. A report on the fiscal union (the MacDougall Report) had already been published in 1977 on behalf of the European Commission, and a mention concerning the economic desirability of a common budget is present even in the 1970 Werner Report. Later on, the technical papers accompanying the 1989 Delors Report and especially European Commission (1993a, 1993b) discussed the topic in depth. On 3 May 1998, when Europe was completing the last steps before the adoption of the single currency, Padoa-Schioppa wrote a column for *Corriere della Sera* highlighting its incompleteness. The debate on a fiscal union for the EA re-started during the crisis, as countries were struggling to cushion against the recession.

There is no shortage of technical alternatives to create a fiscal capacity

---

[24] See also Asdrubali et al. (1996), Melitz and Zumer (2002), and Obstfeld and Peri (1999).

for the EA. A 'rainy day fund' model with common resources allocated inter-temporally and across member participants according to the economic cycle is discussed, among others, in European Commission (2012), Allard et al. (2013) and Caudal et al. (2013). Proposals for a euro-wide unemployment insurance have also been put forward (for example, Lellouch and Sode, 2014; Brandolini et al., 2014; Bénassy-Quéré et al., 2016). Balassone et al. (2014) discuss the possibility of an EA pension scheme.

However, the idea has met with strong opposition and is mainly seen as a long-term project.[25] Critics of the rainy day fund have pointed out the difficulty of identifying the cyclical position of member states in real time. Proposals for a common unemployment insurance scheme have met resistance because of the difficulty in discriminating between cyclical and long-term unemployment, opening the way to permanent net transfers to regions characterized by higher structural weaknesses. The establishment of a common pension system would be a challenging endeavour, in view of the variety of pension arrangements now existing in EA countries. More generally, critics fear that such a common fiscal capacity could foster opportunistic behaviour and weaken the incentives to promote possibly painful growth-enhancing reforms.

Against this background, a second-best solution is to allow fiscal stabilization at the national level in the face of exceptional circumstances. The 'ratification' of such 'exceptional circumstances' cannot be based on numerical criteria. Complete contracts cannot be written and chances are that exceptionality may take different and new shapes over time. After all, even though today deflation is a concrete risk, it was not considered explicitly in any of the provisions of the SGP. A comprehensive evaluation will have to rely on discretion, on the possibility to complement hard evidence with qualitative case-by-case analysis.

To make sure that discretion is properly used, appropriate checks and balances will be necessary. One possibility would be to entrust the national fiscal councils introduced by the Fiscal Compact with this responsibility (Pisani-Ferry, 2016), possibly with the backing of the recently created European Fiscal Board (EFB).[26] Both are independent technical bodies,

---

[25] All official reform proposals put forward since 2012 – though with differences in emphasis – share the conclusion that a fiscal union for the euro area is a medium- to long-run project (Balassone et al., 2014).

[26] The EFB was introduced by a Commission decision in November 2015. It will be composed of five renowned international experts in macroeconomics and budgetary policy-making, nominated by the Commission in consultation with several key stakeholders such as the ECB, the Eurogroup and the national fiscal councils. It is bestowed with the responsibility to evaluate the consistent implementation of the EU fiscal framework, with a particular focus

the national councils with a better knowledge of local conditions, and the European board with a longer safety distance from national politics. Another possibility advocated by Villeroy de Galhau and Weidmann (2016) would be to entrust the EA Finance Minister with the authority to declare the existence of 'exceptional circumstances', again with the backing of national fiscal councils and the EFB. Comparing these two options, the former can be seen as providing more shelter from political bargaining, while the latter has advantages in terms of both democratic legitimacy and political responsibility.

The identification of those circumstances that qualify as 'exceptional times', although not based exclusively on numerical thresholds, should nevertheless be inspired by transparent criteria. The decision should be based on a large information set encompassing, *inter alia*, the monetary policy stance, financial and macroeconomic risks as identified by the European Systemic Risk Board (ESRB) and by the macroeconomic imbalances procedure, the country-specific fiscal space (measured with a view also to the long-term, for example with reference to the Commission's sustainability indicator S2).

In practice, in 'exceptional circumstances' a 'budget of flexibility' would be made available to member states. This would be additional to the flexibility margins already attached to specific clauses in current rules (investment, structural reforms). It would be an exceptional and temporary budget, made available by the Commission or by the EA Finance Minister (with the backing of national fiscal councils and the EFB) when, for example, the fiscal stance is deemed to be unduly restrictive once the overall macroeconomic and fiscal conditions are taken into account. In order to mitigate moral hazard, access to this budget could be made conditional on countries' track record with sound fiscal policy.

Implementing this reform would be easier if it were accompanied by some increase in risk sharing. The change in 'rhetoric' and the backing of European institutions may help reduce the potential for negative market reactions to fiscal expansions in distressed member states. However, an explicit financial backing would be much more effective. As stated in the 5-Presidents' report 'the world's second largest economy cannot be managed through rule-based cooperation alone. [. . .] it will need a shift from a system of rules and guidelines to a system of further sovereignty sharing within common institutions' (Juncker, 2015, p. 5). This could be achieved, for instance, through a mechanism of gradual debt mutualization (German

on the horizontal consistency of the implementation of budgetary surveillance and on cases of particularly serious non-compliance with the rules. It will also advise on the appropriate overall fiscal stance for the EA.

Council of Economic Experts, 2011)[27] by strengthening the financial capacity of the ESM and streamlining its governance, or by providing a leaner set of rules for the OMT.[28] Unfortunately there doesn't seem to be much appetite for further risk sharing at present.

To be a credible insurer against liquidity crises, the ESM should be able to provide financing in sufficient quantity. The extension of unlimited joint guarantees to ESM operations by its shareholders, in addition to their participating capital, could increase the lending capacity of the mechanism substantially. Currently such guarantees are explicitly ruled out by the ESM Treaty, consistent with the no bail-out clause in Art. 125 of the TFEU and with national legislation in some member states.[29] The availability of an autonomous revenue flow would be an alternative which would require no less institutional reform.[30] As it stands, the ESM lending

---

[27] The German Council proposed the creation of a European Redemption Fund to swap national debt in excess of 60 per cent of GDP into common liabilities issued by the Fund and backed by limited joint guarantees pledged by all member states, subject to a pre-defined plan for debt reduction under the form of an amortization scheme covering 20–25 years. The proposal, later dismissed by the German Council, crashed against opposition to the build-up of joint guarantees, sharing this fate with earlier proposals for the introduction of Eurobonds. Parello and Visco (2012), building on an earlier suggestion by Visco, revamped the proposal by envisaging the possibility for the Fund to invest the surplus liquidity generated by the difference between the flow of amortization instalments paid by the member states and the interest bill due by the Fund to the market each year, arising from the very long-term issuance policy of the Fund. Similar proposals have been put forward by Pâris and Wyplosz (2014) and by Corsetti et al. (2015). They also find antecedents in the general debate on Eurobonds (see, for instance, Delpla and Von Weizsacker, 2010, and Boonstra, 2011).

[28] OMT could be allowed to start without waiting for the definition of a fully fledged macroeconomic adjustment programme (for example using precautionary conditioned credit lines), or simply upon the request for assistance to the ESM by a member state. Additionally, macroeconomic conditionality could be taken out of the picture once the OMT has started. On this account, however, great controversy is likely to impede reforms. The current set-up for OMT decided in 2012 is obviously the result of a compromise balancing the concerns over financial stability with those over moral hazard and it is unlikely that positions have changed much thereafter. Moreover, some members of the Governing Council are expressing doubts about the current asset purchase programme (APP) of the ECB (for example, Weidmann, 2016). Although the OMT differs from the APP in its scope and characteristics, these criticisms can make it very difficult to accept changes that would simplify the activation of OMT. It should also be noted that the German Constitutional Court considers itself entitled to reject the decisions or opinions of the ECJ and this does not exclude the reopening of the case concerning the legitimacy of OMT.

[29] ESM Treaty Chapter 3, Art. 8 reads: 'The liability of each ESM Member shall be limited, in all circumstances, to its portion of the authorized capital stock at its issue price. No ESM Member shall be liable, by reason of its membership, for obligations of the ESM.' In 2011 the German Constitutional Court, ruling on financial aid to Greece and the EFSF, clarified that Parliament cannot 'enter in permanent mechanism under international public law which results in an assumption of liability for other state voluntary decisions, especially if they have an impact that is difficult to evaluate'.

[30] For instance, Corsetti et al. (2015) propose bringing forward the future (50-year-long) income stream of specific revenue sources and capitalizing them into a Stability Fund which

capacity could be increased only through new capital subscriptions by member states, which would impact their national debts, or by an increase in the ratio of lending capacity to subscribed capital (currently at about 71 per cent), which would impact on ESM rating and cost of funding.[31]

Besides its quantity, the timeliness and predictability of financing are key to the effectiveness of ESM operations. A revision and simplification of ESM governance could go a long way in this respect. The involvement of the Board of Governors in the operation of ESM could be reduced and most 'routine' decisions left to the Board of Directors (possibly, with a much smaller membership), whose decision could as a rule be taken by qualified majority (set at a lower level than the current 80 per cent). Moreover, the number of actors involved in the decisions could be reduced.[32] Finally, a new very short-term liquidity facility could be introduced for use in an emergency situation, allowing the ESM to provide liquidity without the need to set a fully fledged adjustment programme.

Resistance to increasing the financing power of the ESM, especially under lower conditionality, is, however, strong. Several proposals, both institutional and academic, actually go in the opposite direction, suggesting the introduction of sovereign insolvency procedures associated with ESM assistance – which would reduce the need for additional financial resources – in order to partially deal with moral hazard concerns. The German Council of Economic Experts (2015) has suggested the introduction of a formalized insolvency mechanism to make the no bail-out clause credible (Andritzky et al., 2016a provide more details). Such a procedure would require a maturity extension of government bonds as part of future adjustment programmes if public debt is not deemed sustainable. In the event of severe public debt overhang or a material breach of fiscal rules, an ESM adjustment programme should only be approved after a debt haircut is imposed on private creditors. This line of reasoning was recently echoed in a recent open letter by the president of the Bundesbank and the governor of the Banque de France, underlying the necessity to investigate 'how ESM rescue programmes could better involve private investors and how a sovereign debt restructuring process could be designed which does not put financial stability in the euro area as a whole at risk' (Villeroy de Galhau and Weidmann, 2016, p. 1).

However, these proposals risk exacerbating the very problem the ESM

---

would then allow the Fund to buy a large share of the public debt of the participating countries. To this purpose, the Fund would issue 'stability bonds', collateralized by the expected stream of revenues.

[31]   At present ESM bonds have a AAA rating from Fitch and an Aa1 rating from Moody's.

[32]   Balassone and Committeri (2015), for instance, argue for the separation of ESM and IMF activities.

was set up to address. First, the introduction of automatic triggers may end up facilitating the ignition of crises rather than helping to prevent them. Runs on sovereign bonds may start as soon as debt levels come in the vicinity of thresholds and/or as soon as talks of ESM support begin. Second, triggers may also negatively affect the sustainability of countries' fiscal positions both by further reducing the fiscal space available for stabilization policies (Bofinger, 2016) and by raising their borrowing costs. Third, by increasing the stigma associated with ESM assistance, an automatic link between ESM financing and maturity extension may delay intervention, thus increasing the costs of restructuring. Fourth, and conversely, by creating a relatively easy and less uncertain exit option a sovereign debt restructuring mechanism (SDRM) might incentivize more irresponsible fiscal policy early on. The current setting, in which debt restructuring is possible but is painful because of uncertainties and the accompanying adjustment programme imposed by European institutions, 'might in fact strike the right balance between market discipline and fiscal responsibility' (Bénassy-Quéré et al., 2016, p. 7).

There are further good reasons not to modify the ESM Treaty by introducing more specific terms concerning debt restructuring. First of all, it is not that easy to discriminate between solvency and liquidity crises, and any assessment on the solvency of a sovereign debt requires a significant degree of judgement when considering the several elements involved (deficit and debt dynamics, the maturity profile of liabilities, growth prospects, macroeconomic and demographic risks and so on). It is for this reason perhaps that the recent reform of IMF lending policy, while reducing the degree of allowed discretion compared with previous arrangements, does not entail a degree of automatism comparable to proposals put forward in the European context. Second, and more importantly, the ESM must preserve the stability of the EA as a whole, and systemic issues cannot simply be disregarded when deciding on financial support to member states and whether their debt should be restructured with private sector involvement, which, as clearly pointed out by Bini Smaghi (2011), can entail very high and unpredictable costs.[33]

Finally, there is no agreement on the optimal timing and features of debt restructuring. A consensus appears to be emerging on the correlation between debt crisis and growth slowdown (Borensztein and Panizza, 2009; Furceri and Zdzienicka, 2012; Reinhart and Reinhart, 2015), but the IMF 'too little, too late' claim is not univocally proved yet. For instance, Asonuma (2012), with data as well as a theoretical contribution, highlights

---

[33] Balassone and Committeri (2015) also discuss the merits of the controversial 'systemic clause' abolished by the new IMF lending policy.

a possible trade-off between haircut dimension and subsequent credit conditions, as lower recovery rates for creditors are associated with higher bond spreads in the post-default period. Moreover, causality issues remain to be solved, and the doubt remains if recession is a good time for implementing a restructuring: final restructurings (conventionally, the ones not followed by another debt crisis within four years) usually happen when a country is already recovering from past decline (Reinhart and Trebesch, 2016; Benjamin and Wright, 2009). The evidence is also mixed on the relative merits of debt reprofiling and deeper debt restructuring. For instance, Reinhart and Trebesch (2016) and Schröder (2014) show that the economic landscape and the probability of serial restructurings are worse for reductions in net present value given by maturity extensions and/or interest rate reductions (that is, reprofiling) than for a debt write-off.

COMPLETING THE BANKING UNION AND BEYOND

Severing the link between banks and sovereigns requires the completion of the banking union with the risk-sharing elements foreseen by the original project and still lacking implementation. Member states have to agree on a common backstop (that is, a common financing facility) backing the Single Resolution Fund in case of sudden need, exceeding the available means of the fund. In the short term, while the Single Resolution Fund is progressively built up (until 2024) through contributions from the banking sector, member states also need to provide appropriate bridge financing (for example, through a credit line with the European Stability Mechanism, ESM). Concerning deposits, the approval of the Commission proposal discussed above needs to be complemented by a public backstop for the privately financed deposit insurance fund, which could be needed to support its role in crisis financing.

The crisis management framework should incorporate a macro-prudential approach. This would reassure financial markets that, in the case of crisis, resolution tools that might endanger financial stability will not apply. The new European framework on banking crisis has the overarching purpose to ensure that banks can fail without adverse consequences for financial stability. However, it does not provide for any effective tool to safeguard financial stability when the application of resolution tools – such as the bail-in – may exacerbate rather than alleviate systemic risk.

The European debate is instead increasingly focusing on calls for a revision of the prudential treatment of banks' sovereign exposures, which is argued to be necessary to strengthen the stability of the banking sector and address the sovereign–bank nexus.[34] The Dutch Presidency note for the ECOFIN of April 2016 lists five possible policy options identified by the EFC High Level Working Group,[35] ranging from retaining the current treatment to addressing both credit and concentration risk. A common point in the debate is the necessity of a gradual implementation of any possible revision, to avoid dangerous repercussions on financial markets. However, even if the implementation takes place in the medium to long term, possible issues related to frontloading by banks in terms of sell-off of sovereign bonds should be taken into account.

Such reforms could have disruptive consequences for EA economies, risking being more harmful than helpful. Based on Lanotte et al. (2016), Balassone et al. (2016) provide estimates on the likely consequences on government bonds' yields of the revision of the prudential treatment of banks' sovereign exposures as proposed by the German Council of Economic Experts (Andritsky et al., 2016b). They show that the reform could have significant consequences on the government bond markets of Italy, Spain and, to a lesser extent, Germany. As pointed out by Lanotte et al. (2016), this kind of estimate must be interpreted as lower bounds. First, they are derived from a comparative static exercise, while transitional dynamics in the current circumstances might be highly non-linear. Second, they are based on a partial equilibrium analysis, excluding changes in the riskiness of government bonds

---

[34]   According to Nouy (2012), there is a need to have a better understanding of the sovereign risk and to assess the need for regulatory reform in that regard, in particular to consider regulatory charges differentiated according to the respective credit quality of sovereigns. For Weidmann (2013), a reassessment of the regulatory treatment of sovereign exposures of financial institutions is crucial. Gros (2013) suggests that risk weights on sovereign debt should not be at zero, and should be based on 'objective' criteria, rather than ratings; he points out that more important than risk weighting for sovereign exposure is diversification, which is to be addressed by applying large exposure rules. The Five Presidents' Report (Juncker, 2015) also refers to the possibility of introducing limits on banks' exposures to individual sovereigns as a means to ensure sovereign risk diversification. The European Commission announced that it will come forward with the necessary proposals on the prudential treatment of sovereigns, drawing on quantitative analysis under preparation in the Economic and Financial Committee and the Basel Committee and paying particular attention to financial stability aspects (European Commission, 2015c). Constancio (2015) expressed its disagreement with the idea of introducing caps on sovereign exposure, but sounded more confident about revisions of risk weights, provided they do not create undue turbulence in markets where sovereign debt is used. Visco (2016b) examines in detail pros and cons of a revision of the prudential treatment of sovereign exposures and concludes against it: 'the mere recognition that there is no truly risk-free asset does not per se warrant a change in the regulatory treatment of sovereign exposures. [. . .] At the current stage, a broad agreement has been reached on the pros and cons of different reform options, not on their overall balance. My personal view is that the potential benefits of a reform are uncertain, while the potential costs could be sizeable' (p. 5).

[35]   The EFC HLWG on the prudential revision of sovereign exposures was set up in 2015 to study different dimensions of sovereign exposures and look at the implications of various regulatory changes.

following portfolio adjustments induced by the reform. Third, they exclude repercussions on regulation applicable to other intermediaries (for instance, the insurance sector, which also holds significant amounts of government bonds). Fourth, they exclude possible changes in banks' portfolio composition following the reform, while a more realistic assumption would be that banks rebalance their portfolio towards less risky assets in order to save capital costs. Fifth, there could be significant macroeconomic implications if banks decide to deleverage in order to address at least part of the capital shortfall arising from the revision of sovereign risk weights (any significant deleveraging could cause further credit tightening, reduce economic growth, and eventually also have an impact on fiscal balances).

Sovereign exposures generally receive a more favourable treatment than those towards private companies. In the Basel II framework, 'at national discretion, a lower risk-weight may be applied to banks' exposures to their sovereign (or central bank) of incorporation denominated in domestic currency and funded in that currency' (Paragraph 54). In most advanced countries, banks' exposures to domestic sovereigns in domestic currency receive a zero risk weight (to our knowledge, this is the case in Australia, Canada, Hong Kong, Japan, Singapore and the US). Any possible changes of the regulatory treatment of the sovereign exposures should be discussed in an international context, namely within a reassessment of the Basel framework, so to ensure a level playing field.

There are good reasons for this preferential treatment. Markets need a safe asset that serves as a store of value, as a means to meet regulatory requirements, and as a pricing benchmark.

> To be sure, risk-free must be understood as a behavioural concept. [. . .] there is no such thing as a risk-free asset, strictly speaking. However, we used to live in a world where sovereign risk was so low that investors could behave as if that debt was risk-free. The situation was a bit like air travel: we all know that the risks are not zero when we get on a plane but they are low enough for most of us behave as if they were truly minimal. (Caruana, 2013, p. xxvi)

Governments have a comparative advantage in providing safe assets (even the large production of safe assets before 2008 by private vehicles relied implicitly on the perceived government backstop). In general, their credit, liquidity and market risks are lower than in the private sector. The probability of a default of an AAA-rated sovereign issuer is much lower than one of AAA-rated corporations. According to Moody's (2008), between 1983 and 2007 issuer-weighted cumulative default rates for sovereigns have been on average lower than those for their corporate counterparts, except for BBB-rated issuers at three-year or longer horizons.

A reform of the prudential treatment of sovereign exposure should only be considered if it provides incentives to remedy the current shortage of safe assets, not if it risks worsening it. In the EA, there are only two ways to remedy the shortage of safe assets. First, there is risk reduction: member states should ensure sound fiscal positions to make their sovereign paper safer. Second, there is risk sharing through a fiscal union and debt mutualization with eurobonds. We have already discussed the progress made in risk reduction and the difficulty of making further advances in risk sharing.

Solutions could be envisaged to provide incentives to diversification, resulting in a 'synthetic' alternative to Eurobonds. As suggested by Corsetti et al. (2015), exposures to individual EA sovereigns may indeed be assigned a non-zero risk weight and be subject to concentration limits if both provisions do not apply when a bank holds paper issued by all EA sovereigns in a balanced portfolio (say, in proportion to countries' GDP). For this to work, the same concentration limit and non-zero risk weight should apply to all sovereigns, thus recognizing that excessive demand for a single sovereign can pose risks to financial stability regardless of its riskiness (as was the case with the sharp increase in demand of German bonds during the crisis). Although the proposal may present some conceptual appeal, to assess its viability a more in-depth investigation of its technical features and potential repercussion would be needed. Among several open issues, the following could be mentioned: how to define the diversified portfolio of sovereign bonds; how to account for sovereign bonds in currencies other than the euro; how to deal with non-investment grade securities.

CONCLUSIONS

The unchecked build-up of imbalances during the 2000s exposed the EA to the risk of sudden stops. Such risk materialized in 2009–10 and its consequences were amplified by the absence of adequate institutions. Europe embarked on a thorough process of reforming the economic governance of the EU and the EA. Significant progress was achieved, but a lot of ground remains to be covered.

The poor pre-crisis compliance record warranted a tightening of fiscal rules, but rules should be more flexible in the face of exceptional circumstances, especially in a context where institutional and economic rigidities hamper other sources of macroeconomic stabilization.

The degree of sovereign risk sharing has increased, but remains limited. A strict interpretation of the no bail-out clause has been overcome, but the financial capacity of the ESM is relatively small and, beyond the participating capital, it is not backed by the unlimited joint guarantee of its shareholders. The ECB's outright monetary transactions remain untested and there are concerns as to whether they can be deployed in time. The link with ESM conditionality, while useful to limit moral hazard, may hamper their effectiveness.

The implementation of banking union has so far favoured risk reduction over risk sharing. The single resolution fund is small, privately financed and building up very slowly. The Commission proposal for an EA deposit insurance scheme has the same features and is being put on hold. The success of the SRM will depend on its ability to perform a difficult balancing act between micro- and macro-prudential considerations. The first applications of burden sharing in Portugal and in Italy have already shown their limitations and risks.

The EA needs fiscal tools for macroeconomic stabilization, but fiscal union has met with strong opposition. The only viable second-best option is to allow fiscal stabilization at the national level in the face of exceptional circumstances. To make sure that discretion is properly used, appropriate checks and balances will be necessary. This reform should be accompanied by some increase in risk sharing, by enhancing the lending capacity of the ESM and ensuring it is able to provide timely and predictable financing.

Several proposals, both institutional and academic, actually move in the opposite direction by suggesting the introduction of automatic sovereign insolvency procedures associated with ESM assistance in order to partially deal with moral hazard concerns. They risk exacerbating the very problem the ESM was set up to address.

Severing the link between banks and sovereigns requires that banking union be completed, incorporating the risk-sharing elements envisaged in the original project but still not implemented. A reform of the prudential treatment of banks' sovereign exposures could have a disruptive impact on EA economies, risking doing more harm than good, unless used to remedy the shortage of safe assets by providing a synthetic alternative to Eurobonds.

Europe is at a crossroads, pressured by exceptional economic and geopolitical circumstances. Either it finds the strength to return to its roots and embraces a second (and deeper) round of reforms based on enhanced risk sharing, or it risks running into pro-cyclical excesses that may finally tear it apart. It cannot afford to abandon national stabilization instruments (fiscal and financial) without replacing them with similar tools at the supranational level.

REFERENCES

Allard, C., P.K. Brooks, J.C. Bluedorn, F. Bornhorst, K.M. Christopherson, F. Ohnsorge and T. Poghosyan (2013), *Towards a Fiscal Union for the Euro Area*, IMF, SDN/13/09.

Altavilla, C., D. Giannone and M. Lenza (2014), 'The financial and macroeconomic effects of OMT announcements', ECB Working Paper no. 1707.

Andritzky, J., D. Christofzik, L.P. Feld and U. Scheuering (2016a), 'A sovereign insolvency mechanism for the Euro Area', paper presented at the 18th Banca d'Italia Workshop on Public Finance: 'Current Issues in Fiscal Policy', Rome, 31 March–2 April.

Andritzky, J., N. Gadatsch, T. Koerner, A. Schlafer and I. Schnable (2016b), 'A proposal for ending the privileges for sovereign exposures in banking regulation', 4 March 2016, available at: http://www.voxeu.org/article/ending-privileges-sovereign-exposures-banking-regulation. Accessed 30 March 2016.

Asdrubali, P., B.E. Sorensen and O. Yosha (1996), 'Channels of interstate risk sharing: United States 1963–90', *Quarterly Journal of Economics*, **111** (4), 1081–110.

Asonuma, T. (2012), 'Serial default and debt renegotiation', available at: http://papers.ssrn.com/sol3/papers.cfm?abstract_id=2416482. Accessed 30 March 2014.

Balassone, F. and M. Committeri (2015), 'Europe and the IMF: nec sine te, nec tecum . . .', LUISS Guido Carli – School of European Political economy, Working Paper no. 6/2015.

Balassone, F., S. Momigliano, M. Romanelli and P. Tommasino (2014), 'Just round the corner? Pros, cons, and implementation issues of a fiscal union for the Euro Area', *Banca d'Italia Questioni di Economia e Finanza*, Occasional Papers, No. 245, November.

Balassone, F., S. Cecchetti, M. Cecioni, M. Cioffi, W. Cornacchia, F. Corneli and G. Semeraro (2016), 'Economic governance in the Euro Area: Balancing risk reduction and risk sharing', *Banca d'Italia Questioni di Economia e Finanza*, Occasional Papers, No. 344.

Baldwin, R. and F. Giavazzi (eds) (2016), *How to Fix Europe's Monetary Union: Views of Leading Economists*, London: CEPR Press.

Baldwin, R., T. Beck, A. Bénassy-Quéré, O. Blanchard, G. Corsetti, P. de Grauwe, W. den Haan et al. (2015), 'Rebooting the Eurozone: Step 1 – agreeing a crisis narrative', *CEPR Policy Insight*, no. 85.

Banca d'Italia (2013), Economic Bulletin, No. 67, January.

Banca d'Italia (2016a), Economic Bulletin, No. 2, April.

Banca d'Italia (2016b), Financial Stability Report, No. 1.

Bank for International Settlements (BIS) (2013), *Sovereign Risk: A World Without Risk-free Assets?* Proceedings of a seminar on sovereign risk including contributions by central bank governors and other policy-makers, market practitioners and academics, Basel, 8–9 January, *BIS Papers* No. 72.

Bayoumi, T. and B. Eichengreen (1992), 'Shocking aspects of European Monetary Unification', NBER Working Paper, No. 3949.

Bénassy-Quéré, A., X. Ragot and G. Wolff (2016), 'Which fiscal union for the Euro Area?', Bruegel Policy Contribution, Issue 2016/05.

Benjamin, D. and M.L.J. Wright (2009), 'Recovery before redemption: A theory of delays in sovereign debt renegotiations', CAMA Working Paper, No. 2009-15.

Bini Smaghi, L. (2011), 'Private sector involvement: From (good) theory to (bad) practice', speech at the Reinventing Bretton Woods Committee, Berlin, 6 June, available at: https://www.ecb.europa.eu/press/key/date/2011/html/sp110606.en. html. Accessed 30 June 2011.

Bluedorn, J., D. Furceri, F. Jaumotte, F. Ohnsorge, T. Poghosyan and A. Zdzienicka (2013), 'Fiscal risk sharing: New evidence for the Euro Area', Technical Background Note to IMF Staff, Discussion Note, 13/09.

Bofinger, P. (2016), 'The way forward: Coping with the insolvency risk of member states and giving teeth to the European Semester', CEPR's Policy Portal, 12 February, available at http://voxeu.org.

Boonstra, W.W. (2011), 'Can Eurobonds solve EMU's problems?', Rabobank, Economic Research Department, August.

Borensztein, E. and U. Panizza (2009), 'The cost of sovereign default', *IMF Staff Papers*, **56** (4): 683–741.

Brandolini, A., F. Carta and F. D'Amuri (2014), 'A feasible unemployment-based shock absorber for the Euro Area', *Banca d'Italia Questioni di Economia e Finanza*, Occasional Papers, No. 254, December.

Buti, M., D. Franco and H. Ongena (1997), 'Budgetary policies during recessions – Retrospective application of the "Stability and Growth Pact" to the post-war period', *European Economy, Economic Papers*, No. 121, May, Brussels.

Caruana, J. (2013), *Welcoming remarks*, in Bank for International Settlements, *Sovereign Risk: A World Without Risk-free Assets?* Proceedings of a seminar on sovereign risk including contributions by central bank governors and other policy-makers, market practitioners and academics, Basel, 8–9 January, *BIS Papers* No. 72.

Caudal, N., N. Georges, V. Grossmann-Wirth, J. Guillaume, T. Lellouch and A. Sode (2013), 'A budget for the Euro Area', *Trésor-Economics*, No. 120.

Committee for the Study of Economic and Monetary Union (1989), *Report on Economic and Monetary Union in the European Community*, Brussels: European Commission.

Constancio, V. (2015), 'The role of stress testing in supervision and macroprudential policy', keynote speech at London School of Economics, 29 October.

Corsetti, G., L.P. Feld, P.R. Lane, L. Reichlin, H. Rey, D. Vayanos and B. Weder di Mauro (2015), *A New Start for the Eurozone: Dealing with Debt*, Monitoring the Eurozone 1, London: CEPR Press.

De Groen, W.P. and D. Gros (2015a), 'The Single Resolution Fund: How much is needed', available at: http://voxeu.org/article/size-single-resolution-fund. Accessed 20 December 2015.

De Groen, W.P. and D. Gros (2015b), 'Estimating the bridge financing needs of the Single Resolution Fund: How expensive is it to resolve a bank?', CEPS Special Report, No. 122, CEPS, Brussels, November.

Delpla, J. and J. von Weizsacker (2010), *The Blue Bond Proposal*, Bruegel Policy Brief, 2010/03, May.

Demirgüç-Kunt, A., E. Kane and L. Laeven (2014), 'Deposit insurance database', IMF Working Paper WP/14/118.

Di Cesare, A., G. Grande, M. Manna and M. Taboga (2012), 'Recent estimates of sovereign risk premia for euro-area countries', *Banca d'Italia Questioni di Economia e Finanza*, Occasional Papers, No. 128.

European Commission (1993a), 'Stable money, sound finances: Community public finances in the perspective of the EMU', *European Economy*, No. 53.

European Commission (1993b), 'The economics of community public finance', *European Economy – Report and Studies*, No. 5.

European Commission (2012), 'Blueprint for a deep and genuine economic and monetary union', Brussels: European Commission.

European Commission (2015a), 'Making the best use of the flexibility within the existing rules of the Stability and Growth Pact', Communication to the European Parliament, the Council, the European Central Bank, the Economic and Social Committee, the Committee of the Regions and the European Investment Bank, Strasbourg.

European Commission (2015b), 'Updated version of first memo published on 15/04/2014 – Banking Union: Restoring financial stability in the Eurozone', European Commission Factsheet, November.

European Commission (2015c), 'Communication: Towards the completion of the Banking Union', Communication from the Commission to the European Parliament, the Council, the European Central Bank, the European Economic and Social Committee and the Committee of the Regions, Strasbourg.

European Commission (2015d), Proposal for a Regulation of the European Parliament and of the Council amending Regulation (EU) 806/2014 in order to establish a European Deposit Insurance Scheme.

Furceri, D. and A. Zdzienicka (2012), 'How costly are debt crises?', *Journal of International Money and Finance*, **31** (4), 726–42.

German Council of Economic Experts (2011), 'Annual Report 2011/12: "Assume responsibility for Europe"', Bonifatius.

German Council of Economic Experts (2015), 'Consequences of the Greek crisis for a more stable Euro Area', Special Report, 28 July.

Giordano, R., M. Pericoli and P. Tommasino (2013), 'Pure or wake-up-call contagion? Another look at the EMU sovereign debt crisis', *International Finance*, **16**, 131–60.

Gros, D. (2013), 'Banking union with a sovereign virus: The self-serving regulatory treatment of sovereign debt in the euro area', *CEPS Policy Brief* no. 289, Brussels.

Gros, D. (2015), 'Countries under adjustment programmes: What role for the ECB?', CEPS Special Report, No. 124.

Hohonan, P. (2013), 'Panel remarks', in Bank for International Settlements, *Sovereign Risk: A World Without Risk-free Assets?* Proceedings of a seminar on sovereign risk including contributions by central bank governors and other policy-makers, market practitioners and academics, Basel, 8–9 January, *BIS Papers* No. 72.

Juncker, J.C. (2015), 'Completing Europe's Economic and Monetary Union', report in close cooperation with D. Tusk, J. Dijsselbloem, M. Draghi and M. Schulz, 22 June.

Kenen, P. (1969), 'The theory of Optimum Currency Areas: An eclectic view', in R.A. Mundell and A.K. Swoboda (eds), *Monetary Problems in the International Economy*, Chicago: University of Chicago Press, pp. 41–60.

Lanotte, M., G. Manzelli, A.M. Rinaldi, M. Taboga and P. Tommasino (2016), 'Easier said than done? Reforming the prudential treatment of banks' sovereign exposures', *Banca d'Italia Questioni di Economia e Finanza*, Occasional Papers, No. 326.

Lellouch, T. and A. Sode (2014), 'An unemployment insurance scheme for the Euro area', *Trésor Economics*, No. 132.

Melitz, J. and F. Zumer (2002), 'Regional redistribution and stabilization by the center in Canada, France, the UK and the US: A reassessment and new tests', *Journal of Public Economics*, **86**, 263–86.

Mody, A. (2015), 'Living (dangerously) without a fiscal union', Bruegel Working Paper No. 2015/03.

Moody's (2008), 'Sovereign default and recovery rates, 1983–2007', Moody's Global Credit Research, March.

Musgrave, R.A. and P.B. Musgrave (1984), *Public Finance in Theory and in Practice*, Singapore: McGraw-Hill.

Nouy, D. (2012), 'Is sovereign risk properly addressed by financial regulation?', *Banque de France Financial Stability Review*, **16**, 95–105.

Obstfeld, M. and G. Peri (1999), 'Regional non-adjustment and fiscal policy: Lessons for EMU', NBER Working Paper, No. 6431, National Bureau of Economic Research.

Parello, C.P. and V. Visco (2012), The European Redemption Fund: A comparison of two proposals, *Politica Economica – Journal of Economic Policy (PEJEP)*, **3**, 273–306.

Pâris, P. and C. Wyplosz (2014), 'PADRE: Politically Acceptable Debt Restructuring in the Eurozone', Geneva Special Report on the World Economy 3, ICMB and CEPR.

Pisani-Ferry, J. (2016), 'The Eurozone's Zeno paradox – and how to solve it', *VoxEU*, 10 April.

Reinhart, C. and V.R. Reinhart (2015), 'Financial crises, development and growth: A long-term perspective, *World Bank Economic Review*, **29** (1), 1–24.

Reinhart, C. and C. Trebesch (2016), 'Sovereign debt relief and its aftermath', *Journal of the European Economic Association*, **14** (1), 215–51.

Rossi, S. (2016), 'The Banking Union in the European integration process', speech at the Conference 'European Banking Union and bank/firm relationship', CUOA Business School, Altavilla Vicentina, 7 April.

Schoenmaker, D. (2014), 'On the need for a fiscal backstop to the banking system', DSF Policy Paper, No. 44, Duisenberg School of Finance.

Schröder, C. (2014), 'Haircut size, haircut type and the probability of serial sovereign debt restructurings', ZEW Discussion Papers, No. 14-126.

Villeroy de Galhau, F. and J. Weidmann (2016), 'Europe at the crossroads', *Le Monde* and *Süddeutsche Zeitung*, 8 February.

Visco, I. (2012), 'Address by the Governor of the Bank of Italy at the Italian Banking Association Annual meeting', Rome, 11 July, available at: http://www.bancadi talia.it/pubblicazioni/interventi-governatore/integov2012/en-visco-110712.pdf? language_id=1. Accessed 30 July 2012.

Visco, I. (2013), 'The exit from the euro crisis: Opportunities and challenges of the banking union', Istituto Affari Internazionali and Council on Foreign Relations, Council of Councils Regional Conference: Europe and the Future of Global Governance, Rome, 10 September, available at: http://www.bancaditalia.it/pub blicazioni/interventi-governatore/integov2013/Visco_IAI__09092013.pdf?langu age_id=1. Accessed 30 September 2013.

Visco, I. (2016a), 'Fact-finding inquiry on the Italian banking and financial system and the protection of savings, also regarding supervision, crisis resolution and European deposit insurance', Rome, 19 April, available at: http://www.banca ditalia.it/pubblicazioni/interventi-governatore/integov2016/en-audizione-govern atore-19042016.pdf?language_id=1. Accessed 30 April 2016.

Visco, I. (2016b), 'Banks' sovereign exposures and the feedback loop between banks and their sovereigns', Euro50 Group meeting on 'The Future of European Government Bonds Markets', Rome, 2 May, available at: http://www.bancadita lia.it/pubblicazioni/interventi-governatore/integov2016/en_Visco_Euro50_Bank_ Sovereign_Exposure_02052016.pdf?language_id=1. Accessed 30 May 2016.

Weidmann, J. (2013), 'Stop encouraging banks to load up on state debt', *Financial Times*, 1 October.

Weidmann, J. (2016), 'A look at the euro area from a central bank perspective', Keynote speech at Second Finance Forum, Lichtenstein, 23 March, available at: https://www.bundesbank.de/Redaktion/EN/Reden/2016/2016_03_23_weidmann. html. Accessed 10 April 2016.

8. Adjustments in the balance sheets: is it normal, this 'new normal'?*

Liviu Voinea, Alexie Alupoaiei, Florin Dragu and Florian Neagu

8.1 INTRODUCTION AND PROBLEM DISCUSSION

The adjustments in the balance sheets are one of the 'new normal' after the outbreak of the financial crisis. High level of indebtedness among companies and households calls for debt re-adjustment towards more sustainable levels. Banks shrink their business in order to cope with the new risk environment. Governments strive to consolidate their accounts, amid modest economic recovery.

In some cases, the issue of debt overhang also plays an important role. For instance, companies – in their endeavour to pay down debt – will overlook possible profitable investment opportunities, even though the net income which could be obtained from taking on these projects would facilitate an eventual scale down of their liabilities over time.

In this sense, Koo (2011) argues there are at least two types of recession. The first one is prompted by the normal business cycle, while the second is determined by private sector deleveraging or debt minimization (referred to as a *balance sheet recession* and related to the financial cycle). In an attempt to repair their financial standing, companies and households will increase savings and repay the debt they accumulated, which in turn translates into lower consumption and therefore lower aggregate demand. Koo (2011) also mentions that premature fiscal consolidation can prolong the recession, as it can transform in the long run into even higher public deficits than those which will be required to stimulate demand in the short term.

* The opinions expressed herein are those of the authors and do not necessarily reflect the views of the National Bank of Romania. The authors would like to thank Adrian Codirlaşu, Bogdan Negrea, the participants in the 'Regional Seminar on Financial Stability', jointly organized by the National Bank of Romania and the International Monetary Fund, the participants in the 'Inside public debt: ethical arguments against default' conference organized by the European Center for the Study of Public Choice, and the participants in the 'Risk management' conference organized by the University of Turin for their valuable input.

These debt adjustments might be normal: what goes up must come down. But some questions are brought forward: by how much, how fast, and how to act as a policymaker. To answer these questions, the response of the probability of recession for various levels of indebtedness is investigated in order to obtain the critical thresholds of debt above which economic growth and financial stability might be affected.

This idea is not new. Cecchetti et al. (2011) examine debt thresholds for the OECD countries concerning government, household and corporate sectors. Eberhardt and Presbitero (2013) find some support for a non-linear relationship between public debt and long-run growth across countries, while Neagu et al. (2015) identify thresholds for debt service-to-income and loan-to-income ratios in order to decrease the probability of excessive lending.

Reinhart and Rogoff (2010) look at the relationship between real GDP growth and government debt, showing that there is no discernible connection between the two variables until the debt-to-GDP ratio reaches a threshold level of 90 per cent. If public debt continues to grow beyond this value, then the median growth rate of these countries will be approximately 1 percentage point below that of countries with lower debt levels.

Baum et al. (2013) investigate the relationship between public debt and economic growth by means of a dynamic-threshold panel model in order to assess the non-linear impact of public debt on economic growth. The authors find a level of public debt-to-GDP of approximately 67 per cent, up to which debt has a positive and statistically significant impact on GDP growth in the short run. However, for values surpassing 95 per cent, adding more debt influences economic activity in a negative way.

Furthermore, Caner et al. (2010) also search for a tipping point in public debt level, beyond which debt will have a negative influence on economic growth. By using yearly data, spanning between 1980 and 2008, and a threshold least squares regression model, the authors find that a debt-to-GDP ratio greater than 77 per cent will reduce the average annual GDP growth by approximately 0.0174 percentage points for each additional percentage point of debt.

Clements et al. (2003) analyse the impact external debt has on growth in low-income countries and show that a value of external debt beyond 50 per cent could have a negative effect on growth.

Chudik et al. (2015) revisit the question of the effect of debt on growth and its dependence on indebtedness levels and find no evidence for a universally applicable threshold in the relationship between public debt and economic growth, once the authors take into consideration the impact of global factors and their potential spillovers.

In light of this existing literature, the value added of our chapter is to grasp, jointly, the indebtedness level of all the sectors (companies, households, government, external and total) when searching for the critical thresholds. The chapter focuses on seven emerging European economies, employing both domestic and foreign credit data to study how the probability of recession reacts to a range of debt values in the case of the individual sectors (companies, households and government), as well as at various aggregation levels. The study takes a macroprudential perspective by looking for solutions to reach the intermediate macroprudential objective of preventing excessive indebtedness. In this regard, our chapter strives to identify the optimal level of debt beyond which the economic growth could be negatively affected. The chapter is structured as follows. Section 8.2 deals with the methodology employed in conducting the study. It also contains a description of the data and the variables which form the model. In section 8.3 the results are presented and interpreted. Finally, section 8.4 concludes and suggests further research avenues.

8.2 METHODOLOGY AND DATA

The objective of the study is to determine the optimal levels of debt for various institutional sectors. To this end, data were collected on six distinct debt categories (households, non-financial corporations, government, private, external and total), as well as on gross domestic product dynamics. In order to control for the possible effects of other macroeconomic variables, data are also gathered on gross fixed capital formation, household consumption, exports and imports, inflation and interest rates, together with government balance and unemployment rates. The sample spans a 10-year period between December 2004 and December 2014, while the data frequency is quarterly. With the exception of interest rate, inflation and unemployment, the rest of the variables are expressed as percentages of GDP (see Tables 8A.1 and 8A.2 in the Appendix for summary statistics and correlation matrix).

The information on debt and the other variables was extracted from Reuters, Bloomberg, the European Central Bank, the national central banks, as well as the national statistics institutes.

The recession event indicator, that is, the dependent variable, is constructed as a binary variable based on quarterly GDP data, which takes the value 1 if the annual economic growth remains in negative territory for two consecutive quarters and 0 otherwise:

$$y_{i,t} = \begin{cases} 1, & if\, \Delta GDP < 0\, for\, two\, consecutive\, quarters \\ 0, & otherwise \end{cases} \qquad (8.1)$$

Initially, seven countries were considered to enter the regression analysis, but for Poland no two consecutive quarters of negative growth during the interval December 2004 to December 2014 were reported. Hence, the dependent variable for this country consists only of zeros, which does not allow for the computation of debt thresholds in the panel logit estimations.

A multivariate panel logit model with fixed effects, building on the specification used by Baum et al. (2013), is then employed to assess the response of the recession probability to various threshold values of debt (see Table 8A.3 in the Appendix for estimation results). In order to control for the effect of other macroeconomic variables, which could also have an impact on growth, the model also includes these potential relevant indicators, as established by previous studies on economic growth. Marginal effects on the probability of recession were computed in order to gauge how various debt levels will influence the probability, while the other covariates were kept fixed. In order to deal with the issue of heteroscedasticity, all models were run in a robust manner. After the estimation of each of the model specifications below, the ability of the predictions to follow the actual recession variable was checked to further ensure that the models were properly defined. Moreover, the accuracy ratio was computed to verify that the specifications can accurately discriminate between the two states of the recession indicator.

$$
\begin{aligned}
y_{i,t} = \ &total\_debt_{i,t-4} + gfcf_{i,t-4} + consum_{i,t-4} + trade\_gdp_{i,t-4} \\
&+ govt\_balance_{i,t-4} + ir\_dob_{i,t-4} + hicp\_all_{i,t-4}
\end{aligned} \tag{8.2}
$$

The total debt model was estimated by means of a panel regression in which the dependent variable was considered as the one in equation (8.1). With respect to the regressors, the total debt variable was constructed by adding the liabilities of households, non-financial corporations (both internal and external credit) and those in the public sector (domestic and foreign debt). Other determinants of growth were considered to be gross fixed capital formation, household consumption, the economy's openness (measured as the sum of exports and imports divided by GDP), the government balance, together with inflation and interest rates. All the independent variables were used with a lag of four quarters. In order to check the robustness of the results, model specifications with two quarters and eight quarters lag were also run (see Table 8A.4 in the Appendix). Further explanatory variables were included in the model as well, but the results do not merit their incorporation. Given the superior predictive ability of the four-quarter lag model and the increased statistical significance in this case, it was chosen to move forward with this specification (equation (8.2)).

Similar panel regressions and reliability checks were used for the external debt and private sector debt models (equations (8.3) and (8.4)).

$$y_{i,t} = ext\_debt_{i,t-4} + gfcf_{i,t-4} + consum_{i,t-4} + trade\_gdp_{i,t-4}$$
$$+ govt\_balance_{i,t-4} + ir\_dob_{i,t-4} + hicp_{all\,i,t-4} \qquad (8.3)$$

$$y_{i,t} = private\_debt_{i,t-4} + gfcf_{i,t-4} + consum_{i,t-4} + trade\_gdp_{i,t-4}$$
$$+ govt\_balance_{i,t-4} + ir\_dob_{i,t-4} + hicp_{all\,i,t-4} \qquad (8.4)$$

For the public sector, the debt variable included both domestic and external liabilities. The model also consisted of the unemployment rate, household consumption, government budget balance, the interest rate and inflation (equation (8.5)). Similar robustness checks were performed as in the previous cases.

$$y_{i,t} = govt\_debt_{i,t-4} + unemployment_{i,t-4} + consum_{i,t-4}$$
$$+ govt\_balance_{i,t-4} + ir\_dob_{i,t-4} + hicp_{all\,i,t-4} \qquad (8.5)$$

In order to be able to evaluate private sector debt at a more granular level, this category was split into household and non-financial corporation debt. In the case of the latter, debt consisted of both domestic and foreign claims. The regression models in these two cases follow the specifications below (equations (8.6) and (8.7)):

$$y_{i,t} = nfc_{debt\,i,t-4} + gfcf_{i,t-4} + trade_{gdp\,i,t-4} + govt_{balance\,i,t-4}$$
$$+ ir_{dob\,i,t-4} + hicp_{all\,i,t-4} \qquad (8.6)$$

$$y_{i,t} = hh\_debt_{i,t-4} + unemployment_{i,t-4} + consum_{i,t-4}$$
$$+ import\_gdp_{i,t-4} + ir\_dob_{i,t-4} + hicp_{all\,i,t-4} \qquad (8.7)$$

In order to cross-validate the results, a model-based sustainability approach is also employed, as in Mendoza and Ostry (2007), in order to get further information on those levels of debt which have no negative spillovers for economic growth. This approach was preferred to the so-called ad hoc sustainability analysis promoted by Bohn (2005). Mendoza and Ostry (2007) develop the method described below in order to assess public debt sustainability. Our chapter builds on their work and extends it by considering this approach also for the other debt categories.

The foundations of Mendoza and Ostry's (2007) model are found in Ljungqvist and Sargent (2004), starting from the following Euler-type equation:

$$Q_j(s_{t+j}|s_t) = \beta^j \frac{u'(y(s_{t+j}) - g(s_{t+j}))}{u'(y(s_t) - g(s_t))} f^j(s_{t+j}, s_t) \qquad (8.8)$$

where $Q_j(s_{t+j}|s_t)$ denotes the j-periods ahead pricing kernel, β is the subjective discount factor, y is the output produced in economy, g are the expenditures incurred by government, while u' is the marginal utility. At every moment t, the state of economy s_t is given by the combination of y_t and g_t. Because we are living in an uncertain environment, a Markov process is used to model the economy's dynamics, whose transition function between successive states is given by $f^j(s_{t+j}, s_t)$. The main idea underlined by the Euler equation is to equalize the net present value of consumption across consecutive periods. Thus, considering that allowed consumption results from resource constraint $c(s_{t+j}) = y(s_{t+j}) - g(s_{t+j})$, the above equation states that in a general equilibrium environment, $Q_j(s_{t+j}|s_t)$ denotes the stochastic discount factor required to satisfy the Euler condition. In other words, $Q_j(s_{t+j}|s_t)$ shows the incentive for which an economic agent is willing to give up a unit of consumption today in favour of consumption tomorrow.

On the other hand, the related return R_{jt} required to borrow the government j-periods ahead from now (t) is defined as:

$$\frac{1}{R_{jt}} = \beta^j E_t \left[\frac{u'(y_{t+j} - g_{t+j})}{u'(y_t - g_t)} \right] \qquad (8.9)$$

From here on, the notations expressed in terms of states were changed with a temporal notation. From relation (8.8), alongside standard budget constraints used in general equilibrium optimization, the following asset-pricing type relationship was defined for the optimal level of debt D:

$$D_{t-1}(s_t) = \tau_t - g_t + \sum_{j=1}^{\infty} \beta^j E_t \left[\frac{u'(y_{t+j} - g_{t+j})}{u'(y_t - g_t)} (\tau_{t+j} - g_{t+j}) \right] \qquad (8.10)$$

where τ_t are the government revenues. By manipulating relations (8.9) and (8.10), we obtain a relation for the optimal debt level D with the same philosophy as the consumption-CAPM model of Lucas (1978):

$$D_{t-1}(s_t) = \tau_t - g_t + \sum_{j=1}^{\infty} \left\{ \frac{1}{R_{jt}} E_t [\tau_{t+j} - g_{t+j}] \right.$$
$$\left. + cov_t \left[\frac{u'(y_{t+j} - g_{t+j})}{u'(y_t - g_t)}, \tau_{t+j} - g_{t+j} \right] \right\} \qquad (8.11)$$

If the covariance relation from (8.10) is ignored, the so-called ad hoc sustainability principle results, which implies that the optimal debt level is obtained when the initial debt equals the expected present value of the primary balance. Basically, the presence of $cov_t[\frac{u'(y_{t+j} - g_{t+j})}{u'(y_t - g_t)}, \tau_{t+j} - g_{t+j}]$ ensures an interaction between the government and the private sector in the financial markets. A positive covariance between the primary balance and the marginal utility emphasizes a countercyclical primary balance. Several studies showed that primary balances are countercyclical especially in the case of emerging economies, which means the primary balances usually grow in periods of recession.

Mendoza and Ostry (2007) defined the following relation for the data generating process of the primary balance:

$$PB_t = \rho D_{t-1} + \varphi_t + \varepsilon_t \qquad (8.12)$$

where PB_t is the primary balance, ρ is the response of PB_t to the already existing debt level, while φ_t is used to control for other factors that affect the ratio between primary balance and aggregate output. ε_t is a Gaussian homoscedastic martingale sequence process[1] for innovations. In fact, Mendoza and Ostry (2007) use (8.12) to test if (8.10) is valid as a response to Bohn's observation. This is done by checking if ρ is positive and statistically significant. Several empirical studies proved this for developed countries, as well as for emerging economies.

More exactly, relations (8.10) and (8.11) represent a solvency condition within the sustainability analysis of debt. In that sense, Mendoza and Ostry (2007) derived the following sustainable debt/GDP ratio:

$$E[D_t] = \frac{-\mu + (1 - \rho)cov(1 + r_t, D_{t-1})}{\rho(1 + \bar{r}) - \bar{r}} \qquad (8.13)$$

where r_t is the real interest rate on debt with its long-run mean $\bar{r}$, while μ is the long-run average of the primary balance. In particular, the two authors defined sustainable debt as the level of GDP ratio to which it is expected to converge in the long run under an optimal design. Therefore, for positive long-run mean of the primary balance, as well as for a positive covariance between real interest rate and past levels of debt, the sustainable level is decreasing in ρ. The inverse relationship between $E[D_t]$ and the response of the primary balance to previous debts can be explained as follows: a large existing level of debt will determine the government to obtain a larger primary balance now, affecting instead its capacity to borrow in the future.

---

[1] $E(\varepsilon_t) = 0$, $E(\varepsilon_t'\varepsilon_t) = \begin{pmatrix} 1 & 0 \\ 0 & 1 \end{pmatrix}$.

Based on Bohn (2005), Mendoza and Ostry (2007) assumed zero covariance between the real interest rate and the previous debt level, which transforms (8.13) into:

$$E[D_t] = \frac{-\mu}{\rho(1 + \bar{r}) - \bar{r}} \tag{8.14}$$

Relationship (8.14) was then further used in the computation of the expected debt levels, being also viewed as optimal for the case of private debt. This was possible due to several assumptions implied by the methodology used by Mendoza and Ostry (2007). First of all, since the pricing kernel theory is available for all types of financial assets, the involved formulas can also be applied to private debt. Going further, the approach to which Mendoza and Ostry (2007) resorted makes no connections to the characteristics underlined by benchmark debt, namely no references about its structure and maturity. However, the use of the optimal debt formula above for other types of debt is also done somehow ad hoc, without a rigorous anchoring in the microfoundations.

In fact, the formula for the optimal debt level derived by Mendoza and Ostry (2007) supposes the calibration of four parameters: the primary balance, the response of the primary balance to existing debt, the real long-run interest rate, and the real output growth rate. In order to calibrate the model of Mendoza and Ostry (2007) for the various debt categories and countries, the following actions were taken.

The primary balance, in the case of public debt, was considered to be the quarterly difference between public revenues and expenditures. It is important to note in this case that the primary balance is cleared of any expenditure made to service existing debt. As such, the primary balance denotes the quarterly need for money in order for the government to meet its obligations. Based on this idea, a corresponding proxy was constructed for the private sector. More exactly, the growth rate of private debt was employed as a stand-in for the primary balance. The analogy between the two measures can be expressed as: while the primary balance denotes the government's need for money, the growth rate of private debt denotes the same thing, but for the private sector. A positive unconditional mean or the 50th percentile figures for the growth rate of private debt denotes an increasing need for money, similarly to the negative primary balance in case of public debt. The response of the primary balance to existing debt is calibrated on the base of Mendoza and Ostry (2007). In that sense, given the uncertainty surrounding these two parameters, it was decided to construct grids for each of them. More specifically, different scenarios were considered with respect to the simultaneous values recorded by the long-run primary balance and by the response of the primary balance to existing debt respectively. Therefore, the results will be obtained in terms of surfaces. Bullets are used to indicate the results with the highest likelihood of occurrence in our view. In order to obtain the long-run primary balance, the 50th percentile operator was applied to the underlined empirical distribution. It was observed that between the 50th percentile figures and the sample mean figures there are significant differences in some cases. For this reason, the grid for the long-run primary balance was constructed around the values recorded by the 50th percentile and the sample mean.

Related to the second calibrated parameter, a grid for the response of the primary deficit to existing debt was considered, which ranges between 0.025 and 0.04, in accordance with the results obtained by Mendoza and Ostry (2007) for a pool of emerging economies.

The long-run interest rate was calibrated by using an Ornstein–Uhlenbeck continuous model for the term structure of interest rates. In our case, the model mentioned was estimated by resorting to the Aït-Sahalia (2002) method, which uses Hermite expansions and polynomials. For the long-run real output growth, the 50th percentile was applied to the largest available sample. In that sense, the asymptotic principle was exploited, while the largest available sample for each case was used in order to reduce the potential for bias phenomenon in the long-run figures.

8.3 RESULTS

The present chapter employs a series of multivariate panel logit regressions in order to assess the evolution of the recession probability for various debt levels. In addition, a general equilibrium model is also used in order to gain better insight into debt and growth dynamics. These two approaches strive to identify a debt threshold beyond which the economic activity could be affected. To this end, in the case of the regression models, the marginal response of the dependent variable (that is, the probability of recession) is computed for six distinct debt categories whose values range from 20 to 200 per cent of GDP (see Table 8A.5 in the Appendix). Debt is considered to have an adverse effect on economic growth when the probability of recession surpasses 50 per cent.

In the next subsections, an analysis of the results will be conducted for all six debt classes at the aggregated panel level, but also in the context of each individual country included in the study (Table 8.1). Furthermore, the results of the model-based sustainability approach will also be detailed.

Table 8.1   Comparative results: Regression model (RM) vs. Asset pricing model (AP)

% GDP	Total debt		External debt		Government debt		Non-financial corporations' debt		Households debt	
	RM	AP	RM	GE	RM	GE	RM	GE	RM	GE
Bulgaria	135	64	140	43	30	21	90	23	30	19
Czech Republic	125	88	55	54	45	34	55	28	30	40
Latvia	140		155		25		65		45	
Hungary	195	46	185	173	90	24	75	41	40	48
Poland		148		100		88		8		88
Romania	100	175	90	151	45	39	40	48	25	11
Slovenia	135		100		40		85		25	

8.3.1   Panel Regression Results

First, the relationship between the probability of recession and total debt is investigated by means of a logit model estimated on a panel of seven Central and Eastern European countries. The dependent variable is, of course, the recession event indicator. On the right-hand side of the equation, the model includes as regressors, besides total debt, several other macroeconomic factors in order to control for the impact of these variables on economic growth. In the case of the total debt model, the panel regression results show that most of the variables' coefficients are statistically significant and have the expected sign. Total debt displays a positive and strongly significant relationship with the probability of recession, while a boost in the debt level would materialize in an increase in the probability of an economic downturn. The interest rate, the openness of the economy and inflation also show a direct and statistical significant link to the dependent variable. Even though the consumption coefficient has the expected sign, this variable is not statistically significant, whereas in the case of the gross fixed capital formation and the government balance, the coefficients' signs are opposite to the expected ones.

Marginal effects are then computed with the aim of assessing the response of the recession probability to several total debt levels, while the other covariates are considered to be fixed. The results show that the probability of economic downturn exceeds 50 per cent when the total debt has a value of approximately 140 per cent of GDP (see Figure 8.1). Beyond this level, the probability increases more and more rapidly.

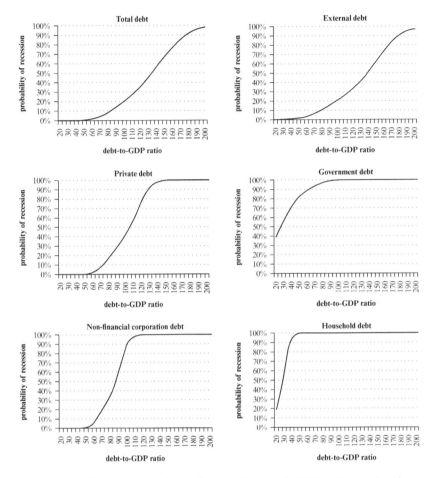

Figure 8.1   Panel results: the evolution of the probability of recession for various debt levels

When analysing the regression results for gross external debt, it can be noticed that the majority of the coefficients are statistically significant. The debt variable influences the recession probability in a positive manner, higher levels of debt resulting in a larger probability of an economic contraction. Applying the same marginal effects technique as above will result in an external debt threshold of 120 per cent of GDP, at which the probability of recession is greater than 50 per cent. After this debt level, the odds of economic decline follow a similar pattern as those of total debt.

Splitting total debt into private and government liabilities indicates that the public sector has a lower capacity to absorb debt than the former. In the case of government debt, the response of the recession probability is swifter, with the debt threshold standing at 50 per cent of GDP, whereas in the case of the private sector the warning rate is approximately 90 per cent of GDP.

Further disaggregating private sector liabilities into non-financial corporation and household debt shows that the reaction of the dependent variable is faster in the case of household debt, with the probability of a downturn exceeding 50 per cent when the debt level for this category is around 30 per cent of GDP. For non-financial corporations, the debt threshold is approximately double, having a value of 60 per cent of GDP. This stands to show that household debt could represent an important vulnerability for economic growth if it increases excessively. Developments in this sector warrant ongoing supervision and a swift policy response, either through the activation of a macroprudential instrument or other available measures, when there are indications that debt levels are heading towards unsustainable values.

8.3.2 Country Analysis

Marginal effects were computed in order to assess the response of the probability of an economic downturn for several debt values and categories at country level (see Figures 8A.1–8A.6 in the Appendix). In this case, results vary quite substantially from one state to another, although one common denominator throughout all regions seems to be the fast response of the recession probability in the case of household debt. In all countries, the debt threshold for this category does not go beyond 40 per cent of GDP in order to register recession probabilities that exceed 50 per cent. In countries like Romania and Slovenia, the threshold values range between 20 and 25 per cent of GDP, whereas Latvia and Hungary record the highest levels of household debt, at approximately 40 per cent of GDP.

These results underline once again the need to properly monitor the developments in this sector in order to ensure that debt does not grow in an excessive manner, especially given the importance of household consumption and confidence in spurring growth in an economy. To this end, Neagu et al. (2015) find that implementing macro prudential instruments such as caps on Debt-Service-to-Income (DSTI), Loan-to-Value (LTV) or Loan-to-Income (LTI) ratios can significantly decrease the probability of excessive credit growth or unsustainable lending.

In the case of non-financial corporations' debt, thresholds range from 40 per cent of GDP in Romania to 85 per cent in Slovenia and Bulgaria. Even though at aggregate level non-financial corporations seem to have a better ability to cope with higher levels of debt, it is important to keep in mind that developments at the microeconomic level are usually quite heterogeneous. As such, credit institutions should focus their efforts on viable companies with a sound financial standing, while companies that prove to be over-indebted should be assisted in improving their financial position.

In most countries the probability of an economic decline exceeds 50 per cent at public debt values that are well below the limit established in the Maastricht criteria (60 per cent of GDP), the only exception being Hungary, for which the calculated threshold reaches 90 per cent of GDP. The most eloquent example for the former is Bulgaria, where general government debt has a negative impact on economic growth when its level surpasses 30 per cent of GDP. In Romania the public debt threshold stands at 45 per cent of GDP, similar to the one recorded for the entire panel, while the current level of government debt is at 39.9 per cent of GDP. In fact, five of the seven countries included in the analysis have public debt thresholds below 50 per cent of GDP.

Caner et al. (2010) argue that the financial crisis and the subsequent sovereign debt crisis have led to a surge in the level of government debt and further increases are to be expected. The authors find that, in the case of emerging economies, a public debt value over 64 per cent of GDP can produce important negative effects on economic growth.

It is therefore necessary to find a proper balance between the level of government deficits, which are ultimately financed either by adding more debt or by increasing taxes on companies and households, and the need to stimulate the economy. Governments could make use of other instruments at their disposal, such as better management of European grants, in order to run key investment projects in transportation, utilities, health or education. Furthermore, additional changes to the public–private partnerships could incentivize private sector involvement in the investment process and therefore reduce the budgetary effort that would otherwise be required from the government should the project be undertaken by the public sector only.

Another argument for the increased involvement of the private sector is this category's better capability to take on larger amounts of debt than the government. The debt thresholds for the private sector in all countries are well above those determined for the public sector, ranging from 55 per cent of GDP in Romania to approximately 110 per cent of GDP in states like Hungary, Slovenia or Bulgaria. As shown above, these results are mainly driven by the non-financial corporations' ability to cope with greater levels of debt, while the case of households this capacity remains rather limited.

High levels of external debt could also hamper a country's ability to harness growth in a sustainable manner, especially due to the possibility of a shock transmission from partner states. In most countries gross external debt thresholds have relatively high values, with the lowest in the Czech Republic (55 per cent of GDP). The country that showed the largest capability to accumulate external debt is Hungary (the estimated threshold is 185 per cent of GDP). For the other four countries, the external debt values at which the recession probability exceeds 50 per cent fluctuate between 90 per cent of GDP (in Romania) and 155 per cent of GDP (in Latvia).

Finally, the assessment regarding total debt consisting of households, non-financial corporations and government sectors reveals a similar pattern to that of external debt. The thresholds in this case range from 100 per cent of GDP in Romania to approximately 195 per cent of GDP in Hungary. The values for the other four countries are positioned around the threshold recorded at panel level (140 per cent of GDP).

8.3.3 An Asset Pricing Model-based Sustainability Analysis

The maximum likelihood estimates for the long-run average real interest rates[2] obtained from the continuous Ornstein–Uhlenbeck model (OUM) were compared to the unconditional means in order to include the most appropriate variable in the overall model. The calibration of the model was based on the estimates obtained from OUM as long as the standard errors determined the rejection of the null hypothesis of a two-tailed T-test for significance. The null hypothesis of the significance test could not be rejected in two cases: Bulgaria and the Czech Republic. In these two instances, the unconditional means were used throughout the calibration exercise. For the remaining countries, estimates of the long-run interest rates proved to be significant from a statistical point of view.

The customized version of the Mendoza and Ostry (2007) approach was then applied in order to compute the optimal debt levels. With respect to the two grids used in the model, for the response of primary deficit to existing debt level (ρ), the highest likelihood scenario was represented by a value of 0.03, while in the case of the long-run primary balance (μ) it resulted in the 50th percentile having the best fit. The figures for μ in the highest likelihood scenario were empirically derived, whereas ρ was set at 0.03 for the purpose of robustness. The mechanics behind the levels, namely the shapes of each debt surface, can be explained as: the optimal debt level determined by the model is increasing in μ and $\bar{r}$ and decreasing in ρ. As such, the differences between the highest likelihood scenarios from country to country related to the computation of $E[D_t]$

---

[2]   Figure 8A.7 in the Appendix shows the maximum likelihood estimates of the long-run average real interest rates.

are explained by μ, as well as by the real return exceeding economic growth. The lowest $\bar{r}$ was recorded in Bulgaria, while Poland registered the highest value. In the ascending order of $\bar{r}$, the other countries were ranked as follows: Czech Republic, Hungary and Romania. Therefore, for comparable figures related to μ, an 'up' effect on $E[D_t]$ for countries like Poland or Romania is observed. Furthermore, it should be mentioned that, in order to be able to consider $E[D_t]$ as a sustainable debt level, it is also necessary to fulfil the condition $E[(1 - \rho)(1 + \bar{r})] < 1$ as Mendoza and Ostry (2007) emphasize. In our calibration exercises, this condition is satisfied for each country when ρ fluctuates within the grid [0.025; 0.04].

If the Maastricht criterion is considered for the public sector as a standard for the optimal public debt value, it can be observed that the calibrated $E[D_t]$, in the highest likelihood scenarios, surpasses that level only in the case of Poland (see Figure 8A.8 in the Appendix). For the other countries, the optimal debt stands firmly below the 60 per cent of GDP benchmark. The surfaces calibrated for Romania and Poland show higher non-linearity as compared with the other three countries. Poland and the Czech Republic post values of the long-run primary balance (μ) almost twice as great as those of Hungary and Romania. Thus, the sustainable level of the public debt calculated for Romania is influenced by the larger $\bar{r}$ when compared to the Czech Republic, for example.

As stated in the methodology section, for private debt, μ was approximated through the growth rate of debt for each institutional sector. When looking at the variable related to the financing need in the Hungarian non-financial sector, data point to decreasing funding pressure. In the case of Poland, the unconditional mean operator shows an increasing need for money, while the 50th percentile operator reveals the opposite. For this reason, in our highest likelihood scenario for Poland, the unconditional mean operator was used instead of the 50th percentile operator. For the other three countries, μ has a similar value, but due to differences in terms of $\bar{r}$ from country to country, $E[D_t]$ in the case of Romania is more than double when compared to the optimal debt level for Bulgaria (see Figure 8A.9 in the Appendix).

If, in the previous two cases, the sustainable levels obtained for Romania were among the largest in the pool of countries, in the case of the household sector, Romania's $E[D_t]$ is the lowest (see Figure 8A.10 in the Appendix). This is explained by the lowest μ among the five considered countries. The Czech Republic has the largest calibrated μ, followed by Poland, Hungary and Bulgaria. On the other hand, in terms of optimal level of debt, Poland has recorded the largest figure, with Hungary and the Czech Republic trailing behind. In the most likely scenario, Poland's

$E[D_t]$ is almost double the optimal levels of debt obtained for Hungary and the Czech Republic.

For external debt, Hungary registered the largest $E[D_t]$ (around 173 per cent), followed by Romania (around 151 per cent; see Figure 8A.11 in the Appendix). For the other three countries, much lower figures were recorded for their respective optimal debt levels. More specifically, $E[D_t]$ is around 100 per cent for Poland, 54 per cent in the Czech Republic, while in Bulgaria it stands at around 43 per cent. The higher $E[D_t]$ figures obtained in the case of external debt, when compared to the previous three cases, are explained by a larger empirical μ. Even though the technical way in which μ was calibrated for the private sector is different from the approach envisaged in the case of the public sector, in terms of economic meanings the two instances are relatively similar.

Last but not least, in the most likely scenario for the total debt case, Romania has recorded the largest optimal debt level, followed by Poland and the Czech Republic (see Figure 8A.12 in the Appendix). At the other end of the spectrum are Bulgaria and Hungary. Conversely, the Czech Republic has the largest μ, relatively close to that of Romania. Although Poland's μ is approximately one third lower than that observed for the Czech Republic, the optimal level of debt obtained for Poland is around 59 percentage points greater compared to the Czech Republic's $E[D_t]$.

8.4   CONCLUSIONS

A series of panel regressions were used in order to assess the effect of debt on economic growth. To this purpose, the marginal response of the dependent variable (that is, the probability of recession) was calculated for six debt categories at values that range from 20 to 200 per cent of GDP. Moreover, an asset pricing model was also estimated in order to better grasp the effects of debt on economic growth. The results vary quite considerably from one category to the other, but also between the methods used. One important conclusion the results bring forward is that 'one size fits all' measures or thresholds (see for example the 60 per cent level of public debt-to-GDP ratio established in the Maastricht Treaty) might not be the optimal solution, as countries can bear various debt levels. Imposing too restrictive a threshold in a country which can sustain higher debt values can lead to opportunity costs through missed investment possibilities. Conversely, setting a threshold above the one which can be afforded can also have negative effects on economic growth. Similarly, the different sectors investigated in this chapter proved to have a contrasting resilience to the different debt levels. Developments in the household sector warrant constant supervision and the policy response should be immediate when there are indications that debt levels are heading towards unsustainable values.

REFERENCES

Aït-Sahalia, Y. (2002), 'Maximum-likelihood estimation of discretely-sampled diffusions: A closed-form approximation approach', *Econometrica*, **70**, 223–62.

Baum, A., C. Checherita-Westphal and P. Rother (2013), 'Debt and growth: New evidence for the euro area', *Journal of International Money and Finance*, **32**, 809–21.

Bohn, H. (2005), 'The sustainability of fiscal policy in the United States', Department of Economics, University of California, Santa Barbara.

Caner, M., T. Grennes and F. Koehler-Geib (2010), 'Finding the tipping point when sovereign debt turns bad', *World Bank Conference on Debt Management*, March.

Cecchetti, S., M. Mohanty and F. Zampolli (2011), 'Achieving growth amid fiscal imbalances: The real effects of debt', *BIS Working Papers*, No. 352.

Chudik, A., K. Mohaddes, M.H. Pesaran and M. Raissi (2015), 'Is there a debt-threshold effect on output growth?', *IMF Working Paper*, WP/15/197.

Clements, B., R. Bhattacharya and T.Q. Nguyen (2003), 'External debt, public investment, and growth in low-income countries', *IMF Working Paper*, WP/03/249.

Eberhardt, M. and A. Presbitero (2013), 'This time they are different: Heterogeneity and nonlinearity in the relationship between debt and growth', *IMF Working Paper*, WP/13/248.

Koo, R. (2011), 'The world in balance sheet recession: Causes, cure, and politics', *Real-World Economics Review*, no. 58.

Ljungqvist, L. and T. Sargent (2004), *Recursive Macroeconomic Theory*, Cambridge: MIT Press.

Lucas, R.E. (1978), 'Asset prices in an exchange economy', *Econometrica*, **46**(6), 1429–45.

Mendoza, E.G. and J.D. Ostry (2007), 'International evidence on fiscal solvency: Is fiscal policy "responsible"?', *IMF Working Paper*, WP/07/56.

Neagu, F., I. Mihai and L. Tatarici (2018), Coping with unsustainable lending: the use of macroprudential instruments in an emerging economy, forthcoming.

Reinhart, C. and K. Rogoff (2010), 'Debt and growth revisited', MPRA Paper No. 24376.

Table 8A.1 Summary statistics

Variable	Explanation	Unit	No. of observations	Mean	Median	Standard deviation	Min	Max	Expected sign
nfc_debt	Non-financial corporation debt	% of GDP	287	50.51	47.85	18.81	19.92	91.73	positive
govt_debt	Public sector debt	% of GDP	287	38.58	38.00	20.33	8.20	84.00	positive
hh_debt	Household debt	% of GDP	287	23.71	23.78	7.95	4.90	47.12	positive
private_debt	Private sector debt, calculated as sum of household and non-financial corporation debt	% of GDP	287	74.22	71.86	22.27	24.83	120.22	positive
ext_debt	Gross external debt	% of GDP	287	85.94	77.12	33.75	34.09	167.20	positive
total_debt	Total debt, computed as sum of private sector and government debt	% of GDP	287	112.80	114.12	29.50	43.05	173.85	positive
gfcf	Gross fixed capital formation	% of GDP	287	24.75	24.03	4.53	17.88	38.74	negative
consum	Final consumption expenditure	% of GDP	287	58.52	61.27	6.40	46.32	69.72	negative
govt_balance	Government balance	% of GDP	287	-3.36	-3.20	5.04	-39.40	12.50	negative
unemployment	Unemployment rate	%	287	8.89	7.80	3.21	4.30	20.60	positive
export_gdp	Exports of goods and services	% of GDP	287	55.82	58.27	16.81	26.16	91.16	positive
import_gdp	Imports of goods and services	% of GDP	287	58.61	60.73	13.06	33.78	83.75	positive
trade_gdp	Openness of the economy, calculated as the sum of exports and imports	% of GDP	287	114.44	118.90	29.24	60.91	174.91	positive
hicp_all	HICP inflation	%	287	3.70	3.20	3.21	-4.00	17.50	positive
ir_dob	Interest rate	%	287	4.00	3.74	2.98	0.08	16.22	positive

Source: Eurostat, ECB, national central banks' statistics, Reuters, Bloomberg.

Table 8A.2   Correlation matrix of the main variables

	nfc_debt	govt_debt	hh_debt	private_debt	ext_debt	total_debt	gfcf	consum	export_gdp	import_gdp	trade_gdp	hicp_all	ir_dob	govt_deficit	unemployment
nfc_debt	1														
govt_debt	−0.15	1													
hh_debt	0.26	0.23	1												
private_debt	**0.94**	−0.04	0.58	1											
ext_debt	0.55	0.35	0.61	0.68	1										
total_debt	0.61	0.66	0.60	**0.73**	**0.76**	1									
gfcf	0.04	−0.66	−0.15	−0.02	−0.21	−0.47	1								
consum	−0.20	−0.42	−0.04	−0.18	0.00	−0.43	0.01	1							
export_gdp	0.44	0.57	0.14	0.42	0.42	**0.71**	−0.29	−0.72	1						
import_gdp	0.51	0.35	0.13	0.47	0.49	0.60	−0.04	−0.52	**0.92**	1					
trade_gdp	0.48	0.48	0.14	0.45	0.46	0.68	−0.19	−0.65	**0.98**	**0.97**	1				
hicp_all	−0.14	−0.32	−0.09	−0.15	−0.05	−0.34	0.51	0.31	−0.30	−0.03	−0.19	1			
ir_dob	−0.41	−0.06	−0.19	−0.41	−0.15	−0.36	0.36	0.24	−0.35	−0.22	−0.30	0.59	1		
govt_deficit	−0.03	−0.25	−0.15	−0.08	−0.09	−0.23	0.13	0.15	−0.01	0.10	0.04	0.17	−0.08	1	
unemployment	0.04	0.24	0.41	0.18	0.44	0.30	−0.56	0.30	−0.03	−0.11	−0.07	−0.32	−0.21	−0.09	1

Source: Eurostat, ECB, national central banks' statistics, Reuters, Bloomberg.

Table 8A.3 Logit estimation results

	Total	External	Private	Government	Non-financial corporations	Households
total_debt$_{t-4}$	0.146*** (0.0302)					
ext_debt$_{t-4}$		0.108*** (0.0231)				
private_debt$_{t-4}$			0.287*** (0.0575)			
govt_debt$_{t-4}$				0.174*** (0.0439)		
nfc_debt$_{t-4}$					0.325*** (0.0677)	
hh_debt$_{t-4}$						0.748*** (0.158)
gfcf$_{t-4}$	0.385*** (0.115)	0.263** (0.132)	0.229** (0.100)		0.269** (0.109)	
consum$_{t-4}$	−0.231 (0.169)	−0.0104 (0.186)	−0.328* (0.191)	−0.211 (0.174)		−0.350 (0.220)
trade_gdp$_{t-4}$	0.0677** (0.0323)	0.0831*** (0.0308)	0.127*** (0.0427)		0.122*** (0.0323)	
import_gdp$_{t-4}$						0.173** (0.0770)
govt_balance$_{t-4}$	0.0274 (0.0386)	−0.0236 (0.0428)	−0.0135 (0.0643)	0.0153 (0.0524)	−0.0176 (0.0588)	
ir_dob$_{t-4}$	0.982*** (0.208)	0.782*** (0.264)	1.135*** (0.225)	0.757*** (0.227)	0.894*** (0.193)	1.152*** (0.287)
hicp_all$_{t-4}$	0.465*** (0.0970)	0.357*** (0.0944)	0.519*** (0.113)	0.333*** (0.101)	0.326*** (0.0972)	0.467*** (0.140)
unemployment$_{t-4}$				−0.467*** (0.162)		−0.382** (0.182)
Constant	−29.95** (12.53)	−35.37*** (11.96)	−38.47*** (14.58)	6.792 (13.15)	−53.94*** (9.263)	−14.50 (11.47)
Observations	222	222	222	222	222	222
Wald chi2	72.13	65.38	54.46	78.02	69.96	48.22
Prob > chi2	0.00	0.00	0.00	0.00	0.00	0.00
Log likelihood	−55.36	−60.64	−47.90	−77.43	−53.88	−47.42
R2	0.57	0.52	0.62	0.39	0.58	0.63
ROC	0.94	0.94	0.96	0.90	0.95	0.96

Notes:
Robust standard errors in parentheses.
*** $p < 0.01$; ** $p < 0.05$; * $p < 0.1$.

Table 8A.4 Logit estimation results: robustness checks

	Total		External		Private		Government		Non-financial corporations		Households	
	lag 2	lag 8	lag 2	lag 8	lag 2	lag 8	lag 2	lag 8	lag 2	lag 8	lag 2	lag 8
total_debt	0.127*** (0.0178)	0.0284** (0.0138)										
ext_debt			0.0987*** (0.0160)	0.0326** (0.0141)								
private_debt					0.214*** (0.0354)	0.0415** (0.0178)						
govt_debt							0.0837** (0.0372)	0.0579** (0.0289)				
nfc_debt									0.260*** (0.0371)	0.0371 (0.0276)		
hh_debt											0.470*** (0.0770)	0.170*** (0.0477)
gfcf	0.157* (0.0853)	0.497*** (0.0914)	0.0981 (0.0749)	0.511*** (0.0954)	0.0317 (0.0912)	0.444*** (0.0835)			0.114 (0.0712)	0.323*** (0.0791)		
consum	-0.405*** (0.133)	0.513*** (0.133)	-0.151 (0.127)	0.600*** (0.147)	-0.418*** (0.161)	0.490*** (0.126)	-0.316*** (0.112)	0.245** (0.100)			-0.340** (0.140)	0.327*** (0.108)
trade_gdp	-0.0106 (0.0215)	0.0249 (0.0219)	0.00704 (0.0209)	0.0206 (0.0223)	0.0321 (0.0243)	0.0238 (0.0209)			0.0359* (0.0217)	0.0204 (0.0189)		
import_gdp											0.0261 (0.0433)	0.0274 (0.0404)
govt_balance	-0.0231 (0.0485)	0.0607 (0.0613)	-0.0638 (0.0432)	0.0536 (0.0574)	-0.0743** (0.0302)	0.0633 (0.0618)	-0.0657 (0.0594)	0.0407 (0.0444)	-0.0813*** (0.0301)	0.0539 (0.0602)		
ir_dob	0.804*** (0.156)	-0.221 (0.136)	0.618*** (0.128)	-0.226 (0.140)	0.790*** (0.173)	-0.214 (0.135)	0.539*** (0.133)	0.0735 (0.115)	0.661*** (0.136)	-0.236* (0.128)	0.632*** (0.133)	0.0368 (0.0957)

Table 8A.4 (continued)

	Total		External		Private		Government		Non-financial corporations		Households	
	lag 2	lag 8	lag 2	lag 8	lag 2	lag 8	lag 2	lag 8	lag 2	lag 8	lag 2	lag 8
hicp_all	0.126	0.144*	0.0693	0.134	0.136	0.129	0.0792	0.0681	0.0387	0.175*	0.0311	0.0299
	(0.0866)	(0.0877)	(0.0881)	(0.0889)	(0.0969)	(0.0878)	(0.0916)	(0.0847)	(0.102)	(0.0907)	(0.0936)	(0.0900)
unemployment							−0.0930	−0.640***			−0.136	−0.631***
							(0.132)	(0.152)			(0.133)	(0.123)
Constant	3.100	−56.22***	−7.963	−61.85***	−4.450	−53.52***	15.61**	−15.04**	−31.28***	−15.73***	5.504	−24.63***
	(9.300)	(11.26)	(8.905)	(12.17)	(9.847)	(10.34)	(7.642)	(6.360)	(5.262)	(3.390)	(8.230)	(7.076)
Observations	234	198	234	198	234	198	234	198	234	198	234	198
Log likelihood	−78.69	−87.25	−84.51	−86.47	−73.63	−86.80	−100.94	−96.22	−79.81	−95.56	−79.14	−87.94
R2	0.40	0.27	0.36	0.28	0.44	0.28	0.23	0.20	0.39	0.20	0.40	0.27
ROC	0.90	0.83	0.88	0.84	0.91	0.84	0.83	0.77	0.89	0.81	0.90	0.82

Notes:
Robust standard errors in parentheses.
*** p < 0.01; ** p < 0.05; * p < 0.1.

Table 8A.5 Marginal effects on the probability of recession

Level (% DP)	Probability of recession for various debt levels				
	Total debt	Private debt	NFC debt	Household debt	Government debt
20	0.0068	0.0024	0.0172**	0.1469***	0.1551***
	(0.13)	(0.33)	(0.01)	(0.00)	(0.00)
30	0.0131**	0.0138**	0.0322***	0.6068***	0.2504***
	(0.00)	(0.00)	(0.00)	(0.00)	(0.00)
40	0.0196***	0.0242***	0.0913***	0.8713***	0.3921***
	(0.00)	(0.00)	(0.00)	(0.00)	(0.00)
50	0.0264***	0.0350***	0.2792***	0.9315***	0.5636***
	(0.00)	(0.00)	(0.00)	(0.00)	(0.00)
60	0.0351***	0.0725***	0.4879***	0.9915***	0.7043***
	(0.00)	(0.00)	(0.00)	(0.00)	(0.00)
70	0.0505***	0.1839***	0.6232***	1.0000***	0.8116***
	(0.00)	(0.00)	(0.00)	(0.00)	(0.00)
80	0.0788***	0.3572***	0.7247***	1.0000***	0.8900***
	(0.00)	(0.00)	(0.00)	(0.00)	(0.00)
90	0.1219***	0.5149***	0.8587***	1.0000***	0.9464***
	(0.00)	(0.00)	(0.00)	(0.00)	(0.00)
100	0.1805***	0.6161***	0.9769***	1.0000***	0.9804***
	(0.00)	(0.00)	(0.00)	(0.00)	(0.00)
110	0.2570***	0.7056***	0.9988***	1	0.9949***
	(0.00)	(0.00)	(0.00)	(.)	(0.00)
120	0.3465***	0.8337***	1.0000***	1	0.9990***
	(0.00)	(0.00)	(0.00)	(.)	(0.00)
130	0.4432***	0.9447***	1.0000***	1	0.9998***
	(0.00)	(0.00)	(0.00)	(.)	(0.00)
140	0.5388***	0.9850***	1.0000***	1	1.0000***
	(0.00)	(0.00)	(0.00)	(.)	(0.00)
150	0.6259***	0.9967***	1.0000***	1	1.0000***
	(0.00)	(0.00)	(0.00)	(.)	(0.00)
160	0.7129***	0.9997***	1.0000***	1	1.0000***
	(0.00)	(0.00)	(0.00)	(.)	(0.00)
170	0.8060***	1.0000***	1.0000***	1	1.0000***
	(0.00)	(0.00)	(0.00)	(.)	(0.00)
180	0.8883***	1.0000***	1.0000***	1	1.0000***
	(0.00)	(0.00)	(0.00)	(.)	(0.00)
190	0.9439***	1.0000***	1.0000***	1	1.0000***
	(0.00)	(0.00)	(0.00)	(.)	(0.00)
200	0.9732***	1.0000***	1.0000***	1	1.0000***
	(0.00)	(0.00)	(0.00)	(.)	(0.00)

Notes:
p-values in parentheses.
*** $p < 0.01$; ** $p < 0.05$; * $p < 0.1$.

Debt default and democracy

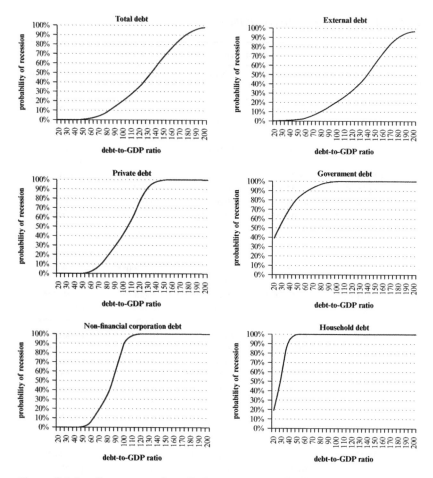

*Figure 8A.1   Country results – Bulgaria: marginal effects on the
            probability of recession for various debt levels*

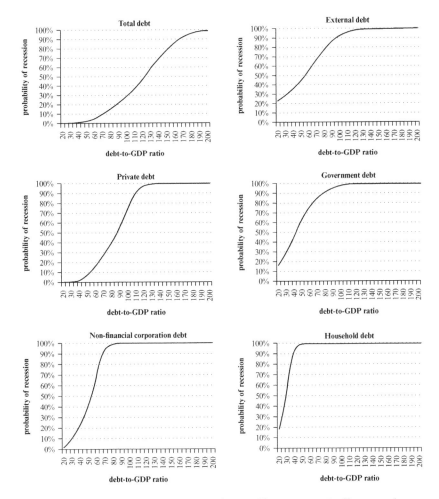

Figure 8A.2   Country results – Czech Republic: marginal effects on the probability of recession for various debt levels

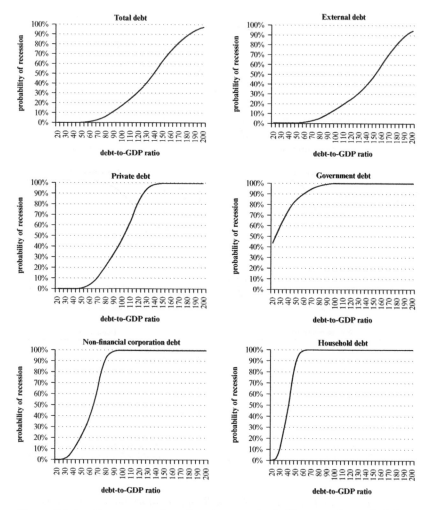

*Figure 8A.3   Country results – Latvia: marginal effects on the probability
of recession for various debt levels*

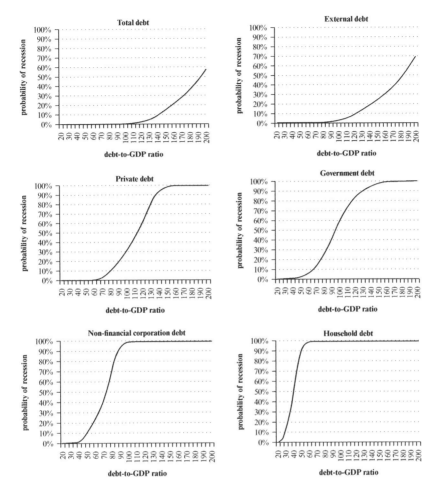

Figure 8A.4 Country results – Hungary: marginal effects on the probability of recession for various debt levels

Debt default and democracy

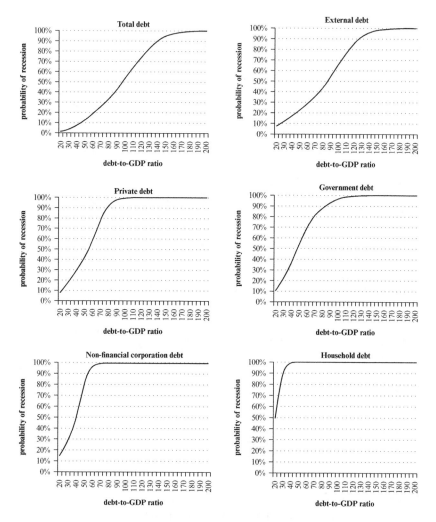

*Figure 8A.5   Country results – Romania: marginal effects on the
            probability of recession for various debt levels*

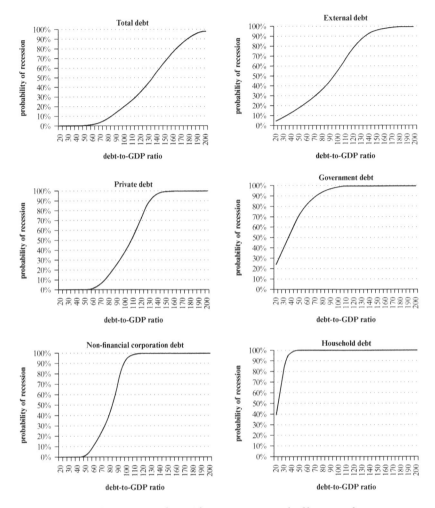

Figure 8A.6   Country results – Slovenia: marginal effects on the probability of recession for various debt levels

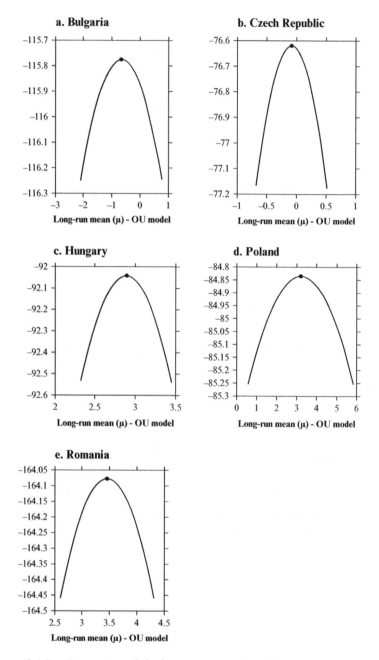

Figure 8A.7   Estimation of the long-run mean in real interest rates using an Ornstein–Uhlenbeck model

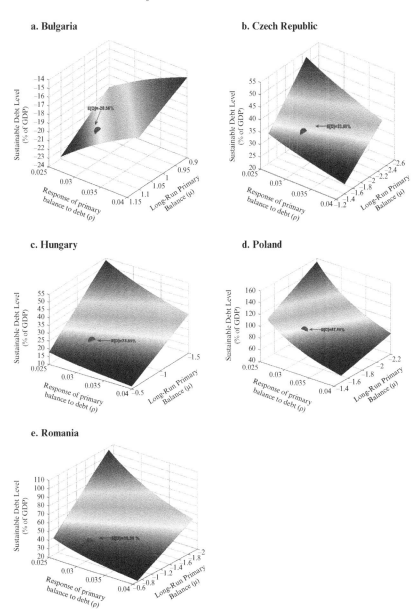

Figure 8A.8   Calibration of the optimal public debt level using the asset pricing approach

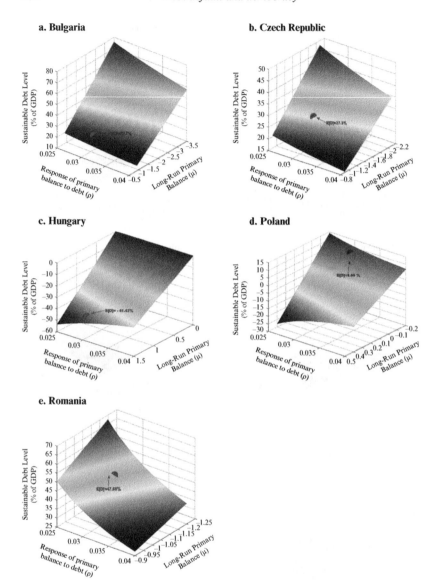

*Figure 8A.9   Calibration of the optimal debt level for the non-financial
corporations sector using the asset pricing approach*

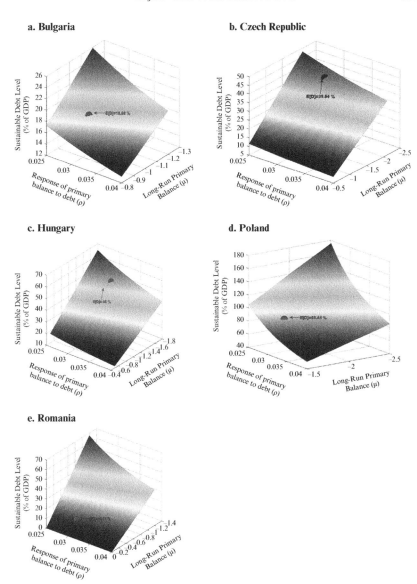

Figure 8A.10   Calibration of the optimal debt level for the household sector using the asset pricing approach

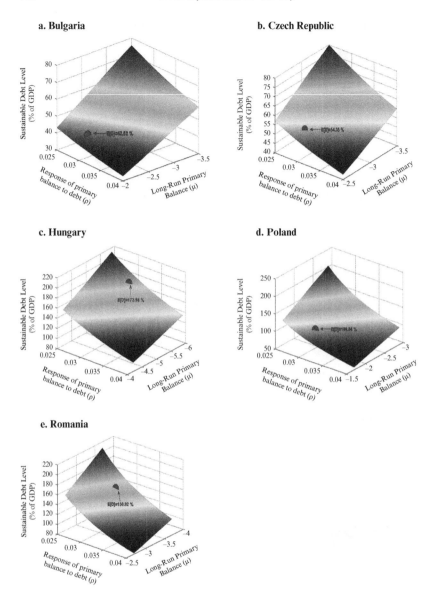

Figure 8A.11   Calibration of the optimal debt level for the external sector using the asset pricing approach

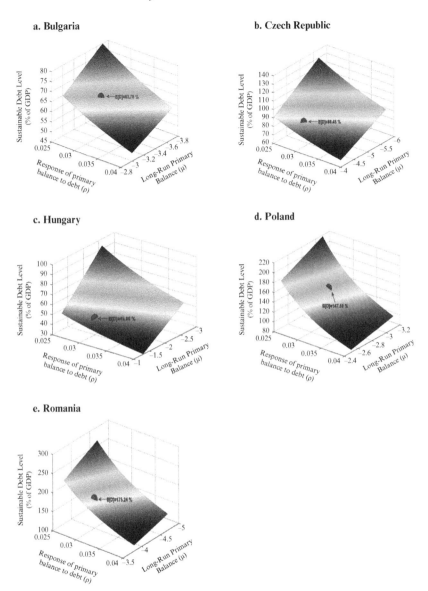

Figure 8A.12   Calibration of the total optimal debt level using the asset pricing approach

Index

Printed and bound by CPI Group (UK) Ltd, Croydon, CR0 4YY

23/04/2025

14660979-0003